D1212679

# Fictions of Resolution in Three Victorian Novels

# Fictions of Resolution in Three Victorian Novels

*North and South*
*Our Mutual Friend*
*Daniel Deronda*

Deirdre David

Columbia University Press
New York 1981

*Printed in Great Britain*

**Library of Congress Cataloging in Publication Data**

David, Deirdre, 1934–
Fictions of resolution in three Victorian novels.

1. English fiction–19th century–History and criticism. 2. Social classes literature. 3. Gaskell, Elizabeth Cleghorn Stevenson, 1810–1865. North and South. 4. Dickens, Charles, 1812–1870. Our mutual friend. 5. Eliot, George, pseud., i.e. Marian Evans, afterwards Cross, 1819–1880. Daniel Deronda. I. Title.
PR878.S6D3 823′.8′09355 80–16262

ISBN 0–231–04980–3

# Contents

*Acknowledgments* vii
*Preface* ix

PART I NORTH AND SOUTH 1

1 The Industrial Novel as Social Tract 3
2 Masters and Men and Ladies and Gentlemen 11
3 Men and Women 31

PART II OUR MUTUAL FRIEND 51

4 Society and its Discontents 53
5 The River 63
6 The Mounds 90

PART III DANIEL DERONDA 133

7 Social Realism and Moral Correction 135
8 Deronda and the Jews 147
9 Gwendolen Harleth as Heroine and Metaphor 176

*Index* 207

# Acknowledgments

Steven Marcus helped me in the initial preparation of this study; I am grateful for his scholarly guidance and invigorating criticism. Michael Wood read my manuscript with careful attention and encouraging responsiveness. In informal discussions about Victorian literature and society and in specific readings of parts of this study, Louise Yelin was unfailingly free with her time and with her lively intellect. As a stimulating teacher and as a kind and generous friend, Edward Said has helped me in innumerable and invaluable ways. John Richetti's intellectual support and affectionate companionship sustained me through all stages of this study, and, indeed, through many stages of my life.

The author and publishers wish to thank the following who have kindly given permission for the use of copyright material: The Hogarth Press Ltd, Sigmund Freud Copyrights Ltd, and the Institute of Psycho-Analysis, for the extracts from *The Standard Edition of the Complete Psychological Works of Sigmund Freud*, translated and edited by James Strachey; *American rights*: W. W. Norton & Company, Inc., for the extracts from *Civilization and Its Discontents* and Basic Books Inc., for *Female Sexuality*; Lawrence & Wishart Ltd, for the extracts from *Capital* and *Economic and Philosophic Manuscripts of 1844* by Karl Marx; and Routledge & Kegan Paul Ltd and W. W. Norton & Company Inc., for the extract from *Totem and Taboo* by Sigmund Freud, translated by James Strachey (1950).

DEIRDRE DAVID

# Preface

We take it for granted that Victorian novels are about "society", and that by the middle of the nineteenth century a vast and complex social system became an urgent topic of representation and analysis for the Victorian novelist. We also take it for granted that Victorian novels were written primarily for the English middle class: the names that dominate a roll-call of mid-nineteenth-century novelists are ones associated, in large part, with middle-class origin and with middle-class readership. And we take it for granted, too, that this relationship between genre and a certain social class originates coevally in the mythic rise of the English novel in the middle of the eighteenth century. But by the middle of the nineteenth century, both social class and genre were in full and profuse bloom, firmly rooted in the solid soil of Victorian commercial dominance, and for modern readers the Victorian novel and the English middle class have come to exist in a given historical and critical symbiosis – it is virtually impossible to talk about one without talking about the other.

As well as providing popular entertainment, many Victorian novels performed an important social function, as they described and sometimes explained the workings of a society in the process of rapid and unprecedented alteration, and as they tried to clarify a proper and satisfactory place for the individual in that society. As a constituent mark of this social function, certain nineteenth-century novels engaged in a complex series of mediations between the social actuality they represented and the desires of their predominantly middle-class readers that things not be the way they were in that actuality. In what follows, I analyse three well-known Victorian novels, *North and South, Our Mutual Friend,* and *Daniel Deronda*, in order to elucidate this particular relationship between fiction and a specific social group, and employ a critical methodology that relies upon historical, social and psychological analysis, as well as upon literary criticism; I suggest that the tension between representation of social actuality and desire for difference is mythically resolved in fictions of one sort or another. Elizabeth Gaskell, Charles Dickens, and George Eliot, each in his or her own historical and artistic province, create fictions of resolution for the problems of pervasive social uneasiness with which they engage themselves.

In Elizabeth Gaskell's Milford-Northern (a barely disguised Manchester), middle-class life is beset by the problems inherent in an industrial community: her lucid combination of social tract and engaging fiction suggests some of these difficulties – the factory working class is restless, the self-made businessman does not exercise the proper stern management and moral leadership founded upon Christian benevolence, and the South is not fully appreciative of Northern commercial aggressiveness. In Dickens' London, discontent and dissatisfaction pervade all social strata: he powerfully satirises the aimlessness, boredom and materialism of the upper classes and movingly portrays the lower-class struggles with shabby poverty, physical and psychological suffering, and oftentimes malevolent class resentment. In Eliot's country-house world, the upper class devotes itself to narcissistic self-display and lives a life empty of intellectual and moral content – for Eliot, and for her fictive agent of moral criticism, Deronda, it is a life representative of all that is wrong with English life. In other words, we see in these three novels various images of Victorian dissatisfaction, doubt, and moral questioning, and these are common enough assumptions we make about Victorian culture. In my readings, however, I have been more interested in seeing how the cultural power enjoyed by the Victorian novelist actually mediates the problems of class conflict, miserable city life and moral malaise that we almost automatically erect as major semiological markers of Victorian experience, than in merely isolating and identifying such problems in each of the novels. In these fictions of resolution, we see the visible authority of the middle-class novelist at work – elaborating the myths of middle-class culture, embroidering middle-class ideology, and mediating between mimesis and desire for transformation of what is represented.

The industrial novel, with its emphasis upon class relationships and upon local working conditions, offers a clear example of how the novel, as a genre, quite nakedly sets out to resolve social conflict and to provide moral lessons. The industrial novels of the 1840s and 1850s responded to a desire for information and guidance in a time that was socially uncertain, and they also engaged themselves with an intense and specific form of a felt absence of coherence in social life, that is to say, with modern man's feeling of alienation from his work. I chose to discuss *North and South*, rather than any other industrial novel, because of Gaskell's skilful and complementary management of didactic documentary about factory life and romantic narrative of Northern mill-owner and Southern clergyman's daughter.

I include *Our Mutual Friend* here, rather than, say, *Bleak House* or *Little Dorrit*, Dickens' other two great novels of the city, because of its implicit insistence upon the relationship between social dissatisfaction and economic situation and its continuous allusion to myth, to fairy-tale, and to making fictions. In the process of undertaking a fictive work of social improvement, where bourgeois domesticity fabulously triumphs over greed and materialism and where resentment of economic lot is mythically dispatched, Dickens ambiguously transcends the social actuality that he so movingly and effectively describes. Depending upon the relation of their fictive experience to his mediations, Dickens selects certain characters for inclusion in the new social order that comes into being at the end of the novel, while he relegates others to death, exile and obsession.

*Daniel Deronda*, a provocatively taxing novel about upper-class manners and mores and the discovery and acceptance of Jewish identity, initially may seem an unusual choice for discussion of middle-class myth-making: *Middlemarch*, Eliot's fine novel of social analysis, her most expansive examination of the mutually decisive and nourishing connection between the individual and society, comes more immediately to mind. Her last novel is formally and thematically problematic, and it is for me, if not for others, uneven. But there is a connection between this unevenness, the irreconcilation between social and psychological realism and moral correction, and Eliot's essentially middle-class, albeit learned and intellectually serious, criticism: *Daniel Deronda* expresses a yearning for a unifying idea of national life, for a decent middle ground where politics, commerce, art and morality might meet and enrich each other. As Eliot mediates between representation and desire for difference, she displaces herself from offering a plausible alternative to all that she finds so lamentable, for she can find no place in English life for Deronda's idealised moral consciousness.

These three novels explore the related meanings of economic situation and class position, and in the sense that the English novel is always, in one way or another, about money and class, this is hardly anything new. But *North and South, Our Mutual Friend* and *Daniel Deronda* were produced in a newly solidified and fully developed capitalist society and many of their mediations between representation and desire for difference are concerned with the problems of class and money inherent in such a social system. In my discussion, I sometimes refer to Marx's theories of class and economic situation where I think they enrich an understanding of the ways these three novels approach matters which he, in different forms, in different language, and certainly with different intentions, concerns himself.

It seems to me that Gaskell, Dickens and Eliot, consciously or unconsciously, draw decisive connections between social and sexual being, and when I think it facilitates an understanding of the social malaise described in these three novels, I have also made use of Freud's theories of culture and discontent, and, especially in my chapter on *Daniel Deronda*, of his theoretical work on female sexuality. In the following pages, I fully discuss what is only suggested in a very condensed way here – a conjunction of economic situation, class position and sexual being which is represented in different ways in each of these three novels, and which works to imaginatively intensify their dominant themes and to amplify the complicated nature of the social life of their characters.

What follows is divided into three parts and each part begins with an introductory critical discussion of the particular novel; for that reason, these remarks have been merely prefatory. In general, I employ an interdisciplinary critical perspective with no desire to make an exact and reductive fit between novel and economic or psychological theory; nor have I wanted to emphasise a disjunction between what we take to be the actuality of life in Victorian England and the mimesis of that actuality in fiction. I have been more interested in seeing a correspondence in the mediation and myth-making that takes place in these three novels, however different their thematic and formal organisation and however dissimilar their fictions of resolution. And in primarily analysing these novels as social products performing a social function, I do not, in any way, want to deny their power to move and to delight us. This reading has been informed by a critical sense of the novel as an inseparable element of the social and historical process: it has also been informed by a consciousness that the fictions of resolution to be discovered in *North and South, Our Mutual Friend* and *Daniel Deronda* were created, respectively, by novelists of superior narrative skill, almost inexplicable comic genius and informed, expansive intellect.

# PART I
# NORTH AND SOUTH

# 1 The Industrial Novel as Social Tract

> ...the proper Epic of this world is not now "Arms and the Man"; how much less, "Shirt-frills and the Man": no, it is now "Tools and the Man": that, henceforth to all time is now our Epic.
>
> Thomas Carlyle, *Past and Present*, Book III, Ch. XII

James Boswell, that indefatigable biographer, traveller, and record-keeper of his own experience, set off in March 1776 for a "jaunt" to the Midlands with Samuel Johnson. Boswell was anxious to see some of the great manufacturing works in the neighbourhood, and his wish was gratified by a visit to the premises of Matthew Boulton, the business partner of James Watt in the production of steam engines. The "vastness and contrivance of some of the machinery" made a great impression upon Boswell, but an even greater impression was effected by Mr Boulton himself. Boswell writes:

> I shall never forget Mr. Bolton's [sic] expression to me: "I sell here, Sir, what all the world desires to have – POWER." He had about seven hundred people at work. I contemplated him as an *iron chieftain*, and he seemed to be a father to his tribe.[1]

Boswell's contemplation of the successful iron-master as a sort of eighteenth-century tribal chieftain is arresting because of the unquestioning confidence in the new system of industrialised manufacture which it suggests, and because of the way in which an individual newly created by that system, the industrialised worker, is seen as regulated and protected by a stern patriarchal figure. Boswell's enthusiasm is partly due to his own enduring, and sometimes endearing, inclination to create and celebrate fathers, and, in a much larger context, to the fact that those workmen whom he so easily fits into a tribal structure had not yet become the disturbing force which threatened and transformed English society in the nineteenth century. Seven hundred people at work producing the source of that power which all the world desires to have, the steam engine, present no problematic situation; for Boswell, they know their place and are disciplined by the iron hand of Matthew Boulton.

Machinery grew vaster and more intricately contrived in the years which followed Boswell's visit to Birmingham, and Boulton's seven hundred workers multiplied to form a large industrial working class. Britain became the foremost industrial nation, and the working conditions for the creation of that technological eminence and the responsibility of an employer to his workers, became matters of pressing social concern. The mass of material attempting to explain the manufacturing system to a curious and ignorant public, the Parliamentary Commissions of Investigation into working conditions, the essays and books designed to educate English society in the life of the working class, and the industrial novels of the 1840s and 1850s, all seek, in their different ideological and formal ways, to confront the question of what it means for a nation and a people to be powerful. They try to explain the rapidly changing structures of a society which, in some cases, was transforming itself at a faster pace than people were able to write about it. While much of this material retains Boswell's delight and fascination with the operations of machinery and men at work, in the main it illuminates in greater detail and complexity the problematic situation between master and worker which he so ingenuously describes.[2]

Some fifty years after Boswell visited Birmingham, Elizabeth Gaskell moved to Manchester as the wife of a Unitarian minister. Her response to industrialised manufacture was to write a novel, *Mary Barton*, and after its publication in 1848 this eminently bourgeois woman who said about herself, "No one can feel more deeply than I how *wicked* it is to do anything to excite class against class",[3] was assailed as a meddling socialist. Her response was to elucidate the mimetic and didactic intentions of her novel:

> My poor Mary Barton is stirring up all sorts of angry feelings against me in Manchester; but those best acquainted with the way of thinking and feeling among the poor acknowledge its *truth*; which is the acknowledgment I most of all desire, because evils being once recognized are half way on towards their remedy.[4]

She looked around Manchester, perceived an appalling disparity between the lives of the middle and working classes, and believed that if her class were only made aware of the miseries of the poor it would do all it could to alleviate them. She was certainly not the first person to believe that the enlightenment of the privileged would propel them into benevolent action. R. W. Cooke Taylor, in his *Notes of a Tour in the Manufacturing Districts of Lancashire* (1842), wrote: "I am as firmly persuaded as I am of my own existence, that, if the noble and wealthy had witnessed the scenes which I have gone through, they would fling all prejudices and selfish interests to the winds . . . the classes into which English society is divided are opposed to each other because they are ignorant of each other."[5] In *Mary Barton* Gaskell sets out to elaborate upon Cooke Taylor's tour, to take the uninformed visitors, as it were, upon expeditions to places they had never seen, and into the lives of people of whom they were essentially ignorant. But she was regarded by some as a traitor to those people whom she hoped to enlighten, and W. R. Greg, a prominent Manchester manufacturer and man of letters, found the author's worst offence was to have "flattered both the prejudices of the aristocracy, and the passions of the populace",[6] and, one might add, to have implicitly ignored the interests and problems of the middle class. It is ironic that he confirms the realisation of her didactic intention to expose the evils of society by saying that were it "to be only read by Manchester men and master manufacturers it could scarcely fail to be serviceable; because they might profit by its suggestions, and would at once detect its mistakes", but he believes Southerners to labour under "extraordinary delusions" regarding Manchester, and the effect of *Mary Barton* upon someone unacquainted with the other side of the picture, that is the manufacturers', might be "mischievous in the extreme". That a novel could be socially "mischievous" suggests something about mid-nineteenth-century attitudes towards the knotty questions surrounding such terms as realism and fiction.

The industrial novels of early Victorian England are very often primarily regarded as a source of information about industrial conditions, and then secondarily as novels in themselves with all the attendant difficulties that have to do with the relationship between the actuality of those conditions and their transformation into fiction. The industrial novel for us, as twentieth-century readers, provides invaluable depictions of a society in the process of unprecedented and disturbing alteration, and, for readers of the time, offered glimpses of unknown territory. It is unlikely that many readers of *Mary Barton* had seen, and least of all smelt, the Davenport cellar, or been inside a mill like Bounderby's in *Hard Times*. The industrial novel served a sociological function for it enabled people to know about things far removed from their own experience. When Dickens ironically describes an outsider's comprehension of Coketown factories as fairy palaces glimpsed from an express train, he powerfully suggests the differing experiences of someone who has never set foot in the manufacturing towns and someone who is condemned to their grim reality. In *Hard Times* he takes the outsider inside, into Stephen Blackpool's poor, weary head where the stopping and starting of the machinery never ceases its long diurnal round. And it is because *Hard Times* is a novel and not a Commission Report that Dickens is able to use one character as a compelling focus of all the misery which Coketown contains. In the same way, *Mary Barton* can focus upon Alice Wilson as a tragic emblem of the consequences upon family life of rapid change, and W. R. Greg's awareness of the didactic possibilities of the novel made possible by the individualisation of misery that we experience in *Hard Times* and *Mary Barton* confirms one of the ways in which novels work. Because of the effectiveness of their mimesis, they can be forceful agents in enabling people to understand certain of the workings of society. But, paradoxically, because of their implausible resolutions of problematic social situations, they subject the novelist to charges of failing to be totally "realistic" in the way he may be said to try to change society.

Perhaps the informative quality of the industrial novels is one reason why so much is expected of them by critics. Dickens and Elizabeth Gaskell have been criticised for not providing remedies for the problems they present, and the perfect industrial novel, we are led to believe, is one in which we find both the logical exposition of a social problem and its feasible resolution. When Maria Edgeworth read *Mary Barton* she looked for exactly this kind of ending, and wrote to one of Elizabeth Gaskell's cousins, "*Emigration* is the only resource pointed out at the end of this work, and this only an escape from the evils not a remedy nor any tendency to reparation or improvement."[7] The circus as a counter to the evils of industrial capitalism is questioned by critics of *Hard Times*,[8] but perhaps we should look less to this, or to any novel, for solutions of social problems than to the novel itself as *part* of such problems. In other words, the "unbelievable" endings of the industrial novels, the prevalence in them of coincidence, their dissolution of class animosity into general benevolence, may all be semiological guides to the psychological and social demands made in the consciousness of both their authors and their readers. To castigate Elizabeth Gaskell for an inability to face up to the implications of what she is doing (as Peter Keating does when he says that she relies "on personalized relationships to make her point, and it is in the contrived relationships – in the unbelievable class balance they are meant to symbolize – that the bias is to be found")[9] is to fail to wonder why Elizabeth Gaskell and her readers found a "class balance" so necessary and so satisfying. The point is not that the novel sometimes simplifies complex social problems into unworkable solutions, but rather that it should be examined as an inseparable element, or symptom, of those same problems with which it explicitly sets out to concern itself, as in the case of *Mary Barton*, or as an inseparable component of the society from which it seeks to separate itself and to represent.

In *The French Revolution*, Carlyle has something to say about the separating and ordering act of narrative which I think can be usefully applied to fiction as well as to the business of historiography in which he was engaged. He asks, "Consider it well, the Event, the thing which can be spoken of and recorded, is it not, in all cases, some disruption, some solution of continuity?"[10] To speak of an event, to record it in a narrative, is to isolate and abstract it from a continuity, and, one may add, were man not separate from the event he would not be able to speak of it, nor, obviously, desire to do so. In other words, the narrative act is symptomatic of man's alienation from his experience. In this connection, I would suggest that the industrial novel may be read as an intensified symptom of such alienation for if, as Georg Lukacs suggests in his seminal study of the meanings of epic and novel, "the epic gives form to a totality of life that is rounded from within; the novel seeks, by giving form, to uncover and construct the concealed totality of life,"[11] then the industrial novel deals with a concentrated form of this problematic in its explicit concern with one of man's most immediately felt modern alienations from his experience, namely his alienation from his work. By an initial establishment of the confused relationship between masters and men, and through the replacement of this relationship by a myth of class cooperation, the industrial novel seeks to do something about this alienation, and the concomitant separation of class from class. In its engagement with an intensified and specific form of a felt absence of coherence, the industrial novel seeks to uncover and construct the more abstract concealed totality of life which the novel, as a genre, seeks.

Elizabeth Gaskell addresses herself to this last situation most specifically in *Mary Barton* and *North and South*. She does not enquire into the economic basis of Manchester misery; she observes, records, attempts resolutions which we now find "unbelievable", and hopes for the best. That John Barton, frustrated Chartist and murderer, dies penitent in the arms of the manufacturer father of the man he murdered, is her way of reconciling master and worker, and offering some kind of solution to the problems of alienation of class from class, and of man from his work. These are improbable and melodramatic solutions, to be sure, but she was a novelist and not a political economist, and the ways in which she manages such explosive issues as class hatred and sexual tension reveal crucial aspects of the social function of the novel, as a genre, at large.

Gaskell felt compelled to do something about the estrangements of her culture. She wanted to reconcile the middle and working classes; she wanted to reconcile Manchester with the south of England; and she wanted to reconcile the Christian ethics of her class with the appalling social conditions she saw around her, that is, to somehow draw into balance the religious imperative to love thy neighbour with the creed of commercial individualism.

She tries to do this in almost all her fiction, and most specifically in *North and South*, the most representative novel of her character, and of her particular location in time and in place. As the yoked title suggests, she tries to facilitate an understanding between a geographically and culturally divided England.[12] She illustrates the difficulties of being a Northern manufacturer, as she has previously illustrated the miseries of being a Northern mill-hand. Along with this endeavour, she mythically facilitates an understanding between master and worker, and in the relationship between Margaret Hale and John Thornton, establishes and then resolves a conflict of will between a man and a woman. The resolution of the sexual tension between them is simultaneous with the resolution of industrial strife.

Shortly before Gaskell began the novel she had discussed with Lady Kay-Shuttleworth the difficulties faced by factory masters, for whom she "could not imagine a nobler scope for a thoughtful energetic man, desirous of doing good to his kind", and declared, "I should like some *man*, who had a man's correct knowledge, to write on this subject, and make the poor intelligent work-people understand the infinite anxiety as to right and wrong-doing which I believe that riches bring to many."[13] She undertook the task, feeling perhaps that her woman's knowledge was not the "correct knowledge", and it was a painful experience for her, marked by what she felt were unreasonable demands for the compression and speedy production necessary for its serialisation in *Household Words*, easily managed by its editor, but incompatible with her more leisurely methods of composition.[14] Despite her dissatisfaction with a novel whose production made her dizzy and gave her headaches, she succeeded in suggesting some of the "infinite anxiety" experienced by the wealthy, and I should first like to examine her depiction of the political, moral and social difficulties of a newly-rich family, the Thorntons, and its relationship with a family which is distinctly inferior to them in wealth, but which has the advantage in background, the Hales.

NOTES

1. James Boswell, *Life of Johnson* (Oxford, 1970), p. 704. Asa Briggs notes that between 1775 and 1800 Boulton and Watt turned out 496 engines, and their new foundry, opened in 1795, was the largest and best managed engineering works in the world. See Asa Briggs, *The Making of Modern England 1783–1867* (New York, 1965), pp. 25–6.
2. For works dealing with the fundamental transformation of human life which occurred during the Industrial Revolution I am especially indebted to Asa Briggs, *The Making of Modern England 1783–1867*; E. J. Hobsbawm, *The Pelican Economic History of Britain*, Vol. III, "Industry and Empire" (Middlesex, 1968), and Peter Mathias, *The First Industrial Nation, An Economic History of Britain, 1700–1914* (New York, 1969).
3. *The Letters of Mrs Gaskell*, ed. J. A. V. Chapple and Arthur Pollard (Cambridge, Mass., 1967), letter no. 36. (All further references to Gaskell's letters will be made by number following the cataloguing procedure of Chapple and Pollard.)
4. *Letters*, no. 39a.
5. R. W. Cooke Taylor, *Notes of a Tour in the Manufacturing Districts of Lancashire* (London, 1842, reprinted Frank Cass, 1968), pp. 37–8.
6. W. R. Greg, "Mary Barton", *Essays on Political and Social Science* (London, 1853), Vol. I. She did, of course, receive praise from some quarters. W. S. Landor was sufficiently inspired to address some lines to the author of *Mary Barton*, the most memorable of which is, I think, his greeting to her as "Paraclete of the Bartons". See *Complete Works of Walter Savage Landor*, Vol. XV (London, 1935).
7. *Letters Addressed to Mrs. Gaskell by Celebrated Contemporaries Now in the Possession of the John Rylands Library* (Manchester, 1935), Maria Edgeworth to Mary Howard, 27 December 1848.
8. See Raymond Williams, *Culture and Society* (Harmondsworth, 1961),

pp. 104–8, and George Orwell's well-known essay on Dickens in *A Collection of Essays* (New York, 1954) for a view of Dickens as a quintessentially bourgeois novelist, and a response to Macaulay's categorisation of *Hard Times* as "sullen socialism".

In *The English Novel from Dickens to Lawrence*, Williams makes an astute point about Orwell's criticism of Dickens as a "change-of-heart man" which revises his own criticism in *Culture and Society*. He says about Orwell that "to see a change of heart and a change of institutions as alternatives is already to ratify an alienated society, for neither can be separated, or ever is, from the other; simply one or other can be *ignored*" (p. 49). If I understand Williams correctly, he is saying that Dickens perceived a total condition and advocated a total change; to advocate a change in one's heart *or* in one's institutions is implicitly to accept things as they are because neither can be changed without the other.

9. Peter Keating, *The Working Classes in Victorian Fiction* (London, 1971), p. 228.
10. Thomas Carlyle, *The French Revolution*, (London, 1900) Vol. I, Book II, Ch. I "Astrea Redux".
11. Georg Lukacs, *The Theory of the Novel* (Cambridge, Mass., 1971), translated by Anna Bostock, p. 60. First published in Berlin in 1920.
12. Actually, Dickens suggested the title for the novel's serialisation in *Household Words* from 2 September 1854 to 27 January 1855. She wanted *Margaret Hale* or *Death and Variations*. The latter was not an inappropriate choice for five deaths occur in the novel; however Dickens' insistence prevailed, and perhaps he knew better than she did what she was up to.
13. *Letters*, no. 420.
14. In a short preface to the first two-volume edition published by Chapman and Hall in 1855 she writes that she had tried to remedy the defects caused by the demand "to hurry on events with an improbable rapidity towards the close" by the insertion of various short passages and the addition of several new chapters; the concluding chapter of the twenty-first part published in *Household Words* was expanded to form Chapters 44 to 48.

    For a full discussion of the difficult working relationship between Gaskell and Dickens see A. B. Hopkins, *Elizabeth Gaskell: Her Life and Work* (London, 1952), Ch. VII.

# 2 Masters and Men and Ladies and Gentlemen

In *North and South* Elizabeth Gaskell openly questions the power of men and machinery to which Boswell had accorded enthusiastic acceptance, and in place of Boswell's benign chieftain and happy tribe, she tends toward an imagery of conquest and force of arms. Technologically armed man, in the shape of Thornton, battles with nature in the assertion of industrial power over her raw and crude materials; this battle is extended to the internecine competition of the market place; and war is conducted between masters and workers in the form of strikes and lockouts. And last, but certainly not least, because of its complementary place on all the other battlefields, the relationship between Thornton and Margaret is a sequence of skirmishes on the sexual front; they confront each other in "one continued series of opposition".[1]

An intense struggle is also conducted between the three principal families in the novel, the Hales, the Thorntons, and the Higginses, whose names are suggestive of their respective histories and place in the English class system at the time Gaskell wrote *North and South.* The Hales come from the once hale and hearty English gentry, the contentious and prickly Thorntons spring from the new-rich commercial middle class, and the Higginses, whose graceless and stubborn sounding name belongs with the miserable Wragg's in Matthew Arnold's 1864 dilation on the phrase "Wragg is in custody", are members of that class which Karl Marx describes in an article he wrote for the *New York Daily Tribune* on 10 August 1852, as the "arising enemy of the middle class", just as the aristocracy is "their vanishing opponent".[2] The three families may be said to represent past, present and future in the dynamics of power in English society as it was perceived in mid-century. The dynamic connection between them, their confluence at a particular time and place, comes about as follows.

The Rev. Hale, while back at his country parsonage on the edge of the New Forest, suffers a religious crisis which leads to the removal of the Hale family from the South and from any significant role in modern England. Mr and Mrs Hale die; a son, Frederick, who has been forced into exile because of his participation in a mutiny, settles in Portugal and marries a Roman Catholic. And Margaret marries Thornton. She brings to her marriage the best of the Hale morality, which is essentially composed of a finely developed sense of responsibility towards the needy, and the haughty, snobbish and unforgiving strain in her character is leached out in the trials she undergoes before she finds her home in the North and with Thornton. She experiences a loss of what may be seen as a semblance of a meaningful life in the South, and in her reconciliation to this loss she recognises the substance of her life in the North.

Thornton in turn, and through Margaret, establishes a humane working relationship with his men, of whom Higgins is the principal spokesman, and he thereby appropriates both the genteel past of Margaret and the potentially disruptive future represented by Higgins and his class. That things turn out this way is an instance of how novels often create fables which mediate between a distressing social reality and the desires and fantasies of their authors and readers. Here, the commercial middle class progresses, having annexed a class it hopes to supersede in the balance of power in English society, and having defused the explosive animosity of the working class and appropriated its energy for the mythic amelioration of all.

An examination of what the Hales stand for, their connection with their London relatives, their social values when they come to Milton, is a way of understanding what is rejected and what is retained in *North and South*. The novel opens with a discussion of love and marriage. Edith Shaw, with whom Margaret has lived since childhood in a sort of dependent-cousin relationship, is about to be married and the ladies have retired after a meal composed of "those extra delicacies of the season which are always supposed to be efficacious against immoderate grief at farewell dinners" (Ch. I). The ironical tone suggests that we are in the world of Jane Austen, as does the note that Mrs Shaw's "friends" are people she happens to dine with more frequently than others; however, the resonances of Austen's acerbic prose do not continue beyond Chapter I and Margaret's departure from the house. This is not to be a novel of manners, and Gaskell's abandonment of London society and the ironic mode indicates, on the one hand, that Margaret has no place in the South, and, on the other, that she is not to be treated ironically by Gaskell. And, moreover, she is not an ironic character. She does not belong in the world of Harley Street materialism and neither can she assume a pose of ironic detachment from it. She belongs in Milton where one's energies are almost totally engaged by work in one form or another, and where there is no possibility of their reservation in ironic dissociation.

When Margaret returns to her father's parsonage after her cousin's wedding she is greeted by the alarming news that he feels he can no longer be a Church of England clergyman.[3] Unfortunately for Margaret the resolution her father displays in his decision to give up his living does not extend to his dealings with his wife, and he is unable to break the news of the impending drastic change in their family life. He asks Margaret to do it for him, and absents himself from the house for the day. To be sure, he keeps his religious doubts a secret from his wife partly out of a deep and protective love for her, just as she keeps the secret of her wasting illness from him for the same reason, but the point to be made here is that Margaret is made of different and more resolute stuff than her parents, and in this particular situation she demonstrates a masculine quality one conventionally expects from fathers (at least in Victorian novels), that is to say, the ability to take charge of one's wife and one's household. And it is interesting that at her mother's death she supports her father with a stamina never displayed by the dead woman. In a sense, she is both mother and father to her parents. She is not really like them: "Sometimes people wondered that parents so handsome should have a daughter so far from regularly beautiful." Her irregular beauty, her height, her firm handshake, her straightforward and non-hysterical dealings with the family doctor when she learns of her mother's approaching death, all mark her as having qualities which are not conventionally associated with feminine behaviour (again, at least in Victorian novels). This psychological and physical strength is nicely complemented by the surprising presence in Thornton of what is explicitly spelled out as a maternal instinct. When Margaret's mother dies, his impulse is to console her and to experience that "same kind of strange passionate pleasure which comes stinging through a mother's heart, when her dropping infant nestles close to her, and is dependent upon her for everything" (Ch. XXXIII). Now Elizabeth Gaskell certainly knew all about the "strange passionate pleasure" of motherhood, and she obviously writes out of her own experience when she speaks of this pleasure, but in her descriptions of the feelings which men and women have for each other, she does more than merely translate her experience into fiction: she expands it to give us an unexpected sense of the feminine and masculine inclinations which are common to both sexes.

The fourth member of the Hale family, Frederick, is considered by most commentators on *North and South* to have little function in the novel except to keep the story moving.[4] But it seems to me that he is not a gratuitous character; his presence in the novel has a larger significance than as a technical device to keep things swimming along. He is a social exile by virtue of his immaturity and impetuosity – qualities which render him unfit for life in modern England.

His story is the conventional saga of the mutiny of a brave young officer against his cruel captain. Shortly after Margaret learns the details of this story from her mother, the antagonism between Thornton and his workers erupts into a riot at the mill. The scene of the riot, the implications of Gaskell's language in describing it, and Margaret and Thornton's part in it, demand greater examination than the present context of a discussion of the meaning of Frederick's part in the novel permits, and for the moment I want to jump ahead to a conversation between Margaret and Higgins' daughter Bessy after the explosive events. They are discussing the absence of Bessy's father from the riot and his role as committeeman for the Union in negotiations with Thornton, as well as the incitements to violence of another worker, Boucher. Bessy relates that her father had decreed:

> . . . above all there was to be no going against the law of the land. Folk would go with them if they saw them striving and starving wi' dumb patience; but if there was once any noise o' fighting and struggling – even wi' knobsticks – all was up, as they knew by th' experience of many and many a time before. They would try and get speech o' the knobsticks, and coax 'em, and reason wi' 'em, and m'appen warn 'em off; but whatever came, the Committee charged all members o' th' Union to lie down and die, if need were, without striking a blow; and then they reckoned they were sure o' carrying th' public with them. . . . He'd show the world that th' real leaders o' the strike were not such as Boucher, but steady thoughtful men; good hands, and good citizens, who were friendly to law and judgment, and would uphold order.
>
> (Ch.xxv)

Bessy describes the by now familiar tactics of non-violent resistance. She makes Gaskell's appeal to reason and speech in place of chaos and action, in very much the same way that *North and South* as a whole is a rational argument for cooperation between classes in place of distrust and antagonism. Frederick has disobeyed the law and has committed a violent act by depositing his senior officer in a longboat. He is not a good citizen, as Higgins is, and I think one of Frederick's functions in the novel is to demonstrate Gaskell's belief that to disobey the law is to exile oneself from reason and reconciliation; because Frederick does so, he is permanently exiled from his country and his family.

He lacks discipline, resembles a wilful child more than a rational man, and possesses none of the resilient maturity to live in the North of England. Higgins' strike plan, we feel, is one that should have been adopted by Frederick; even though the strike and the mutiny are not strictly analogous situations, it is better to lie down and die in the collapse of reason than to fail to be "steady", "thoughtful" and "a good citizen". Gaskell's remedy for discontent, whether in a cotton mill or on board ship, is a good long talk, preferably around a tea-table, and even though we can dismiss this as ridiculous and unworkable, we can see that Frederick's actions in the novel have more meaning than merely to creak the plot along.

Another criticism levelled against *North and South*, which is related to plot manipulation, and to the character of Frederick, is the use of coincidence. But Gaskell's use of coincidence is related to her firm sense of the inseparable connection between personality and social circumstance: she arranges two coincidental situations when Frederick returns as a fugitive to Milton to visit his dying mother and Margaret accompanies him to the station on his departure. They stop and talk together, Thornton rides by at this moment, and having been rejected by Margaret and having no knowledge of a fourth member of the Hale family, assumes that they are sweethearts. They hurry to the station, are seen by Leonards, a draper's son who is from the Hales' old village and who drunkenly attempts to apprehend Frederick. Frederick trips him, he falls by the side of the railway and dies as a consequence. Margaret is questioned by the police and denies that she was present at the scene in order to protect her brother, and Thornton, in turn, protects her by instructing the police in his role as magistrate to close the investigation. Leonards is a lower-middle-class malcontent and in apprehending the handsome and privileged son of a genteel family, he asserts a power and control previously denied him by his class position. His coincidental presence in Milton with Frederick suggests the inescapability of two things: that Frederick can never be free of his past and responsibility for his transgressions, and that one class, by the very nature of its existence *as* a class, can never be free of another. What may appear to be gratuitous coincidence is related to one of the central themes of *North and South*, namely, the dynamics of power in the English class structure.

Perhaps the most important thing to be said about novelistic coincidence, apart from its origin in technical necessity, is that it suggests the possibility of discoverable meaning in the world.

Coincidence implies coherence in a society in which people very often left their families to seek work in other parts of the country and were never heard of again; in which apprentices were taken from provincial workhouses and set to work as indentured mill-hands, disappearing forever into the confusion and neglect of teeming cities, and in which social change proceeded at an extraordinary and incomprehensible rate.[5] The Victorian novel, as well as frequently giving us horror stories of social suffering, also creates a world or society of connection and meaning: it shows that people are not finally lost, that children are eventually restored to their parents, even if they are beyond saving in this world, like Smike, and beyond redemption, like Ralph Nickleby. And coincidence turns out for the best in *North and South*. Thornton happens to get into the same railway carriage on a journey from London to Milton as an old friend of the Hale family, Mr Bell, and learns of Margaret's attempts to protect her brother. Coincidence, which has first created a misunderstanding between the lovers, is employed by Gaskell to resolve their difficulties.

When confronted by the necessity of leaving his parish, Mr Hale chooses to go to Milton because there, he says, "I shall find a busy life, if not a happy one, and people and scenes so different that I shall never be reminded of Helstone." He wants to forget the past in the process of being engrossed by the present. The present is to be found in men like Thornton, and the future in how they undertake their responsibilities to those who are powerless to accompany them on their triumphant march of technological progress. Thornton, too, has a past, but it is not one he wishes to forget: he hangs on to it as a reminder of what may happen to a man if he abandons a regimen of self-denial and self-advancement. In one of the innumerable tea-table debates in the novel he responds to Margaret's high-minded criticism of his ethic of competitive individualism with an autobiographical defence:

> Sixteen years ago, my father died under very miserable circumstances. I was taken from school, and had to become a man (as well as I could) in a few days. I had such a mother as few are blest with; a woman of strong power, and firm resolve. We went into a small country town, where living was cheaper than in Milton, and where I got employment in a draper's shop (a capital place, by the way, for obtaining a knowledge of goods). My mother managed so that I put by three out of these fifteen shillings regularly. This made the beginning; this taught me self-denial. . . . Now when I feel that in my own case it is no good luck, or merit, nor talent – but simply the habits of life which taught me to despise indulgence not thoroughly earned – indeed, never to think twice about them – I believe that this suffering, which Miss Hale says is impressed on the countenance of the people of Milton, is but the natural punishment of dishonesty – enjoyed pleasure, at some former period of their lives. I do not look on self-indulgent, sensual people as worthy of my hatred; I simply look upon them with a contempt for their poorness of character. (Ch. x)

Thornton here sounds like a disciple of that legendary Victorian optimist, Samuel Smiles, who wrote that commercial success "is the representative of patient industry and untiring effort, of temptation resisted, and hope rewarded; and rightly used it affords indications of prudence, forethought, and self-denial – the true basis of manly character".[6] Prudence, forethought, and self-denial make the man and the successful manufacturer: to spend is to waste one's reserves of masculine energy, as anyone who has taken a cursory look at that monumental Victorian account book of expenditure, *My Secret Life*, can immediately appreciate.[7]

Smiles's extraordinarily popular creed of self-help was advocated for the working class, and they were told that if they applied themselves and restrained their inclinations to self-indulgence in drink and lassitude they could not only improve their own station in life, but improve the condition of their class as a whole. Temperance and Religious Societies advertised competitions for the best essay offering counsel to the working class as to the best means of their own elevation, and the prize money offered in one 1849 competition, for example, can be usefully compared with the working-class wages of the time. Andrew Ure, in his *Philosophy of Manufacture*, one of the books designed to illuminate the previously shrouded mysteries of industrialised manufacture, gives the highest weekly wage of a Lancashire cotton hand in 1835 as £1 2s 2½d,[8] and allowing for raises over a period of fourteen years and the ideological bent of Ure's work (it is an unwavering celebration of industrial capitalism), it is ironic that a prize offered for suggestions as to the "Improvement of the Social, Intellectual, and Moral Conditions of the Working Classes", namely fifty pounds, equals about three quarters of the annual wage for a member of that class requiring such improvement. The prize-winner of this competition, a Rev. Samuel Green, himself describes an agricultural labourer who earns nine shillings per week and supports eight people therefrom.[9]

The patron of this competition was a temperance advocate, John Cassell, and, as might be expected, the demon drink lies at the root of working class misery. Green advises the poor to be "patient, calm, resolute and frugal", and above all to stay out of the public house. Money spent there should be saved for "it is astonishing what a sum even a common workman can contrive to get together in a few years if he is only frugal – saving, for instance from the tobacconist and the publican". While he was hardly a "common workman", Thornton's rehabilitation of the family name and reconstitution of the family wealth, achieved through diligence and thrift, presents a fine model for the Rev. Green's readers. His subsequent experience, however, seen in the light of this ethic of self-application, presents a paradoxical situation and an example of Gaskell's confusion and ambivalence when she comes to grips with the idea of the self-made man.

Thornton's autobiography makes it clear that he believes he did not succeed because of "good luck", "merit" or "talent", but because he learned "good habits", and that every man, regardless of an initially unpromising economic condition, can become a successful capitalist. Nature, then, is ruled out because Thornton's rise to financial eminence has nothing to do with "talent", and we can assume that his success has everything to do with disciplined self-application. But Thornton's experience in the novel, crucial in a modification of his harsh judgment of others who do not possess the "character" to be as resolute and successful as himself, is to be subject to the historical and economic determinant of a slackened demand for cotton. He is rescued from near ruin by Margaret's money, and not by "good habits".

Thornton's childhood was in fact a good deal more miserable than he indicates. Mr Hale learns from his old college friend, Bell, that Thornton's father "speculated wildly, failed, and then killed himself, because he could not bear the disgrace. All his former friends shrunk from the disclosures that had to be made of his dishonest gambling – wild, hopeless struggles, made with other people's money, to regain his own moderate portion of wealth" (Ch. XI). In the depths of his financial depression Thornton has a chance to gamble in the cotton market; his brother-in-law invites him to speculate, and if the gamble paid off it would put him "high above water-mark", but he refuses because his creditors' money would be at risk. And the psychological risk would be even more terrifying, for if he gambled he would become like his father, something he has spent his entire adult life trying to avoid, and yet, of course, in a paradoxical way also trying to be. He becomes the ideal patriarchal figure which his father never was, strong and loving with his mother, stern with his dizzy sister, and firm ruler of the women in his household.

The quest in Victorian novels for rehabilitation of a disgraced father is familiar, and especially so in Dickens. Steven Marcus points to Nicholas Nickleby's efforts in this regard and to Dickens' compulsion to "rehearse all over again the fable of the child whose life is loyally dedicated to a disastrously improvident father".[10] One might add that this quest is not abandoned at the end of the century. Charles Gould's efforts in Joseph Conrad's *Nostromo* to knit together all the past incoherence and despair of his father's experience in dealing with Costaguana, that imaginary Central American province, constitutes a dominant concern of the novel, and the San Tome mine becomes a concrete manifestation of Gould's obsession with rehabilitation. Thornton, Nicholas Nickleby and Gould undertake an aggressive form of devotion and rehabilitation which is, in a sense, to replace their fathers with themselves, to substitute present success for past failure. It is interesting that their aggressive self-assertion marks them as different from their female counterparts in the person of, say, Florence Dombey or Amy Dorrit, who, through passive and unwavering devotion, hope to rehabilitate fathers who are deficient in responsibility and love. And Margaret's role in Thornton's financial rehabilitation is also passive; she is merely the agent of money inherited from Mr Bell.

Mr Bell was born in Milton but he only visits the town "every four or five years" and when he does, gets lost "among the very piles of warehouses that are built upon my father's orchard". To show how property changes, and changes hands, as Gaskell does in *North and South*, is an effective way of showing how a particular place and particular people change through time and social upheaval. Mr Bell is a sort of closet-capitalist. He lives very comfortably as a fellow in his old Oxford college on the income from his Milton property, which is now the site of cotton mills, and he is, among other things, Thornton's landlord. He leaves his property and the income therefrom to Margaret, and she, in turn, finances Thornton's schemes for a humane manufacturing system, which he has begun in the form of a factory kitchen, buying meat wholesale for nourishing Lancashire hot-pots for his men. She brings Thornton into full and proper ownership of his mill, something for which he now seems fitted because of the double ordeal he has gone through of near financial ruin and rejection by the woman he loves. By having him suffer, Gaskell manages to make it seem that he deserves his restoration to financial eminence because of what he has experienced, and, in so doing, she never has to tackle the complex question of why Thornton should live in infinitely better comfort than his men: that is to say, she never questions the economic structures of industrialised society. This is not meant as a political criticism of the novel, in the sense that one should chide Gaskell for a failure to provide a remedy for economic inequality, but rather to show that novels try to resolve mythically the conflict between moral doctrines which is inherent in a highly developed society. In the society which Gaskell represents in *North and South*, the imperative of competitive individualism competed, as it were, with the imperative to love thy neighbour as thyself. At the end of the novel, Gaskell manages to suggest quite skilfully that Thornton deserves to be a rich capitalist by virtue of his ordeal and chastened attitude towards his workers, and she thereby mythically resolves a tension between competition and benevolence by making him succeed through self-help, fail through historical circumstance, suffer from unrequited passion, and having him restored to financial and psychological wholeness through fortuitous inheritance. She tries to have it all ways, and, finally, of course, she has it no way at all.

Before Thornton can say at the end: "My only wish is to have the opportunity of cultivating some intercourse with the hands beyond the mere 'cash-nexus,'" (Ch. LI) he revises his ideas about his function in a capitalist society. He learns, also from Carlyle, that "Supply and Demand is not the one Law of Nature"; he begins as a merchant-prince and becomes a fit candidate for Carlyle's Captain of Industry. When Margaret declares that she is unable to reconcile his ethic of independence and his refusal to acknowledge the same right of independence for his men, he announces:

> I choose to be the unquestioned and irresponsible master of my hands, during the hours that they labour for me. But those hours past, our relation ceases, and then comes in the same respect for the independence that I myself exact. (Ch. xv)

This fairly moderate assertion of the fiction of mutual independence of master and worker is one of the principal litanies of the gospel which Carlyle attacks in *Past and Present*, that of Mammonism, and Thornton learns to abandon it, and put in its place the creed of a relation with his men which is conducted "face to face, man to man . . . out of the character of master and workman" (Ch. L). This doctrine, of course, is as mythical as the belief in the mutual independence of master and worker, for as long as the economic relationship of employer and employee pertains between Thornton and his men, they can have no intercourse with each other which is not affected by it. And Gaskell's dissolution of one fiction into another indicates how *North and South*, when confronted with the social actuality of class animosity, embroiders the mystification of class relationships which has partially constituted that animosity.

Thornton lives with his mother and sister in a handsome house right next to his mill, and when Margaret first visits the family she wonders "why people who could afford to live in so good a house and keep it in such perfect order, did not prefer a much smaller dwelling in the country, or even some suburb; not in the continual whine and din of the factory" (Ch. xv). According to Alexis de Tocqueville, to walk the streets of Manchester in 1835 was a cacophonous ordeal:

> The footsteps of a *busy* crowd, the crunching wheels of machinery, the shriek of steam from boilers, the regular beat of looms, the heavy rumble of carts, those are the noises from which you can never escape in the sombre half-light of these streets.[11]

The fact that the Thorntons choose to live within such close range of these noises, which surely must have multiplied along with the population by mid-century, suggests a moral and psychological compulsion to do so, for there is certainly no economic pressure upon them. And their choice is even more surprising when seen in the light of contemporary descriptions of middle class homes in Manchester in the mid-1840s.

For example, Friedrich Engels, in describing the layout of Manchester, says that middle-class and working-class districts are quite distinct. The middle class live beyond the belt of working-class poverty where they "enjoy healthy country air and live in luxurious and comfortable dwellings which are linked to the centre of Manchester by omnibuses which run every fifteen or thirty minutes".[12] Mrs Thornton rejects the protective screens established for the sensibilities of the middle class in choosing to expose herself to what Engels calls the "misery and squalor which are part and parcel of their own riches and luxury",[13] and it is interesting that while Gaskell felt that this rejection was appropriate for a woman of Mrs Thornton's character and compulsion, she knew that it would not do for Margaret. While working on the novel she wrote to a friend, "What do you think of a fire burning down Mr Thornton's mills *and house* as a *help* to failure? Then Margaret would rebuild them larger and better and need not go and live there when she's married."[14] We don't exactly know at the end of the novel where Margaret and Thornton will live, but it is a fair assumption that it will not be with his mother. The tension between the two women is never really relaxed: in Mrs Thornton, its roots lie in a *nouveau-riche* resentment of the gentry and in a fiercely protective attitude towards her son when Margaret rejects him; in Margaret they lie in a lingering snobbishness towards people in trade. Gaskell has a fine way of indicating the essential class differences and animosity between these two women and their families in her descriptions of dress and household furnishings.

Margaret's taste is formed by the shabby-genteel elegance of the Helstone parsonage and the comforts of Harley Street, and her lady-like qualities appear in full and refined bloom at a Thornton dinner-party. Even though she is compelled to wear a year-old white silk and some small pieces of coral, her self-possession impresses Thornton when he sees her standing next to his sister Fanny, who goes in for decorating herself in extravagant fashion. Fanny is constantly bored, fidgety and tired, and the object of some pity to her mother, who finds it difficult to admire her because of her shallowness, and yet easy to love her because she is so pathetically unsubstantial. Fanny exhibits the Milton taste for ornament, to which Margaret is exposed when she sees the Thornton drawing room for the first time:

> It seemed as though no one had been in it since the day when the furniture was bagged up with as much care as if the house was to be overwhelmed by lava, and discovered a thousand years hence. The walls were pink and gold; the pattern on the carpet represented bunches of flowers on a light ground, but it was carefully covered up in the centre by a linen drugget, glazed and colourless. . . . The whole room had a painfully spotted, spangled, speckled look about it, which impressed Margaret so unpleasantly that she was hardly conscious of the peculiar cleanliness required to keep everything so white and pure in such an atmosphere, or of the trouble that must be willingly expended to secure the effect of icy, snowy discomfort. Wherever she looked there was evidence of care and labour, but not care and labour to procure ease, to help on habits of tranquil home employment; solely to ornament and then to preserve ornament from dirt or destruction. (Ch. xv)

The museum-like quality of the room is related to the reason Mrs Thornton gives for living so close to the mill, "I am not become so fine as to desire to forget the source of my son's wealth and power." (Ch. xx). She lives in an interminable devotion to the past, and turns her house into a monument where everything is frozen in cold tribute to her son's power to overcome disaster. And even when the covers are removed from the furniture, the room is overwhelming, comfortless, a fully revealed display of acquisition and achievement: "the apartment blazed forth in yellow silk damasks and a brilliantly-flowered carpet. Every corner seemed filled up with ornament, until it became a weariness to the eye, and presented a strange contrast to the bald ugliness of the lookout into the great mill yard . . ." (Ch. xx)[15]

This room is not designed to be lived in; it is to be viewed in a symbiotic relationship to what is to be seen from its windows. The carpet is covered so that it may be preserved for presentation to visitors, and in another of Gaskell's novels, *Cranford*, a carpet is covered for a significantly different reason. Mary Smith recalls preparation for a party:

> We were very busy too, one whole morning, before Miss Jenkyns gave her party, in following her directions, and in cutting out and

> stitching together pieces of newspaper so as to form little paths to every chair set for the expected visitors, lest their shoes might dirty or defile the purity of the carpet. (Ch. II)

Here there is no show, no pretence. The Cranford ladies are painfully aware of the cost of a new carpet and accept the necessity of care and conservation; covering the carpet is a ritual in which they all participate and thereby acknowledge the economic realities of their life. They are able to perform this acknowledgment because they share a common experience of declining wealth and power in English society, whereas Mrs Thornton and her son stand alone as competitive individuals. In other words, Gaskell regards a class which shares a past experience of economic and social superiority as bound together by the present experience of the decline of that power; but she also regards the aggressive individual, seeking to replace that class in the social structure, as being unable to share past or present experience with others, because by the very nature of his aggressiveness he seeks to isolate himself from them, to leave them behind, in his climb to power. Mrs Thornton seems to have no friends, and her taciturnity, her mode of conversation with her son which is always about "facts, not opinions, far less feelings", forms a linguistic analogue to her thrift and self-enclosure. She is reluctant to go into society, and when she does only finds satisfaction in "criticizing other people's dinners". Thornton has virtually no friends, apart from the Hales, and he maintains an uneasy relationship of alternating rivalry and cooperation in the face of a strike with his fellow manufacturers. At the end of the book, his aggressiveness muted both by commercial failure and by love, Thornton makes friends with Higgins and his other employees and joins them for jolly meals in the factory dining-room. He begins the transformation from isolated individual to partner with Margaret in marriage, and partner with his men in the common enterprise of restoring Thornton's Mills to their former profit and glory.

Gaskell also implies that marriage will change the material way in which Thornton lives. His mother's *nouveau-riche* pride in her yellow damask will be replaced by Margaret's taste for homely chintz, and when Thornton first visits the Hale house he is immediately impressed by its difference from his own, and the implications of cultural experience which it reveals:

> Here were no mirrors, not even a scrap of glass to reflect the light,

> and answer the same purpose as water in a landscape; no gilding; a warm, sober breadth of colouring, well relieved by the dear old Helstone chintz-curtains and chair covers. An open davenport stood in the window opposite the door; in the other there was a stand, with a tall white china vase, from which drooped wreaths of English ivy, pale green birch, and copper-coloured beech-leaves. Pretty baskets of work stood about in different places: and books, not cared for on account of their binding solely, lay on one table, as if recently put down .... (Ch. x)

This description, the sort of thing which Elizabeth Gaskell does extremely well in all her novels, sets up an antithesis between display and comfort, the most noteworthy aspects of which are the presence of books and the absence of mirrors in the Hale household. The possession of books is integral to the culture which the Hales inhabit, and they require no mirrors to observe themselves in their own setting. They have lived with their furniture, books and work baskets for years – in effect, with themselves and their position in English society – and they require no reflection of themselves to tell them who they are.

Thornton's mother is immensely proud of him, jealous of him, has sustained him with her thrift and self-denial, and he is her "pride, her property", but his perception of the at once utilitarian and ostentatious qualities of her household, and its unfavourable comparison with that of the Hales, suggests his readiness to leave her. Even before this moment, he has become dissatisfied with the concentrated materialism of his life; his resumption, with Mr Hale as his tutor, of those classical studies that he had abandoned on his climb to the commercial top is one demonstration of this dissatisfaction. And he was obviously not singular in wishing to study classical literature.

The middle-class acquisition of "a smattering of Greek and Latin" is taken by Matthew Arnold as a gross misconception of culture, and in *Culture and Anarchy* he would, without question, place Thornton with the Philistines because of his complacent equation of material wealth with the greatness of England. However, there is one way in which Gaskell points her novel in an Arnoldian direction, and that is in her mitigation of the doctrine of competitive individualism. Arnold in writing about culture says that it admits "the necessity of the movement towards fortune-making and exaggerated industrialism, readily allows that the future may derive benefit from it; but insists at the same time, that the passing generation of industrialists, forming, for the most part, the stout main body of Philistinism, – are sacrificed to it."[16] Thornton's subjection to historical and economic determinants, and the failure of self-help to surmount them, suggest that Gaskell does not entirely believe in the predestined march of industrialism, and we can say that Thornton *is* sacrificed, perhaps not exactly to the idea of culture which Arnold speaks of, but at least to an idea of cultural life which channels his time and energy into other areas besides profit-making. Bell has taunted him with the assertion that Milton men are only concerned with making money as an end in itself, "I wonder when you Milton men intend to live. All your lives seem to be spent in gathering together the materials for life" (Ch. XL). And Thornton learns at the end of *North and South* to do a little more with his capital than merely to reproduce it.

What I am trying to suggest here is that Gaskell's efforts to reconcile competitive individualism with some idea of culture, to find a mediating idea or scheme of things which appropriates and transcends them both, can be considered in the larger context of Victorian social criticism. Her industrial novels can be read as specific critiques of local conditions, but her efforts to transcend the immediate material conditions of industrialised society deserve a larger context, for they are related to the extreme social distress to which her fellow Victorians addressed themselves.

When Gaskell wrote *North and South* England had survived the Chartist movement, had coped with the dangerous unrest stemming from the dreadful hunger among the working-class population of the manufacturing districts during the slumps of the 1830s and 1840s, had escaped revolution in 1848, and had celebrated herself as the workshop of the world in 1851 at the Crystal Palace. Contrary to numerous predictions of anarchy, society had not dissolved. But the working class remained an irritant, a force which required containment, a reservoir of passions which needed to be ordered if the middle class was to retain the power it had gradually acquired in the political life of the nation. The working classes had multiplied at an alarming rate, and when Cooke Taylor undertook his tour in 1842, he was stunned by the density of the population collected in the manufacturing districts, and most especially in Manchester, to which, as Asa Briggs notes, all roads led, for it was "the shock city of the age".[17] Cooke Taylor describes his impressions as follows:

> As a stranger passes through the masses of human beings which have been accumulated round the mills and print-works in this and the neighbouring towns, he cannot contemplate these crowded hives without feelings of anxiety and apprehension almost amounting to dismay. The population, like the system to which it belongs, is NEW: but it is hourly increasing its breadth, and strength. It is an aggregate of masses, our conceptions of which clothe themselves in terms that express something portentous and fearful. We speak not of them indeed as of sudden convulsions, tempestuous seas or furious hurricanes, but as of the slow rising and gradual swelling of an ocean which must, at some future and no distant time, bear all the elements of society afloat upon its bosom, and float them – Heaven knows whither. There are mighty energies slumbering in those masses.[18]

The working classes are "masses", accumulating by the hour at an alarming rate and likened to a tidal wave. He suggests that a sudden convulsion such as a hurricane could be endured, the damage catalogued and the work of restoration begun, but the rising and swelling population is ultimately apocalyptic in its effect.[19] His book, and others which try to cope with the threat posed by the working classes by either depicting them as sensual ruffians unlikely ever to revolt because of their addiction to beer, tobacco and sometimes opium, or by exhorting them directly to emulate their middle-class superiors in habits of thrift and restraint, may all be said to be engaged in defensive manoeuvres. For Cooke Taylor to write about the apocalyptic moment is one way of fending it off; he tries to order those energies which he sees gathering force. And if we accept writing, among other things, as some form of incorporation and containment of social conflicts which are potentially dangerous, then *North and South* may be seen as a novelistic structure of such incorporation and containment. But Elizabeth Gaskell, in wanting to do justice to the commerical middle class, gets herself into very deep waters in her fictional containment of their antagonists.

She is reasonably safe in dealing with the declining gentry and the ascending middle class, but when she gets to the working class, whose potential for destructive activity was inseparable from any consideration of the future, she gets confused, relies less upon observation of manners and more on received myths of working-class behaviour. She ends up, on the one hand, by placating the critics of *Mary Barton* to a satisfactory degree, and, on the other, by creating a new myth of her own of a class purged of its political consciousness.

NOTES

1. Elizabeth Cleghorn Gaskell, *North and South* (Everyman's Library, London, 1968), Ch. VIII. (All further references in the text to Gaskell's works will be to Everyman editions, unless otherwise noted.)
2. Karl Marx, "The Chartists", *Surveys From Exile*, edited and with an Introduction by David Fernbach (New York, 1974).
3. Gaskell's own father had been a Unitarian minister at Failsworth, near Manchester, but he resigned his ministry on conscientious grounds some years before she was born in London in 1810. Gaskell's mother died when she was a thirteen-month-old baby, and she was brought up and mothered by her Aunt Lumb in Knutsford. Her father remarried when she was four, and apart from a visit to his home in Chelsea when he was dying, she had little or no contact with him, her stepmother or her half-brother and sister. She reveals something of the pain of this estrangement in a short memoir written for her friends, William and Mary Howitt, "Long ago I lived in Chelsea occasionally with my father and stepmother, and *very, very* unhappy I used to be; and if it had not been for the beautiful, grand river which was an inexplicable comfort to me . . . I think my child's heart would have broken." (See "Stray Notes from Mrs. Gaskell", *Good Words*, September 1895, XXXVI, pp. 604–12.) The support which Margaret affords her father in his difficulty, his pride in her moral strength and her recognition of his frailty, suggest, perhaps, that Gaskell's creation of this bond between them is a fictional reparation for the deprivation of her father which she felt as a child.
4. Frederick's introduction is seen by Edgar Wright, for example, as "pure plot-spinning". Wright has a highly tendentious view of Gaskell's work and for him *North and South* is but a stopping place on the progressive way to *Wives and Daughters*. He believes that when she reached her last novel, "her writing carried steadily few traces of being written with a sense of obligation towards ideals of moral or public duty"; *North and South* is far too contrived for his liking, and he sees it as "her last full attempt at forcing her creative work to emphasise the sense of duty which was prodded by her religious and social conscience". (See Edgar Wright, *Mrs. Gaskell: The Basis for Reassessment* (Oxford, 1965), pp. 144–6.)

   Gaskell's critics tend to attribute her formal clumsiness to the pressure of her material and her essential distaste for it, or, in contradiction to this explanation, they invent a myth of Gaskell being compelled to write for the pleasure of the act itself and remaining undisturbed by what she represents in her fiction. For example, John McVeagh believes that "the more leisured and less engaged later work comes out of the wish to write rather than the sense of social responsibility or moral outrage". (See *Elizabeth Gaskell* (New York, 1970), p. 6.)

Being a good novelist has nothing to do with social and historical determinants, one is "born" to it, and when another critic of *North and South*, Vineta Colby, says that Gaskell resorts to "stiff lecture-discussion clumsily introduced into her fine and sensitive study of purely human relationships", she implies that "human relationships" can be separated from their context in society, that they can be "pure" in some way, and so implicitly separates the novelist from history. (See *Yesterday's Woman: Domestic Realism in The English Novel* (Princeton, 1974), p. 222.)

5. For two first-hand accounts of the trip from workhouse to factory, and its consequences, see John Fielden, *The Curse of the Factory System* (London, 1836), and *A Memoir of Robert Blincoe, an Orphan Boy: sent from the Workhouse at St. Pancras, London, at seven years of age, to endure the Horrors of a Cotton Mill, through his infancy and youth, with a minute detail of his sufferings, being the first memoir of the kind published*, by John Brown (Manchester, 1832).
6. Samuel Smiles, *Workmen's Earnings, Strikes and Savings* (London, 1862), p. 63.
7. In *Capital*, Marx invents an ironic response on the part of labour to these exhortations to practise self-denial and restraint. In discussing the commodity of labour-power which the workman sells by his daily hire to the capitalist, he creates a monologue for the labourer who sells this commodity on the market:

> To you, therefore, belongs the use of my daily labour-power. But by means of the price that you pay for it each day, I must be able to reproduce it daily, and to sell it again. Apart from natural exhaustion through age, etc., I must be able on the morrow to work with the same normal amount of force, health and freshness as today. You preach to me constantly the gospel of 'saving' and 'abstinence.' Good! I will, like a sensible saving owner, husband my sole wealth, labour-power, and abstain from all foolish waste of it.

Karl Marx, *Capital*, Vol. I, Part III, Ch. X, Sect. I (Moscow, n.d. English edition of 1887, edited by Friedrich Engels).

8. Andrew Ure, *Philosophy of Manufacture* (London, 1835), p. 474.
9. Rev. Samuel Green, *The Working Classes of Great Britain: Their Present Condition, and the Means of Their Improvement and Elevation* (London, 1850), p. 14.
10. Steven Marcus, *Dickens: From Pickwick to Dombey* (London, 1965), p. 128. Financial failure was a very real cause of worry in a time of alternating boom and panic, and Walter Houghton notes that in the mid-nineteenth century "there was no such thing as limited liability, the business magnate and the public investor were haunted by specters of bankruptcy and the debtor's jail". See his chapter on "Anxiety", *The Victorian Frame of Mind 1830–1870* (New Haven, 1957).
11. Alexis de Tocqueville, *Journeys to England and Ireland*, translated by George Lawrence and K. P. Mayer (New Haven, 1958), p. 107.

12. Friedrich Engels, *The Condition of the Working Classes in England*, translated by W. O. Henderson and W. H. Chaloner (California, 1970), p. 55.
13. Ibid.
14. *Letters*, no. 211.
15. In *Elizabeth Gaskell and the English Provincial Novel* (London, 1975), W. H. Craik makes an extraordinary connection between the proximity of Thornton's house to the mill and Bessy Higgins' lung disease. She writes that Gaskell perceives work and personal life as inextricable and that "the noise and business of the mill pervade the Thornton house, as much as the fluff of the carding-room does Bessy Higgins's lungs" (p. 119). The Thornton family obviously have a choice here, whereas Bessy Higgins has no option. The Thorntons *choose* to make work and personal life inextricable; the imposition upon Bessy of this inextricability causes her death.
16. Matthew Arnold, *Poetry and Prose*, edited by John Bryson (Cambridge, Mass., 1953), p. 490.
17. *Victorian Cities* (London, 1963), p. 92.
18. R. W. Cooke Taylor, *Notes*, pp. 4–5.
19. And the working class began, quite early in the century, to become conscious of its reproductive function in the capitalist body of English commercial life. It realised that by restricting its numbers it might increase its wages; for instance, it was advised in 1825 by Richard Carlile to practise a primitive method of birth-control involving a sponge,

    It is a great truth, often told and never denied, that where there are too many working people in any trade or manufacture, they are worse paid than they ought to be paid. . . . How are you to avoid these miseries? The answer is short and plain: the means are easy. Do as other people do, to avoid having more children than they wish to have, and can easily maintain. . . .

    From Richard Carlile's article in *The Republican*, Vol. XI, 7 January to 1 July 1825, pp. 262, 264.

# 3 Men and Women

At a certain point in *Mary Barton* when Elizabeth Gaskell is trying to excuse the use of opium by a class reduced to near starvation by unemployment, and to account for the hatred of one member of that class, John Barton, for its oppressor, she is moved to talk about the fear with which the poor are regarded by those who have never experienced such extreme hopelessness and desperation:

> The actions of the uneducated seem to me typified in those of Frankenstein, that monster of many human qualities, ungifted with a soul, a knowledge of the difference between good and evil.
>
> The people rise up to life; they irritate us, they terrify us, and we become their enemies. Then, in the sorrowful moment of our triumphant power, their eyes gaze on us with a mute reproach. Why have we made them what they are; a powerful monster, yet without the inner means for peace and happiness? (Ch. xv)

Adopting Mary Shelley's myth for her didactic effort,[1] she sees the labouring population as the monstrous progeny of the middle class, grown to full physical power, but deficient in moral education and denied spiritual comfort because of an implicit failure of responsibility on the part of its progenitor. In *North and South* she transforms this monster into a rational human being; she channels its potentially destructive power into a constructive partnership between the working classes and their morally responsible betters. And in a manner which serves to affirm the desirability of the monster's final containment and confinement, she allows it to reappear in a more terrifying form than the reproachful creature of *Mary Barton* before she tames and chastens it forever. In the quasi-riot at Thornton's mill the threat posed to society by working-class dissatisfaction is intensified by what seems to me to be a working-class potential for sexual assault; that is to say, there is a latent meaning to be extracted from Gaskell's manifest description of the events. However, before discussing this episode in some detail and trying to point to some of its implications, it is important to set the scene and to discuss the charged atmosphere of class antagonism which leads to the strike and its culmination in violence.

In the first place, Gaskell was certainly not alone in perceiving that something monstrous had been let loose in English society. For example, from a radically different viewpoint, Marx reverses her structure of engenderment, and rather than seeing the bourgeoisie as giving life to a monstrous creation (the working class), he establishes in *Capital* a recurrent image of the bourgeoisie *taking* life from the working class. Borrowing the vampire myth from folklore and popular fiction, and also from Engels, who describes a body of parasitic middle classes which "first suck the wretched workers dry so that afterwards they can, with consummate hypocrisy, throw a few miserable crumbs of charity at their feet",[2] Marx writes that capital is "dead labour, that vampire-like, only lives by sucking living labour, and lives the more, the more labour it sucks".[3] Marx is dealing in metaphor, and it is a sobering experience to come across a piece of social history which bears close connection to the figurative relation he establishes between the bourgeoisie and labour. In September 1856, Robert Lowery, a Chartist delegate, who after the collapse of that movement became an advocate of temperance as a means of working-class self-improvement, described the privations of a fellow delegate and handloom weaver, one Richard Marsden of Preston. Marsden's wife was literally starving and Lowery writes that as she was "unable to supply nature's nutriment to her sucking babe, the infant had drawn blood from her breasts instead".[4] In Marx's metaphor the bourgeoisie sucks the blood from the labouring classes who have no other function but to produce this sustenance for their oppressors; in Lowery's story the labouring classes, in the last and extreme stages of their exploitation, can *only* literally produce blood. They are disabled from the performance of any other function by virtue of their extremity, and the vampire metaphor is given a bizarre and extended actualisation. The primal symbiotic relationship in human life, that of the nourishing mother and her sucking infant, is broken; this can be seen as a terminal break, for if the working-class mother is debilitated to the point of being unable to nourish her working-class child, there may, in fact, be no more working class. And if there is no more working class there can be no more capitalism, for, as Marx writes elsewhere in *Capital*, "the reproduction of the working class is, and must ever be, a necessary condition to the reproduction of capital".[5]

It is in the context of the dire predictions of the end of society, the monstrous exploitation of Marx and Engels' parasitic bourgeoisie, the constellation of exploitation and misery which cohere in Lowery's anecdote, and her own monstrous working class from *Mary Barton*, that Gaskell creates her mythic resolutions of social distress in *North and South*.

By giving the working class as she imagined it, something to believe in, something to attach itself to, Gaskell attempts to dissolve its alienation and aggression; and the anarchic violence exemplified in John Barton, which can only find its resolution in murder, is replaced by the intelligence and receptiveness to middle-class liberalism of Nicholas Higgins, which finds its resolution in cooperation and reform. Barton is driven to opium and violence because he has nothing left to believe in: his participation in the Chartist march to London of 1848 leaves him disillusioned; the reasonable presentation of grievances is negated by Parliament's rejection of the third Chartist petition; he has no work, and the dead and dying are all around him. He has no faith left in his society.

When we first meet Nicholas Higgins he holds one firm article of faith, and that is faith in the power of unionisation: he believes there is no help for the working man "but by having faith i' the Union". The effectiveness of such belief in *North and South* is ultimately uncertain, and the ambiguity with which unionisation is treated is an indication of the ambivalence which Gaskell maintained towards working-class solidarity, and concomitant isolation from the middle class, as a means of bettering its lot. She does not go to the extreme of inventing a manipulative demagogue like Dickens' Slackbridge in *Hard Times* because she wants to leave the door open for rational social reform. For Gaskell, unionisation is not entirely ruled out as a means of resolving social conflict; she is more conciliatory, as it were, to the idea of institutions, of systems, whereas Dickens, at least in *Hard Times*, is more opposed to any kind of system which imposes a deadening regularity upon the individual, than he is critical of the *way* in which institutions function. But Gaskell is very hedgy on how to manage the union issue. She introduces the possibility of unionisation and then plays it both ways by making the union responsible for both Thornton's moral regeneration and Boucher's death. The strike is a partial cause of the problems which lead to Thornton's financial demise and re-entry as a changed man into the commercial world: the ineptitude of his Irish workers causes him to lose an edge in the market, and thus the employment of scab labour exacerbates his vulnerability in the recession. But the strike is also responsible for Boucher's suicide. Unable to feed his family and ostracised by the union for his violation of the code of peaceful petition and passive resistance, he drowns himself in a dye-stained pond. It is interesting that his death has a meaning similar to that of Stephen Blackpool's in *Hard Times*; both suggest that there can be no escape from a system which is so totally encompassing that it determines the manner of death as well as life. Stephen falls down an abandoned mine shaft on his way back to Coketown; his death is the consequence of an irresponsible system, and it also suggests that he can never be free of that system, as it is fully expressed in Coketown, because he must come back to that dispiriting place even to die: and Boucher is marked by industrialism in death, as he was in life, by the fabric dyes which stain his bloated body.

Thornton's economic suffering, then, which is a condition of his moral development, and Boucher's suicide, both result from unionisation and the strike, and the positive and negative implications of these events work to cancel each other out. Gaskell leaves herself and her readers up in the air. But not for long, because her belief in some kind of ultimate cooperation between masters and men overrides any *need* for unionisation, and at the end of the novel there is no more talk of it. I think the ambiguities of Gaskell's approach to unionisation suggest how novels, and particularly ones which are explicitly engaged in the affirmation of middle-class achievement, can both admit and then despatch problematic social situations through the creation of their own myths. Unionisation is toyed with here; it is introduced as a possible means of reducing social conflict; and it is then treated ambiguously by virtue of Gaskell never really saying – or even suggesting in some indirect mode – whether it is a good thing or a bad thing. *North and South*, as a self-consciously realistic novel, must address itself to unionisation as an inescapable constituent of the social situation with which it is concerned. And because it is a novel it is able to effect such imaginative hedging of the issue as we see manifested in the connection made between Thornton's moral development and Boucher's suicide. In treating the whole issue so ambiguously Gaskell really sets the stage for something else, something which will do away with all ambiguity, and that something else is her myth of class cooperation which puts the whole union issue out of the picture.

The bond which men form through unionisation is not only designed to present a unified front to their employers: it works to gratify an emotional need as much as it tries to satisfy a material one. Higgins complains to Mr Hale that the working class is inculcated with the creed of political economy, but left to its own devices when it comes to matters of salvation in the hereafter:

> If salvation, and life to come, and what not, was true – not in men's words, but in men's hearts' core – dun yo' not think they'd din us wi' it as they do wi' political 'conomy? They're mighty anxious to come round us wi' that piece o'wisdom; but t'other would be a greater convarsion, if it were true. (Ch. XXVIII)

Higgins' complaint is not only that the working man is "dinned" with middle-class propaganda, but that he has no religious belief, no message of "salvation", to sustain and console him in his miserable life on earth.

It is interesting that he finds this emotional satisfaction in a life of meaningful work rather than in any kind of conventionally religious experience. The disappearance of the union and its replacement by class cooperation suggest that the gratification which Higgins once found in working-class solidarity will be replaced by the affectionate respect pertaining between masters and men. And the grand reconciliation at the end of the novel of competitive individualism and Christian ethics, however inconsistent we may find it when we examine Thornton's experience as a failed capitalist, suggests that Higgins' wish to be convinced of "salvation, and life to come, and what not" will also be gratified. His emotional needs which expressed themselves in a wish for religious conversion and which found satisfaction in the union, will be taken care of by his secular conversion to class cooperation and its attendant relationships of affectionate respect. In this sense, *North and South* is remarkable for its emphasis on secular rather than religious gratification of the demand for hope in this world and for help in dealing with fears of the hereafter.

Edgar Wright believes that the absence of religious faith in the lives of those Gaskell saw around her in Manchester was for her a greater impulse to writing novels than the appalling social conditions; he also believes that she takes an existing structure of conflict, that between workers and employers, and uses it to dramatise the effect upon society of the breakdown of religion. He says that her emphasis is on "the need for religion, not for social reform, she sees the latter as one desirable outcome of the former when she begins to write".[6] This seems to me to be a simplification of something quite complex. Gaskell tries to do several things all at once; she wants both social reform and some form of liberal Christianity, and to say that she wants one more than the other fails to take notice of how novels are often over-determined in the multiple fantasies which go into their making. And, one might add, even a cursory reading of *North and South* does not bear out Wright's conclusions. If anything, *North and South* demonstrates that giving up a religious life does not lead to disaster (in fact it ultimately results in social unification), and the need for religious belief which Higgins expresses is gratified in a distinctly non-religious manner. The formal impetus for the events which culminate in Gaskell's dissolution of social conflict is Mr Hale's abandonment of religious for secular instruction. And the one moment of prayer in *North and South* takes place in the Hale sitting room rather than in a church, as "Margaret, the Churchwoman, her father the Dissenter, Higgins, the Infidel" all kneel down together.

*North and South* is considered by most critics to be a vast technical improvement over *Mary Barton* because the crude juxtaposing by a didactic narrator of working-class misery and middle-class ease is replaced by a dominant single consciousness, Margaret Hale's. But Margaret's unifying consciousness does more than filter the impressions of North and South: she is Gaskell's rational and mediating ally and the vehicle of Gaskell's plea to the working class to adopt a course of social reform rather than social destruction. But before she can properly emerge as a figure of social unification she must be educated in the life of the working class. This education begins as she tries to accustom herself to the "open, fearless manner" of the labouring men who do not hesitate to comment on her looks and dress when they pass her on the Milton streets; she soon realises that their "very outspokenness marked their innocence of any intention to hurt her delicacy". Shopping becomes a less taxing experience, and one day she impulsively offers a bunch of wild flowers to a girl she has frequently seen walking with an older man, whom she correctly assumes to be her father. They are Bessy and Nicholas Higgins. Margaret's immediate inclination is to treat them in the same Lady Bountiful fashion in which she had visited the poor cottagers of her father's parish. She has never questioned the benevolent patronage dispensed by her own class to the poor, and she asks for Higgins' name and address with something of this sort in mind. He wants to know why she asks, and her realisation of the impertinence of her question marks the beginning of a change: she realises that even though these people are poor they are not to be patronised, and that the attitudes of her class towards them require revision. And she realises, too, the importance of knowing someone's name in a teeming city; her reconciliation to Milton begins with an awareness that her alienation is reduced by knowing that the bustling crowds are not entirely anonymous to her.

Bessy Higgins is dying of lung disease contracted in the carding-room of a Milton cotton mill. She educates Margaret in the negative (to say the very least) aspects of industrialised cotton manufacture, and this lesson forms a counter-weight to Thornton's celebration of its glories. Bessy describes the insidious fluff which flies off the cotton when it is being carded, causing workers to fall into a "waste, coughing and spitting blood", and Margaret in her innocent and rational fashion, wonders why these debilitating conditions are not remedied. Bessy's response belongs with the horror stories related to Parliamentary Commissioners in their investigations of factory life:

> Some folks have a great wheel at one end o' their carding-rooms to make a draught, and carry off th' dust; but that wheel costs a deal of money – five or six hundred pound, maybe, and brings in no profit: so it's but a few of th' masters as will put 'em up: and I've heard tell o' men who didn't like working in places where there was a wheel, because they said as how it made 'em hungry, as after they'd been long used to swallowing fluff, to go without it, and that their wage ought to be raised if they were to work in such places. (Ch. XIII)

The matter of fact manner in which she imparts the shocking bit of information that men are so underfed (and clearly underpaid) that they depend on the ingestion of fluff suggests that to her there really isn't anything very shocking about it; the quality of life has become so degraded in her world that things like this are taken for granted. And the reader is shocked into a consciousness of such extreme degradation by this disjunction between tone and content: Bessy's casual relation and implicit acceptance of suffering which has become commonplace draws the attention of the reader to the appalling conditions which create such a response.

Her casualness can also be related, of course, to her general passiveness, and, taken overall, she is a tedious and taxing character.

She admires Margaret's manners and clothing to a sycophantic degree and consoles herself with dreams of cities with "golden gates and precious stones". She knows the Book of Revelation by heart, never doubts "all the glory" she is to come to, and consciously desires an end to her life as an end to her earthly sufferings. Gaskell obviously intends her to work in some way as a lesson in humility for Margaret, as an essential part of her education in Northern life, and also as a lesson for the reader. However, Bessy's lachrymose acceptance of her plight makes us wish for, say, the caustic and embittered response to physical pain and class deprivation of Rose Muniment in *The Princess Casamassima*, or for the extraordinary combination of individualism and acceptance of psychological or physical suffering which we find in Dickens' characters such as Miss La Creevy in *Nicholas Nickleby*, Miss Mowcher in *David Copperfield*, or Jenny Wren in *Our Mutual Friend*. But Gaskell was not Henry James or Charles Dickens, and it was not in her imaginative province to create such idiosyncratic and alarming characters. And it may not have been in her historical province either, as Peter Keating suggests in writing about the depiction of working-class characters in Victorian fiction. He presents a cogent reason why characters like Bessy Higgins are rarely interesting beyond providing a focus for the human misery resulting from industrialisation.

Keating divides the representation of working-class characters in Victorian novels into two periods, and draws a distinction between them. The first period came in the 1840s and 1850s when novelists were impelled by social conditions to write about the industrial working classes, and the second in the 1880s and 1890s when they directed their attention to urban slum conditions, primarily in the East End of London. For Keating, the industrial novels tend to focus upon a conflict between capital and labour, to deal with class rather than character because, he suggests, "in real life the industrial labourer was the product of a new kind of environment. No one really comparable with him had existed before, and in writing about him novelists had no literary tradition to draw on."[7] Novelists dealing with urban working-class characters are enabled, because of the absence of a specific conflict between classes and because of the individualism conventionally associated with city life, to create bizarre and sometimes grotesque types. His argument accounts for a good deal of Bessy's pallid passivity in the face of class exploitation.

Bessy Higgins also has no significant part to play in the transformation of relationship between master and worker which is Gaskell's primary concern in *North and South*, and it may be for that reason, too, that Gaskell relegates her to such an unengaged and unengaging role in the novel. It is her father who is destined to represent his class in a reconciliation with its antagonist. It is significant that he is an intelligent and proud representative of that class. His intelligence and his class pride serve to intensify the meaning of his transformation from opponent of the middle class into its respectful adherent. He is a worthy enemy for Thornton in the warfare which exists between their respective classes, and in a consideration of the complex myth of middle-class achievement which the Victorian novel, and *North and South* in particular, is engaged in creating or elaborating, his intelligence, dignity and pride can only strengthen the union of classes which comes about at the end of the novel. What is taken from him in his appropriation by the middle classes can only leave them enriched and him depleted: to have had an unstable and erratic working-class character such as Boucher endorse middle-class values would do little to affirm those values. Higgins' proud defence of unionisation as a way of "withstanding injustice, past, present, or to come", when seen in the light of his later abandonment of the union, indicates that such injustices will no longer be perpetrated and will no longer be possible in the class cooperation faciliated by Gaskell's myth of reconciliation. After the death of Bessy and the responsibility which he undertakes for Boucher's fatherless children, Higgins becomes sober and well-regulated in his manners, he enters "a little more on the way of humility", becomes "quieter and less self-asserting"; he becomes less of a drinker, less of a vivid spokesman for his class, and, implicitly, less of a man. It is true that Thornton also loses something of his conventional masculine identity in his financial humiliation and acceptance of a woman's inheritance as restitution, but Higgins suffers a greater loss of vitality.

Unlike Higgins, Thornton has very little to lose and a great deal to gain from Gaskell's myth of class cooperation. At the beginning of the novel he is preoccupied with his reputation and adamantly opposed to the suggestion that the workers have a say in how a master should dispose of his capital. He has dreamed of universal power by the mere mention of his name. "Far away, in the East and in the West, where his person would never be known, his name was to be regarded, and his wishes to be fulfilled, and his word pass like gold" (Ch. L). His fantasy is a series of multiple screens that will separate him from the actual application of his power, and it constitutes a telling analogue to the barriers which he has erected between himself and his men. In his fantasy he abstracts his commercial power into his name, and the power of that abstraction, in turn, facilitates the implementation of his command, "his word", which will "pass like gold". His fantasy of absolute power which will be operative in all corners of the earth, which will dominate in imperial fashion, finally finds its expression in a self-reification; he will become made of money because his word is to have the power and fluency of that currency. The abandonment of this fantasy is simultaneous with the demolition of the barriers which he has built up between himself and his employees; he learns to think no more about the power of his name in the East and in the West, but to concentrate upon his responsibilities in Milton. However, before this happens he is prepared to fight his men on all fronts, is committed to the policy of lowering cotton prices because he believes this is the only way for English goods to survive in the face of American competition. A lowering of prices signifies a lowering of wages as far as the mill owners are concerned, and, as might be expected, this is untenable for a labouring population already pushed to the limit in rampant inflation. A strike ensues which leads to the violent events at his mill, and it is here that Margaret becomes most fully involved with the North, with Thornton, and with the working class.

Margaret's involvement comes about in the most prosaic fashion; she sets off to borrow an invalid bed from Mrs Thornton for her mother. As she nears the mill she becomes conscious of a strange, portentous atmosphere which is not entirely attributable to the hot and sultry August afternoon:

> ... she was struck with an unusual heaving among the mass of people in the crowded road on which she was entering ... there was a restless, oppressive sense of irritation abroad among the people; a thunderous atmosphere, morally as well as physically, around her. From every narrow lane opening out on Marlborough Street came up a low distant roar ... she looked around and heard the first long far-off roll of the tempest – saw the first slow-surging wave of the dark crowd come, with its threatening crest, tumble over, and retreat, at the far end of the street, which a moment ago seemed so full of repressed noise, but which was now ominously still; all these circumstances forced themselves on Margaret's notice, but did not sink down into her

> preoccupied heart. She did not know what they meant – what was their deep significance; while she did know, did feel the keen sharp pressure of the knife that was soon to stab her through and through by leaving her motherless. (Ch. XXI)

The ominous circumstances are "forced" upon her notice, although they do not "sink down" into her heart, and these verbs foreshadow two kinds of invasion to which Margaret is to be subject. She becomes directly involved in the invasion of the mill by the mob, and some few days afterwards is penetrated by the pain of loss, the death of her mother, which pierces with a "keen sharp pressure". Because of the language which is used to describe it and because of the way in which Gaskell structures the events, the first manifest form of penetration may be seen to carry with it a latent sexual meaning. The political invasion by the working class of the middle-class system of manufacture, exemplified in the mill, may in part be read as the symbolic rape of a middle-class woman by the working class. At the same time, Margaret's manifest experience of her defence of Thornton and attack by the working-class mob acts as an emotional trigger for the release of her latent sexual feelings for Thornton. In this crucial scene, Gaskell symbolically displaces political incursion into sexual violation, and also begins the process of converting the relationship of political opposition between her lovers into one of their conscious recognition of the sexual feelings which they have for each other.

As Margaret enters the house she notices the absence of the engine at work with "beat and pant": this is suspended and replaced by the "deep clamouring and ominous gathering roar" of the crowd. The regularity imposed upon the working class by machinery, making them beat and pant in time with the steam engine, is abandoned and they can resume the clamorous roaring of their previously unregulated existence. The battering ram composed of their bodies makes the gates quiver, and when they hear Thornton's voice they set up a "fierce, unearthly groan", regressing to their monstrous, inhuman condition in *Mary Barton*. And when they see Thornton they begin to yell, a yell which Gaskell describes as so terrible that "to call it not human is nothing – it was as the demoniac desire of some terrible wild beast for the good that is withheld from his ravening" (Ch. XXII). All this furious ramming and animalistic yelling is viewed by the women enclosed in the safety of the house, "fascinated to look upon the scene which terrified them".

They are inside a building which is under threat of violation, and it is significant that Thornton is not among these watchers. The women are passive, mesmerised by the possibility of being overwhelmed by the demonic fury of the workers, while he is active, securing his property and ensuring the safety of the women who are, for the moment, effectively his.

Women are passive watchers in another riot scene in Victorian fiction, and that is in Charlotte Brontë's *Shirley*. There Caroline Helstone and Shirley Keeldar watch as an enraged mob of workers bent on machine breaking attack Robert Moore's woollen mill. The rioters are repelled by soldiers, and the two women try to make out these events from the safety of a hillside. They are not threatened as the women are in *North and South*, but are rather set apart and physically uninvolved. Brontë sets her novel in the Luddite events of 1812, and in some ways it is not really a novel of industrial strife at all; the felt reconciliations are between the two sets of lovers rather than between classes. In fact, Terence Eagleton, in his study of the Brontës, notes that the raid on Robert Moore's mill is "curiously empty – empty because the major protagonist, the working class, is distinguished primarily by its absence".[8] Caroline and Shirley can barely make out what is going on, and all is heard rather than seen; they are extrinsic to the action and are not terrorised directly by the working class because the working class poses no threat to anyone in *Shirley*; Brontë is more concerned with problems of individual loneliness and unrequited passion than with class conflict. *North and South* seeks to show the threat which an uneducated and undisciplined working class presents to middle-class culture, and Gaskell, in choosing to have her women overtly menaced, intensifies the meaning of this threat. Woman as the protectress of middle-class ideals, as the centre of family life, is implicitly under attack, and that she can come so close to the threat of physical violence serves as a dramatic indication of how close Gaskell felt the working class could come to violating the system of which woman was the matrilineal guardian. An intuitive awareness of the latent meaning of this threat is revealed by one of the women, Fanny Thornton, who collapses into hysterical sobbing at the sight to be seen from the windows, and falls into a dead faint at the sound of "the one great straining breath; the creek of wood slowly yielding; the wrench of iron; the mighty fall of the ponderous gates" (Ch. XXII). She mistakes her mother for an intruder when she recovers from her swoon and cries, "I thought you were a man that had got into the house". It is as if her unconscious swooning state facilitates a conscious articulation of the implications of Gaskell's description of the events.

Margaret, as we know from her dealings with her parents, is made of sterner stuff than Fanny; she has some spirit, and some concern for the slaughter which she knows is to be enacted by the soldiers whom Thornton is anxiously awaiting. She perceives no threat to herself, but is anxious for the men and for Thornton, especially when she sees that the former are as "gaunt as wolves, and mad for prey", and are taking off their clogs as preparation for attack. She runs outside into the yard and throws her arms around Thornton, thus making herself into a shield between him and the working class. This physical gesture of imposition between antagonists forms an analogue to her sustained moral imposition between them; she puts her body, as it were, where her morality is. Her gesture is effective, for the sight of a "thread of dark red blood" upon her face when she is hit by a flying pebble wakens the men from "their trance of passion". By having Margaret hit and by having her bleed, and by having the aggressors retreat, Gaskell sustains the sexual implications of the battering ram and the fascinated women, and brings them to something which symbolically suggests defloration. The men are chastened by the sight of Margaret's "pale, upturned face, with closed eyes, still and sad as marble, though the tears welled out of the long entanglement of eyelashes, and dropped down; and heavier, slower plash than even tears, came the drip of blood from her wound" (Ch. XXII). Their passion is exhausted by the sight of a bleeding woman: literally, they are moved to rational action by the image of womanly self-sacrifice; symbolically, they are emptied of their passion by the defloration which is a consequence of their sexual attack. They could very well have been shown the meaning of authority by the arrival of the soldiers, but they are not. Gaskell chooses to have them chastened by the sight of a wounded woman and she thereby shows them to be susceptible to conventional middle-class notions about protection of women (and therefore capable of moral regeneration by proper middle-class leadership), while at the same time she intensifies the political threat of the working class by symbolically suggesting sexual attack.

The involvement of a middle-class woman in a scene of working-class aggression serves, as I have already mentioned, as a warning to the middle classes; if they do not assume a moral responsibility for the class which they have implicitly created, their Frankenstein's monster, it will ultimately destroy a society whose vulnerability to such destruction is demonstrated by the events at Thornton's mill. In line with her melodramatic attempts at class reconciliation in *Mary Barton* and the reconciliation of competitive individualism with Christian ethics in her depiction of Thornton as a self-made man, Gaskell tries in this situation to reconcile working-class dissatisfaction with middle-class celebrations of the essential soundness and stability of English society. She does it by sexualising the explicit expression of working-class resentment in *North and South*, namely the riot.

By showing that working-class political action takes the form of animalistic passion, she converts what is historically determined, the class structure, into something which is a given, a naturally uncivilised working class. The political threat which challenges the foundation of middle-class control is thereby deflected. To depict the working class as beasts, mad for prey and setting up fierce and unearthly groans, denies the historical determination of middle-class culture and suggests its origin in a natural order of things. If the working class is by implication naturally bestial, but capable of rational action by adhering to middle-class values in regard to the sacred position of women, then the middle class by the same implication is naturally civilised, but liable to neglect its proper role as moral leader. The middle class, then, deserves to remain in control of things, provided, of course, that it heeds the warnings of *North and South* and undertakes the moral education of its employees.

In a different form, this conversion of history into nature emerges in Gaskell's depiction of the Boucher family; their Irish blood is posited as the reason for their weakness which expresses itself in the father's suicide and the morbid self-pity of the mother.[9] Margaret remarks to her father that there are "grand makings of a man" in Higgins, but that there is no "granite" in someone like Boucher because of his Irish genes. This is a very neat way of accounting for Boucher's miserable demise and Higgins' eventual success: Boucher commits suicide because he is Irish, and not because he is driven to it out of desperation in the face of the economic realities of his existence.[10] And it is interesting that while in Margaret's eyes Higgins' emergence as a man requires his cooperation with and fidelity to the middle class, an examination of the conditions of this cooperation and fidelity seems to require the relinquishment of much that is manly in his character, namely his vitality and his class pride.

For a woman publicly to throw her arms around a man means only one thing to Thornton and his household – that she loves him – and the next morning he sets off to propose. The recollection of her "clinging defence" of him seems "to thrill him through and through – to melt away every resolution, all power of self-control, as if it were wax before a fire" (Ch. XXIV). He perceives the power of her sexuality as a dissolvant of his resolute identity. He is glowing and trembling with anticipation of a repetition of the scene of yesterday, for the feel of her body against his. She, on the other hand, is wan and guilty "like some prisoner, falsely accused of a crime that she loathed and despised, and from which she was too indignant to justify herself". She is a prisoner of her feelings, at this point, or reluctant to recognise them, while he seems to be liberated by his. She rejects him immediately. She has been the aggressor in the past, challenging his raw assertion of power and his complacent celebrations of Northern life, and her aggressiveness has led her nowhere. Underneath the pride and shame that she advances to herself as the reason for rejection of his proposal, she resents the inference that her morality has meant nothing to him and that it is her physical presence which has jolted his self-satisfaction.

Gaskell is remarkably effective in suggesting the reality and power of sexual attraction. She is often thought of as staid and stuffy, but the episode early in the novel in which Thornton wishes he, and not Mr Hale, had the privilege of using Margaret's fingers as sugar tongs, and in which he is fascinated by a bracelet which keeps tightening around the soft flesh of her arm, is not the creation of a staid and stuffy woman. Margaret may resent Thornton's desire for the acquisition of her body over the adoption of her moral standards, but Gaskell's sexual realism happily contravenes the separation of sexual vitality and moral rectitude into paired heroines like Fanny Price and Mary Crawford in *Mansfield Park* and Amelia Sedley and Becky Sharp in *Vanity Fair*, for example, which one encounters so often in Victorian novels. Margaret is both sexually attractive and morally correct.

Thornton now becomes the aggressor in their relationship, and Margaret is forced not only to examine her feelings for him, but also the attitude of her class to people like him. Her feelings and her attitudes are revised. Her life has been an exercise of control over her feelings, necessitated by her dependent relationship with the Shaw family and by the weakness of her parents. When she first returns to the Helstone parsonage, Gaskell writes that "her keen enjoyment of every sensuous pleasure was balanced finely if not over-balanced, by her conscious pride in being able to do without them at all, if need were" (Ch. II). She is highly conscious of her impulses and she clearly wants to be in charge of them, and in this way she is somewhat like Dorothea Brooke in *Middlemarch*, who enjoys riding "in a pagan sensuous way", but really enjoys more the possibility of renouncing it. Margaret abandons her pride in renunciation, along with her belief that the only people worth bothering about are those "whose occupations have to do with land". She marries an authentic capitalist, in fact the only authentic one in the novel, for Thornton's money is locked up in machinery or floating at risk while this fellow manufacturers have converted their capital into land, and are on the way to becoming *nouveau* landed gentry.

When she is compelled to lie for her brother's protection, it is before Thornton that she feels humiliated, and not before God, which is a further indication of Gaskell's secularisation of social experience. She seeks a secular restoration of her self-respect, a restoration of dignity in Thornton's eyes, and it is interesting that Gaskell weaves together Margaret's guilt for her deceit with her acknowledgment of the possibility of decent and honourable dealings in the commercial world. She has objected to trade in her verbal assaults upon Thornton's values because it too often leads "to the deceit of passing off inferior for superior goods", and it is in this light that she begins to view herself, as if she has passed herself off as superior moral goods when in fact her lie has proved her to be inferior. By a complex process of association, Gaskell arranges it so that Margaret changes her views of commerce because she has lied, and because she is discovered in that lie by Thornton. She asks herself how she can criticise him for deceit when she herself is deceitful, and eventually, in her financial support of him at the end of the novel, endorses commercial dealings which she has previously thought to be unworthy of her approbation.

Gaskell seems to be fudging things here rather, in somewhat the same way as she evades an overt endorsement or condemnation of unionisation, and fails to carry through the implications of Thornton's failure as a self-made man. The deceptions of the commercial world are ratified by the deceptions in which we all, as frail vessels, engage as a means of our own survival, and of protecting our families. Gaskell does not exactly condemn Margaret's lie, for it is a means of her self-education, and she does not exactly condemn commercial deceit either, because of the analogy which is made to the exigencies which impinge upon the individual. For Gaskell, we are all frail and we are all guilty, and the best we can hope for is that we become better persons, as Margaret and Thornton do in their respective educations in the self and in society. The hope of *North and South* is that all our dealings with each other, private and public, will be marked by affectionate understanding rather than by deceitful self-engrossment.

All that is necessary before Margaret can settle in the North, is that she relinquish the South. And after the misunderstandings with Thornton become unbearable she yearns for the placid tranquillity of her old well-ordered life, for the rest and refreshment of Helstone. She sets out with Mr Bell for one last visit, and the visit turns out to be one of discovery and acceptance of change in herself and in her society.

The social change at Helstone is a microcosm of the social change which is taking place everywhere in English life. The ethic of "improvement" is in full gear; "tidy and respectable dwellings" are replacing decayed trees and picturesque, but rickety, cottages, and all the village children now attend the parish school. Mr Hale's former study is now tuned to "action" rather than to "thought"; a window has been built so that the new vicar, a teetotaller, can apprehend any of "the wandering sheep" of his flock who may be tempted to straggle to the beer-house; and his wife, a woman of alarming energy and commitment to new ideas, dispenses "recipes for economical cooking", conducts the village school on utilitarian principles, and is busy converting the parsonage into a suitable home for her seven vigorous children.

In this chapter about past and present, the key word is change:

> There was change everywhere; slight, yet pervading all. Households were changed by absence, or death, or marriage, or the natural mutations brought by days and months and years, which carry us on imperceptibly from childhood to youth, and thence through manhood to age, whence we drop like fruit, fully ripe, into the quiet mother earth. Places were changed – a tree gone here, a bough there, bringing in a long ray of light where no light was before – a road was trimmed and narrowed, and the green straggling pathway by its side enclosed and cultivated. A great improvement it was called; but Margaret sighed over the old picturesqueness, the old gloom, and the grassy wayside of former days. (Ch. XLVI)

Two kinds of change are perceptible at Helstone; the natural changes brought about by time which man must accept as a condition of his mortality, and the changes which he makes in his surroundings in the name of "improvement". Margaret's visit reconciles her to the first kind of change, to the death of her parents which is strongly borne in upon her by the changes in their old home, and the visit also enables her to live with her ambivalence in regard to the second. That night she is overwhelmed by a loss of identity, which I think is a necessary prelude to her final discovery of herself as a woman:

> A sense of change, of individual nothingness, of perplexity and disappointment, overpowered Margaret. Nothing had been the same; and this slight, all-pervading instability, had given her greater pain than if all had been too entirely changed for her to recognize it. (Ch. XLVI)

In the morning the anxiety is replaced by a recognition that she must look outside herself, that if "the world stood still, it would retrograde and become corrupt", and her awareness of her altered mood, of the capacity of the human psyche to adapt itself, to remain flexible, reconciles her to the notion of change itself. She gives up her moral absolutism, accepts the loss of a grassy wayside as a condition of enlightenment, and sees that the "reality" of Helstone, change and all, "is far more beautiful" than she had imagined it. All that remains is her reconciliation with Thornton. The ending is thought to be precipitous, principally because of the way in which Gaskell felt she was "huddled and hurried up", and she tried to slow down the hasty conclusion in the first edition. But she still felt there was something appropriate in the way it ends, and wrote to a friend, "I am not sure if, when the barrier gives way between two such characters as Mr Thornton and Margaret it would not go all smash in a moment."[11]

I think this is what she hoped for if the barrier could somehow give way between the working and middle classes: antagonism and resentment would "go all smash in a moment", and masters and men would learn to work together in affection and respect. However, the fiction of resolution of sexual tension between her lovers seems more plausible than the fiction of resolution of class conflict. Perhaps this is because the industrialised working class did not, at the time Elizabeth Gaskell wrote *North and South*, enjoy the freedom of her heroine. It did not have the privilege of "answering" for its own life, which is one of the resolves which Margaret makes for herself. Maybe for that reason Gaskell's fiction of resolution of sexual tension seems a more acceptable fiction – there is an element of choice, of freedom, in it, a choice unimposed by authority – whereas we sense the authoritative, if benevolent, hand of middle-class novelistic authority at work in Gaskell's resolution of class conflict.

NOTES

1. She makes the common error of confusing the name of Victor Frankenstein with his nameless creation.
2. *The Condition of the Working Class in England*, p. 313.
3. Volume I, Part III, Ch. X, Sect. I. In *Varney the Vampire*, one of the most successful Penny Dreadful serials by James Malcolm Rymer, Varney joins five fellow vampires on Hampstead Heath to resuscitate a corpse and exhorts them in the following fashion, "Brothers . . . you who prey upon human nature by the law of your being, we have work to do tonight." Varney describes the concrete business of the vampire which Engels and Marx adopt and convert into metaphor for political effect. See *The Penny Dreadful*, edited by Peter Haining (London, 1975).
4. Quoted in *Class and Conflict in Nineteenth-Century England*, edited by Patricia Hollis (London, 1973), p. 227.
5. Part VII, Ch. XXIII.
6. *Mrs. Gaskell: The Basis for Reassessment*, pp. 29–30.
7. *The Working Classes in Victorian Fiction*, p. 8.
8. *Myths of Power* (London, 1975), Ch. 3.
9. The Irish seemed to get it from all sides. In *The Condition of the Working Class in England*, Engels writes that the "Irish are less bound by social convention than some of their neighbours and on occasion actually seem to be happy in dirty surroundings". (p. 40)
10. I realise that I have given his suicide another meaning in the context of my discussion of unionisation: the fact that an event can bear several meanings seems to me to indicate the over-determination which is common to such "dreams" as novels.
11. *Letters*, no. 225.

# PART II
# OUR MUTUAL FRIEND

# 4 Society and its Discontents

> ... after all that romancers may say, there is no doing without money.
>
> Jane Austen, *Northanger Abbey*

When Dickens began writing the first numbers of *Our Mutual Friend* at the end of 1863,[1] London was in the throes of two projects designed to cope with the urban problems contingent upon a metropolitan population which was close to three million. The river Thames was being embanked and a new sewer system was being channelled underground.[2] In November 1865, the date of the last number of *Our Mutual Friend* and of its publication in book form, Dickens sent his annual greeting to a correspondent of long standing, M. de Cerjat, and wrote, "... if your honour were in London, you would see a great embankment rising high and dry out of the Thames on the Middlesex shore, from Westminster Bridge to Blackfriars. A really fine work and really getting on. Moreover, a great system of drainage. Another really fine work, and likewise getting on."[3] It seems to me that there is an interesting relation between this really fine work of metropolitan improvement and the really fine work which is *Our Mutual Friend.* The novel is about the river and it is about money accumulated from the collection of dust. Dust-contractors also undertook to empty cesspools, and while one can make a symbolic reading of the novel having to do with excrement and money, I think it is important to remember that old Harmon's money, whose inheritance is the mainspring of Dickens' plot, was partly accumulated by this sort of work. Among other things, Harmon collected real shit because there was, as yet, no "great system of drainage" in London, and he made real money out of this collection.

Besides writing a book about the river and about the inheritance of money made from rubbish collection, Dickens may be said to have undertaken a kind of novelistic embankment and drainage project of his own. In *Our Mutual Friend* he represents a society permeated by dissatisfaction and inhabited by malcontents, some passive and benign and others aggressive and disruptive. At the same time, he transcends his own representation of this dissatisfied society, in which economic situation is an important cause of dissatisfaction, by making an idiosyncratic selection of certain characters for escape from the social situations which determine, to a very large degree, their discontent, and by establishing highly ambiguous conditions for such escape. In the process of representing and transcending social reality, Dickens tries to embank society, to channel it into a fable of regenerated middle-class culture, and, in so doing, to drain it of its pollutants. He is engaged in a fictive improvement of society which, in a sense, parallels the actual work which was going on along the Thames and underneath London at the time he was writing his novel.

The representation and the mythic transcendence of social discontent is, of course, what Elizabeth Gaskell attempts in *North and South*; that novel, in its dissolution of class antagonism into general benevolence, may also be seen as a work of social improvement. But there is a crucial difference between *North and South* and *Our Mutual Friend.* Gaskell describes in a severely antithetical fashion a purely local conflict. Nicholas Higgins laments the cold and mechanical relationship which pertains between masters and men, and Margaret Hale disdains a Northern culture founded upon the profit motive. The conflicts are neatly established and neatly resolved, and we get no sense in reading the novel of a general malaise which infects all of society. One aspect of society, middle-class culture and its discontents, is located firmly in time and in place, and once John Thornton learns to replace the cash nexus with Gaskell's liberal decency, we know that North and South, and middle and working class, will come together.

Dickens' novel, on the other hand, describes a pervasive dissatisfaction on the part of all its characters with the society in which they live, and when we finish it we remain troubled by its representations of the class resentment, hypocrisy, boredom, and general psychological misery which are the signs of this dissatisfaction. *Our Mutual Friend* begins with the words, "In these times of ours, though concerning the exact year there is no need to be precise," and this incipient note of imprecision is related to the ubiquitous unease which is felt by all the characters, and which prevents the gratifying "closure" we experience in finishing *North and South.* Discontent and its dissolution is local in Gaskell's novel. In *Our Mutual Friend* it is as diffuse and inescapable as the river which runs throughout London and the home counties, and which, in one way or another, runs throughout the lives of its characters. Where Gaskell's voice tries to be rational, and tries to order the fragmentation of life in a teeming industrialised city into a coherent vision, Dickens' voice is brooding and mythic, speaks for the collective restlessness of his characters, and eventually appropriates that restlessness for the novel's resolution of it.

In the following pages, I hope to show how he makes this appropriation and how he creates a fable of regenerated bourgeois culture. For the moment, I want briefly to suggest two important ways in which *Our Mutual Friend* both represents and transcends the social reality which is a pervasive determinant of the restlessness and dissatisfaction of its characters.

First, a system of class which limits economic and social ambition is transcended through the marriage of two young women to men of higher economic and social stations. The upward class movement of heroines through marriage has been a feature of the English novel since its beginnings in the eighteenth century, and Samuel Richardson's *Pamela* is, perhaps, the earliest example of the novel's prevailing concern with marriage and with class. The full title of *Pamela* is *Pamela*, or *Virtue Rewarded*, and the novel makes it entirely clear that virtue equals virginity and reward equals marriage. In *Our Mutual Friend*, however, the virtues which lead to marriage, and the marriages which constitute the rewards of virtue, are of a much more complicated and provocative nature. The union of Bella Wilfer and John Harmon nullifies Bella's astute, if sometimes petulant, resentment of an economic situation which restricts her to making do with her life, rather than taking charge of it. The other important marriage in the novel, that of Lizzie Hexam and Eugene Wrayburn, illustrates that love can, indeed, overcome class. *Our Mutual Friend* acknowledges money and class as social determinants, but the consummation of these marriages shows that such determinants may be eluded. The conditions for such an outcome are highly ambiguous.

In the case of the first, Bella's realistic and sustained acknowledgment of the economic character of the world in which she lives seems to be a necessary condition for her elevation to fairy-tale wealth. Her marriage to John is preceded by a constant affirmation of the power of money before that power is mythically undermined: for Bella, the recompense of realism is release from being controlled by what is realised. "Talk to me of poverty and wealth, and there indeed we touch upon realities," she announces to her Pa.[4] Such announcements, and there are many, are dialectically related to her final establishment as mistress of a kind of West End wonderland, replete with tropical birds, water-lilies and a fountain. Although it is true that Bella believes herself to be converted from "mercenary wretch" to blissful "mendicant's bride" (and Dickens may have believed it, too), she remains essentially unchanged until the end of the novel. She is a clever, warm and vital young woman with a firm grasp of social reality. She is the "boofer lady" who responds with sweet kisses to Little Johnny's charms; she is the tender woman who comforts, and is comforted by Lizzie; and she is the canny lower-middle-class girl who cries, "I hate to be poor, and we are degradingly poor, offensively poor, miserably poor, beastly poor." Her aggressive resentment of an economic situation which determines the shabbiness of the Wilfer family affirms the power of money, while at the same time she dramatises a passive compliance which facilitates her mythical release from that situation, and, needless to say, from that family.

The second marriage, which transcends social status even more than it crosses economic boundaries, is strangely exhausted of its instigating passion. After an extraordinary amount of psychological and physical suffering on the part of Lizzie and Eugene, Lizzie becomes nurse rather than sexual partner to her upper-class husband.[5] This muted union is preceded by the constant iteration of the inescapability of social status before social status can be mythically eluded. "Think of me as belonging to another station, and quite cut off from you in honour . . . I am removed from you and your family by being a working girl. . . . If my mind could put you on equal terms with me, you could not be yourself," announces Lizzie to Eugene (IV, vi). Such resolute awareness of the social realities ultimately leads to their marriage. That is to say, Lizzie's flight from Eugene is motivated by a realistic recognition of the disastrous consequences which would ensue for both of them from a marriage so clearly in violation of the standards imposed by Eugene's upper-middle-class culture. His pursuit of her triggers Bradley Headstone's last desperate attempt to *deny* reality; he refuses, or is unable, to recognise that Lizzie will not have him, and so the marriage performed by Eugene's sickbed paradoxically may be said to have come about, through a complex process of cause and effect, because Lizzie has insisted upon the impossibility of such an event. Like Bella, Lizzie affirms in her words and in her actions a powerful determinant of social situation, and her affirmation leads to its ambiguous transcendence.

A second way in which *Our Mutual Friend* creates a fable of regenerated middle-class culture may be seen in the exclusion of certain characters from the new social order which comes into being at the end of the novel. These characters have no place in the sunny world of sparkling money presided over by John and Bella, and Mr and Mrs Boffin. The reasons for their exclusion, which I think vary according to social status, are as problematic as the conditions which are set for the two important marriages in the book. The bourgeois characters who are excluded merely fade out from the novel in disrepute (the Veneerings and the Lammles, for example, take up residence in France): the working-class and lower-middle-class characters who are excluded make violent exits in the form of death or humiliating defeat, or they become more deeply fixed in their isolation from family and society. The experiences of Bradley Headstone, Silas Wegg, and Mrs Wilfer are especially pertinent in this regard.

For instance, the self-denial which has been required for Bradley's escape from working-class ignorance exacts its final terrible price in attempted murder, successful murder, and suicide. "Suppression of so much to make room for so much" makes him a constrained bundle of class resentment and sexual jealousy. He refuses, in a sense, to make the acknowledgment of reality which seems to facilitate the escape of Bella and Lizzie from the confinements of their social situations. To be sure, his defeat has something to do with Dickens' criticism of an educational system which he thought was weighted in favour of the rote acquisition of useless information, and deficient in moral development. Bradley has "acquired mechanically a great store of teacher's knowledge", and has arranged his "wholesale warehouse that it might be always ready to meet the demands of wholesale dealers" (II, i). He is a product of the commercial world, described in the language of commerce and money, which is the language of the novel.

Bradley tries too hard, as it were, to effect his escape. It seems to me that the manner and the consequences of Bradley's struggle constitute one of the novel's most important mediations between the representation and the desire for transformation of distressing social reality. Bradley's resentment of class confirms the existence of a powerful class system. But the destructive consequence of his aggressive class feeling, when compared with the outcome of the essentially passive acceptance of social reality exemplified in Bella and Lizzie, seems to show that the individual who undertakes an active expression of his social discontent can only fail. Such failure is an example of how *Our Mutual Friend* tries to resolve society's unease with itself, how it tries to resolve the problem presented to society by, on the one hand, the imperative to advance oneself, and, on the other, the implicitly disturbing consequences if all and sundry undertake such self-advancement. The mid-Victorian creed of competitive individualism, carried to its fullest expression, carries with it the threat of disruption of established social structures. Bradley's excessive and ultimately destructive consciousness of class, his attempt, in fact, to escape his class, illustrate such dangers. The failure of his aggressive struggle may, perhaps, be seen as a palliative for the anxiety about competition which existed in a society committed to the ethos of self-improvement.[6]

Silas Wegg's desire to escape his marginal existence as ballad-monger and keeper of a fruit stall, is another example of struggle which leads to failure. His life is so destitute of human relations that he invents an attachment for himself to the imagined inhabitants of the house in front of which he sets his stall. If one considers the aridity of his existence (he is pitched on an easterly corner, and "the stall, the stock, and the keeper, were all as dry as the Desert"), it is not difficult to understand his latching on to Boffin as that strange figure comes trotting down the street and into Wegg's life. Boffin represents escape from Wegg's rootlessness, a cosy home in the Bower, a way to use his street cunning and linguistic skills to advantage. However, to be aggressive, to try to escape one's place, even if that place is on a dry and dusty corner, doesn't work in *Our Mutual Friend*. It seems that one must remain passive in order to be released from debilitating social reality and remain firmly in touch with that reality in order to be taken into the fabulous world of shiny, rehabilitated money.

Wegg becomes an aggressive concocter of plots to put Boffin's nose to the grindstone, and takes off into a fantasy world where he has been "passed over" in his rights to Boffin's inheritance. I realise that there are characters in the novel, Riah and the Rev. Frank Milvey for example, whose passivity does not necessarily accord with my description of the relation of passivity to release from a miserable existence. I also realise that the aggressive nature of John Harmon and Boffin's plot to test Bella does not exclude them from the novel's resolution of discontent into the "golden" circle of domesticity (they are, in fact, the principal originators and constitutents of that circle). However, I think that the complex nature of passivity and aggression in *Our Mutual Friend* is related to the novel's ambiguous resolutions of social discontent, and in the pages to follow I hope to elucidate some of this complexity.

Mrs Wilfer, the "tall, angular, stately wife" of R. W., does not fail in the same fashion as Headstone and Wegg, for the area of her operations is much different. It is the family, and it is there that she asserts herself and manipulates those around her as consolation for her miseries. She is a highly interesting case of social paranoia born of class resentment. She is so mindful of the slights she feels she is accorded by her social comedown in marriage to R. W., so conscious of her disregard of her Papa's admonition that "a family of whales should not ally themselves with sprats", that she retreats into majestic and frozen splendour, sitting in corners and enacting a one-woman tragedy of self-sacrifice. By tyrannising her family, she tries to exercise the power she imagines she would have enjoyed had she married above, rather than below her. She has no friends, she merely presents herself to her neighbours when she can impress them with her imagined social superiority, and at the end of the novel, despite and because of her daughter's miraculous transformation from "mendicant's bride" to Portman Place princess, she is even more isolated than she was at the beginning. Her resentment of class has been deflected into resentment of her family, and she is eventually exiled from that family. A special place will always be kept for Pa in Bella's home, but we can be sure that Mrs Wilfer will continue to project her gloomy majesty into the confines of Holloway, rather than into the spaciousness of the Harmon mansion. She is, of course, a superbly comic character (as is Wegg), and it is interesting that the source of her comic presence, the ludicrous disjunction between her social pretensions and her social situation is, in fact, what undoes her. Through her comic presence, Dickens shows that an exaggerated consciousness of class leads to a kind of malevolent dottiness: her inflexibility does not make her a candidate for transcendence of the class system of which she is so fiercely and unforgivingly aware.

Dickens begins his work of improvement by describing two different social worlds. The first chapter of the novel is about the ancient river, the East End, and the working class. The second is about new money, a "bran-new" quarter of the West End, and the middle class. The rest of the novel is, in great part, about the connections between these two worlds, and its two great themes, money and literacy, constitute a unifying thread which runs throughout, and between them. The struggles of the characters to escape the social situations which seem to determine their discontent and dissatisfaction are enacted, on multiple and various levels, within the framework of these themes and within the two mythical kingdoms into which London is transformed, that of the river and that of the dust-heaps.

In saying that Dickens sets up two worlds and then arranges his novel around the direct and indirect connections between them, I do not mean to say that *Our Mutual Friend* is formally based upon a neat and antithetical movement between these two worlds. The novel moves in a quite different way; it covers a highly circuitous and meandering route before it arrives at its mythical terminus. After Dickens has established these two worlds, he creates a fluid and amorphous mingling of them. I think that the initial dichotomy exists in order to demonstrate the depth and diffusion of the discontent which *Our Mutual Friend* describes. Dickens seems to set up two separate societies so that he may show their indissoluble connection. These connections are immediately apparent in the second chapter when Mortimer Lightwood recounts the story of the "Man from Somewhere", and then receives word of the retrieval by Hexam of what is thought to be this man's body from the river. Discontent reaches from Limehouse Hole to St James's, from St Mary Axe to Smith Square; it is present in the lives of all the characters in the novel, and each of the two worlds which Dickens sets up in Chapters i and ii is constantly made aware of what is happening in the other. It is as if Dickens means to show, consciously or unconsciously, that a system of class means that one class, by the nature of its very existence, must always be conscious of the other.

When I talk about one world I will inevitably talk about the other, for when one talks about the working class I think one is compelled to do so in terms of its relation to the middle class. And, needless to say, in talking about the middle class, one is compelled to do so in terms of its relation to those people who do its washing, collect its rubbish, work in its offices, make dresses for its children's dolls, and try to earn a living by scouring the river for its flotsam and jetsam. *Our Mutual Friend* is a fiction of resolution of social discontent which is determined and pervaded by different class experiences coexisting in a constantly reverberating relationship.

NOTES

1. He was very pleased with his efforts, and wrote to Wilkie Collins, "Of the new book, I have done the two first numbers, and am now beginning the third. It is a combination of drollery with romance which requires great deal of pains and a perfect throwing away of points that might be amplified; but I hope it is *very good*. I confess, in short, that I think it is." *The Letters of Charles Dickens*, edited by Walter Dexter (London, 1938), 1864, Vol. III, p. 378.
2. For a detailed discussion of these improvements, and a general picture of how London appeared in the 1860s, see Priscilla Metcalf, *Victorian London* (London, 1972), Ch. 4.
3. *Letters*, Vol. III, p. 445.
4. Charles Dickens, *Our Mutual Friend* (Oxford Illustrated Edition: Oxford, 1952), Book II, Ch. viii. (All further references in the text to Dickens' works will be to the Oxford Illustrated Edition, unless otherwise noted, and will take the form of the book number followed by the chapter number.) Bella's intuitive apprehension of the workings of her society affirms Karl Marx's well-known and much-discussed theory of the base and superstructure, which he outlined some six years before *Our Mutual Friend* made its first monthly appearance:

   > In the social production of their life, men enter into definite relations that are indispensable and independent of their will, relations of production which correspond to a definite stage of development of their material productive forces. The sum total of these relations of production constitutes the economic structure of society, the real foundation, on which rises a legal and political superstructure, and to which correspond definite forms of social consciousness. The mode of production of material life conditions the social, political and intellectual life process in general. It is not the consciousness of men that determines their being, but, on the contrary, their social being that determines their consciousness.
   > (Preface to *A Contribution to the Critique of Political Economy*, Selected Works, Karl Marx and Frederick Engels (Moscow, 1968), p. 182.)

   *Our Mutual Friend*, with different metaphors and with different intentions, that is to say, with everything that marks it as a novel and not as a work of political economy, represents a society whose economic structure is indeed its "real foundation", a society in which the legal and political superstructure is built upon this foundation, and a society in which social consciousness bears a correspondence to the superstructure.
5. Edmund Wilson suggests that the "final implication" of the novel is "that the declassed representatives of the old professional upper classes may

unite with the proletariat against the commercial class". "Dickens: The Two Scrooges", *The Wound and the Bow* (New York, 1947), p. 81. It would seem, however, that Lizzie and Eugene are so physically and psychologically depleted by their experience, that the only thing which does unite them is a shared experience of suffering. Eugene certainly vows to Mortimer that he will confront society rather than take his wife off to the colonies, but there has been such a depletion of energy for the marriage to come about at all, that it hardly seems likely they embody a force strong enough to confront the new Veneerings and Podsnaps who will come along.

6. It is ironic that he implements some advice which Dickens offered to the working man just before the first number of *Our Mutual Friend* appeared. In giving instructions for an article which was to appear in *All The Year Round* on working men's clubs, Dickens writes in an office memorandum that it should "impress upon the working man that they must originate and manage for themselves". *The Letters of Charles Dickens*, edited by Walter Dexter (London, 1938), 2 March 1864, Vol. III, p. 381. Bradley does just this. He hides his "pauper lad" origins, and undertakes his own management.

# 5 The River

In Chapter iii of Book III of *Our Mutual Friend*, the "dank carcase" of Rogue Riderhood lies wet and insensible in Miss Abbey Potterson's first-floor bedroom: it is a scene of rebirth into social existence that powerfully suggests the novel's dominant theme of social discontent. Riderhood has been run down by a steamer, and at this point in the novel it is only as a sodden mass of half-dead humanity that he can have access to the warmth and order of the Six Jolly Fellowship Porters. Miss Abbey, that regal disciplinarian of Limehouse Hole, has forbidden him the house – he is an outcast, eccentric to the novel's various circles of social organisation, and while delivering self-righteous litanies in celebration of his honesty, he slinks through *Our Mutual Friend* in a fog of blackmail and intimidation.[1] But as he struggles between life and death his despicable history is forgotten by the crowd clustered around his body, and Dickens' use of the present tense intensifies the immediacy of a situation in which Riderhood has no past, and possibly no future:

> He is struggling to come back. Now he is almost here, now he is far away again. Now he is struggling harder to get back. And yet – like us all, when we swoon – like us all, every day of our lives when we wake – he is instinctively unwilling to be restored to the consciousness of this existence, and would be left dormant if he could.

The meaning which Dickens gives to Riderhood's oscillation between life and death may be expanded to suggest the struggle of all the characters in the novel. Their restlessness and indecision are synonymous in their social implications with the psychological ambivalence which Dickens attributes to the nearly dead Riderhood; what is implicit and diffuse throughout the novel becomes explicit and concentrated in Riderhood's struggle. It is as if the scene in Miss Abbey's is an epitome of what it means to be alive in the world of *Our Mutual Friend*, what it means to wrestle with discontent and dissatisfaction – as if, at this one moment, Dickens' dark apprehension of the nature of human existence suddenly surfaces from the flow of events.

Riderhood's restoration to life after his immersion in the Thames also constitutes a negative form of mythical rebirth into society (in the experiences of John Harmon and Eugene Wrayburn mythical rebirth takes a positive, if problematic, form). Riderhood is not only returned to life in "an uncommonly sulky state"; he also appropriates his experience for yet another attempt at extortion. He declares that he "ain't a-going to be drownded and not paid for it", and rather than being reborn into life and society with a new moral being, he emerges from the water as an even more mendacious rogue than he was before he fell in. The next time he goes into the river he does not come out, and in the context of Dickens' work of bourgeois improvement in *Our Mutual Friend* which, I have suggested, is a kind of fictive parallel to the work of metropolitan improvement going on in London at the time of the novel's monthly appearances, the manner of Rogue Riderhood's death is grimly appropriate. When he and Bradley Headstone are found locked together in their deathly embrace, they are lying in the ooze and scum at the bottom of the river. This time there is no mythical rebirth for Riderhood; he is sucked down into the primeval ooze and scum where he metaphorically belongs, and Dickens expunges his poisonous and infectious presence from the novel.

Miss Abbey's is also the disciplined centre of working-class society in the river world. Gaffer Hexam has been exiled from this centre along with his "ex-pardner", Riderhood, and he is also exiled rather quickly from the novel. His life in *Our Mutual Friend* is short and not too sweet, partly because he is anomalous in the society which the novel describes, and partly because he implicitly represents what is left behind in his daughter's move away from the river world into literacy and finally into marriage with an upper-middle-class barrister.

While Hexam demonstrates a full awareness of his burdensome existence, he never expresses a desire to change it. He lives in a kind of stoical stasis; he has "no fancies" of self-improvement, and he considers himself "scholar enough" to know who is described in the grisly handbills that function as wallpaper for the Hexam shack. Hexam is a misfit in a novel about social dissatisfaction. He is not exactly a jolly paterfamilias, but he is very tender with his daughter and content with the meagre comforts afforded by his sinister trade. He has his moral priorities straightened out (one does not rob a live man), and, a body in tow, he is quite satisfied to sit back, light a pipe, and contemplate an evening at the Fellowships.

Hexam is a "half-savage creature", his whole body begrimed with the mud which in his son's social consciousness represents the working-class mire from which one escapes as soon as one is able. Hexam's occupation is initially unspecified, and when Dickens details his actions in the first chapter of the novel in a series of negatives, it is as if the reader must interpret the meaning of Hexam's movements as he interprets the movements of the tide. He is not a fisherman, not a waterman, not a lighterman, and not a river-carrier. His business is not nameable, it is carried on at the very lowest level of waterside life, and it takes place amid the primeval slime and ooze with which his boat is covered, and to which Rogue Riderhood is returned at the end of his nefarious career. Hexam is a vulture who survives by picking over the sodden carrion of society, and his marginal and predatory occupation is a fit expression of a system in which everything may be turned to profit.

His restless son, Charley, is deeply resentful of the river life: he wants to dissociate himself from his father and from the East End. And he wants his sister to marry the man whom he has taken as a surrogate father and a model for his aspirations: his own father's distrust of education and dour resignation have been replaced in Charley by Bradley Headstone's aggressive social self-advancement. Charley wants, in a sense, to create a new family unit in which the sister who has replaced his mother will become the wife of the man he has taken as a father-figure. He urges Bradley's suit upon Lizzie, and her refusal is a blow to his fantasies of recreation of self and of family. He tries to persuade her of the social advantages in marrying Headstone; she will achieve "a most respectable station", "a far better place in society"; she will "at length be quit of the river side". But Lizzie, apart from her intuitive and immediate distrust of Headstone, knows that she will never be rid of the river (her "old bold life and habit" inspire her to row "as never other woman rowed on English water" and to rescue Eugene); in her own uneducated fashion, she knows that one can never entirely escape one's history, and she is impervious to her brother's arguments.

Charley Hexam is a minor character in the novel, but the problematic outcome of his struggle to escape the East End is of major importance in Dickens' resolutions of class resentment. He is obviously an intelligent boy; his father's harshness has, to some degree, been alleviated by his sister's tender affection; yet we have to ask ourselves why he is so nasty, why Dickens insists that Charley Hexam remain confined by his sterile obsession with self and respectability – in essence, confined by his class feeling. I think the answer lies in the fact that in the world of *Our Mutual Friend*, nobody can escape from its confining structures without a transcendence of those structures being effected for them by forces they in no way control. In other words, escape from social misery is fabulously effected by the naked, authoritarian hand of the novelist rather than achieved by the individual character in ways we find convincing in terms of a plausible relationship to all that has preceded that escape. Aggressive characters who attempt to engineer their own social advancement get nowhere in *Our Mutual Friend*, and the characters who escape the confinements of social class and poverty are released by virtue of Dickens' mythical transcendence of those confinements. By determining that Charley Hexam shall remain obsessed by his debilitating class resentment, and by determining that Lizzie Hexam shall transcend her social class, and by making Charley's unexplained aggressiveness and Lizzie's unexplained passivity the conditions for this outcome, Dickens may be said to do two things.

In the first place, the failure of Charley Hexam's egregious self-advancement, which he undertakes in the culturally licensed spirit of competitive individualism, may be seen as a balm for the fears, conscious or unconscious, present in a society committed to this spirit: unfettered expression of the ethos of competitive individualism carries with it an implicit threat of social disruption. Lizzie Hexam presents no threat to established social structures, and it seems as if she is allowed by Dickens to escape the East End and marry her social superior *because* she does not undertake the pushy course adopted by her brother. To be sure, Charley Hexam does not fail in the dramatic and absolute way that Bradley Headstone does; but at the end of the novel, even though Charley may be on the road to getting his own school, he has lost the love of his sister and he is exiled from the warm circle of bourgeois domesticity of which Lizzie is a member in perfect standing.

In the second place, by the naked exercise of his powers as omnipotent novelist, by arbitrarily determining that Charley Hexam shall remain a small-minded, class-ridden bundle of resentment, Dickens may be said to possess a power which is similar to the determinative powers of the society that he describes in *Our Mutual Friend.* The power enjoyed by all novelists to decide the social being of their characters is emphatically employed by Dickens to create *and* to mythically transcend an ensemble of economic and social processes that decides the lives of the particular characters in his last completed novel.

Charley's sister is remarkably untouched by her environment. She has none of her brother's fierce determination to escape Limehouse, partly because she is tied to her father, and partly because she is graced by Dickens with a magical immunity from the taint of East End experience as a prelude to her release from the dismal conditions that torment her brother. She exhibits a plausible and realistic awareness of the almost insurmountable obstacles to a marriage which violates bourgeois priorities, but she is also a highly implausible character in the context of Dickens' other representations of East End life and character in *Our Mutual Friend*, most particularly in the person and experience of Pleasant Riderhood.

Pleasant has a "swivel eye", she looks "anxious, meagre, of a muddy complexion", and "as old again as she really was". The only marks which Lizzie bears of her work upon the river are her ruddy complexion, which serves to enhance rather than to diminish her attractions, and her rough hands. She has no swivel eye, no meagre look, and she has clearly remained immune from the hazards of a working-class diet. She also seems to possess none of the working-class social consciousness which Dickens ascribes to Pleasant. In a wonderfully rich and ironic passage, he describes how the principal rituals of human existence appear to Rogue's daughter:

> . . . observe how many things were to be considered according to her own unfortunate experience. Show Pleasant Riderhood a Wedding in the street, and she only saw two people taking out a regular license to quarrel and fight. Show her a Christening, and she saw a little heathen personage having a quite superfluous name bestowed upon it, inasmuch as it would be commonly addressed by some abusive epithet; which little personage was not in the least wanted by anybody, and would be shoved and banged out of everybody's way, until it should grow big enough to shove and bang. Show her a Funeral, and she saw an unremunerative ceremony in the nature of a black masquerade, conferring a temporary gentility on the performers, at an immense expense, and representing the only formal party ever given by the deceased. Show her a live father, and she saw but a duplicate of her own father, who from her infancy had been taken with fits and starts of discharging his duty to her, which duty was always incorporated in

> the form of a fist or a leathern strap, and being discharged hurt her. All things considered, therefore, Pleasant Riderhood was not so very, very bad. (II, xii)

This is a fine, if depressing, apprehension of what it means to grow up in the dark and deep recesses of Limehouse Hole, and I have quoted it at length because it demonstrates an ample awareness of how Pleasant's social consciousness is determined "according to her own unfortunate experience". Lizzie Hexam has surely been exposed to these same events -- she has been "shown" a Wedding, a Christening and a Funeral – yet Dickens never considers Lizzie according to *her* own "unfortunate experience". We can say that Gaffer is never the despicable rogue that Rogue is, and that he had never lifted a finger against his daughter, but it is hardly feasible to isolate that one fact in a working-class life which bears a close resemblance to Pleasant's, and to use it to account for Lizzie's refined sensibility, handsome good looks, and genteel speech.[2]

Besides bearing no significant stigma of the dismal effects of East End life, Lizzie Hexam possesses absolutely no sexual vitality. I think that her lack of the sexual energy with which, say, Bella Wilfer is so plumply endowed and which serves to bring new life to the desiccated Harmon family tree, is integral to Dickens' myth of marriage that contravenes social convention. Dickens creates a fable of attraction between an upper-middle-class man and a working-class woman which is founded less upon the flesh than upon the spirit. Eugene certainly finds Lizzie attractive, but Dickens takes care to show that her appeal for him lies initially in the character she displays in loneliness and adversity, rather than in her physical presence. And she runs away from London not so much because of *her* attraction to Eugene, but because of Bradley Headstone's threats to harm him. Her moral superiority, and accompanying implicit fitness for social elevation through marriage, is demonstrated by this selfless concern. Furthermore, Lizzie is not subject to the temptations attendant upon female loneliness and poverty. In the joyless exigencies of survival in London in the 1860s, a working-class girl like Lizzie, with no parents, few friends and a pitiful amount of money could have been had for a few sweet words, or, failing that, a few useful shillings.[3]

*Our Mutual Friend* also skims over the difficulties which a girl of Lizzie's class and capabilities might have encountered in obtaining employment: she makes a smooth transition from Limehouse to her job as seamstress, and she is exposed to none of the hazards in being female and unskilled in London in the 1860s. In this connection it is illuminating to look at a passage from Arthur J. Munby's diaries written in July 1864 (the month of the third number of *Our Mutual Friend*). Munby records a stroll through St James's Park:

> *Friday, 15 July* . . . walking through S. James's Park about 4 p.m., I found the open spaces of sward on either side the path thickly dotted over with strange dark objects. They were human beings; ragged men & ragged women; lying prone and motionless, not as those who lie down for rest and enjoyment, but as creatures worn out and listless. A park keeper came up: who are these? I asked. They are men out of work, said he, and unfortunate girls; servant girls, many of them, what has been out of place and took to the streets, till they've sunk so low that they cant get a living even by prostitution. . . .
>
> *Wednesday, 30 July* . . . back across S. James's Park; and I counted 79 of these forlorn prostrate outcasts, in half the space I observed last week. I went up to one group, all girls, and some of them healthy and ablebodied. . . . One girl lay in her rags at my feet, her face hidden between her outstretched arms. I spoke to her: but it was at least a minute before she heeded. When she did lift her dirty sodden face, she seemed halfmazed: answered, that she was about twenty; a shawlfringemaker; out of work; no father nor mother; no home; comes here to lie down, every day; wouldn't come if she had anywhere else to go to, of course not.[4]

It is not my intention to criticise Dickens for his failure to produce a certifiable record of the conditions attendant upon female unemployment in London in 1864. Dickens was a novelist, not a sociologist, and it is clearly a reductive exercise to examine literature in terms of its fidelity to what we understand to have been the historical reality of the time in which it was produced. I am much more interested in pointing to Dickens' rejection of a nasty social situation in which Eugene Wrayburn's class would have licensed him to have Lizzie Hexam (Eugene openly refers to this possibility in discussion with Mortimer), and where she could well have ended up prostrate in St James's Park. *Our Mutual Friend* describes a society in which money is the prime means of facilitating human relationships, and apart from the fact that Eugene provides a tutor for Lizzie and

Jenny Wren, the relationship between Lizzie and Eugene is one in which money really plays no part. Lizzie supports herself, however meagrely, as seamstress and paper-mill worker. Dickens rejects the negative social reality in which a vulnerable young woman could become the prey of a privileged man and while this certainly caters to bourgeois sensibilities and makes Lizzie as pure as can be, it also reveals Dickens' implicit distaste for a class structure which endorsed the sexual exploitation of working-class women.

In his examination of the sexual nether world of Victorian society, Steven Marcus contrasts an anecdote from *My Secret Life* in which the author visits a dockside public house with Dickens' description of the Fellowships:

> What Dickens does, of course, is to suppress any reference to prostitutes and to censor his report on the language of the dockside. The first thing we learn, then, from such scenes (and there are hundreds of them in *My Secret Life*) is what did not get into the Victorian novel, and what was by common consent and convention left out or suppressed.[5]

Marcus goes on to say that this censorship "does not merely have a distorting and negative effect; in Dickens' imaginative abstraction from and reconstruction of such an establishment certain positive values, already inherent in it, are brought into view and focussed upon". It is certainly true that these values are positive, but I think their presence also serves to create a bourgeois myth of working-class life, just as the positive values with which Lizzie Hexam is endowed (her tenderness and her finely balanced combination of selflessness and self-esteem) serve to create a bourgeois myth of working-class womanhood.

Dickens' description of the Fellowships propagates a myth of the working class as childlike and disciplined by one of their worthy own. Miss Abbey is a stern schoolmistress in firm charge of her pupils, and her schoolroom/pub is run along very strict lines of codified behaviour. I am not suggesting that a more realistic picture of dockside life would be one which corresponded to that reported on by the author by *My Secret Life*. *My Secret Life* perpetuates one great myth of the working class; the lower orders are perceived entirely in terms of their constant availability for all varieties of sexual performance, polymorphous perverse and other. The reality of Limehouse Hole probably lay somewhere between the randy anarchy of the pub in

*My Secret Life* and the pedagoguish order of the Fellowships in *Our Mutual Friend.*

But one meaning of myth is that it gives fantastic form and gratification to desires which are both generated and denied by exigent reality. The myth of the working class in *My Secret Life* gratifies a desire for the total sexualisation of experience and of the world. And, to return to the positive values to which Marcus refers, the myth of the working class in *Our Mutual Friend*, as manifested in Lizzie Hexam, gratifies a desire for the transformation of a sordid social reality, and, as manifested in the Fellowships, for the embankment of random and fragmented urban experience into a coherent system of social organisation.

In 1844, Engels observed life on the London streets, and it is as if he created the descriptive lineaments of a social alienation which Dickens enriches with the first few unforgettable paragraphs of *Bleak House*, and with his descriptions of a grey, dusty, and withered London in *Our Mutual Friend*; a London where the grating wind saws instead of blows, and where "melancholy waifs and strays" stoop and poke among the waste paper looking for anything to sell. Engels writes:

> Hundreds of thousands of men and women drawn from all classes and ranks of society pack the streets of London. Are they not all human beings with the same innate characteristics and potentialities? Are they not all equally interested in the pursuit of happiness? And do they not all aim at happiness by following similar methods? Yet they rush past each other as if they had nothing in common . . . The disintegration of society into individuals, each guided by his private principles and each pursuing his own aims has been pushed to its furthest limits in London. Here indeed human society has been split into its component atoms.[6]

Dickens' myth of the Fellowships exists in the context of a human society "split into its component atoms" which Engels perceived in 1844; Miss Abbey's is a small unit of human warmth and connection set in the vast indifference of sprawling London.

The building itself is animated; it is in a "state of hale infirmity", the wood forming the "chimney-pieces, beams, partitions, floors and doors" seems "in its old age fraught with confused memories of its youth". And this wood, in its "state of second childhood", seems to hold within itself its own history:

> Not without reason was it often asserted by the regular frequenters of the Porters, that when the light shone full upon the grain of certain panels, and particularly upon an old corner cupboard of walnut-wood in the bar, you might trace little forests there, and tiny trees like the parent-tree, in full umbrageous leaf. (I, vi)

The wood in the Veneering household has no history, no parentage. The furniture is "bran-new", smells of the workshops, and, needless to say, holds no pictures of nature, but rather gives back a reflection of its owners, who are themselves without history and without parents. In his description of the Fellowships, Dickens blends man and nature into a harmonious human snuggery, rich with history and tradition; he creates a positive alternative to the West End world of self-regard and self-reflection, and, incidentally, to Pleasant Riderhood's cynical perspective on Limehouse Hole.

To return to the myth of Lizzie Hexam, Dickens establishes her attraction for Eugene in spiritual, rather than sexual terms, from the moment Eugene spies upon her through the windows of the Hexam abode:

> She had no other light than the light of the fire. The unkindled lamp stood on the table. She sat on the ground, looking at the brazier, with her face leaning on her hand. There was a kind of film or flicker on her face, which at first he took to be the fitful firelight; but on a second look, he saw that she was weeping. A sad and solitary spectacle, as shown him by the rising and falling of the fire. . . . He looked long and steadily at her. A deep rich piece of colour, with the brown flush of her cheek and the shining lustre of her hair, though sad and solitary, weeping by the rising and falling of the fire. (I, viii)

Eugene is certainly susceptible to Lizzie's attractions as a "deep rich piece of colour" – his pallid existence in the Temple and his lacklustre attendance at the Veneering dinner parties are colourless in the extreme – but it is Lizzie's "sad and solitary" state which moves him. I think he is initially drawn to her because, quite simply, she has the power to make him feel something. He describes himself to Mortimer as "constantly" and "fatally" bored, and his ennui is exacerbated by his father and by his culture.

Eugene's Respected Father has nullified the independence of his children by, as Eugene says, "having always in the clearest manner provided (as he calls it) for his children by pre-arranging from the hour of the birth of each, and sometimes from an earlier period, what the devoted little victim's calling and course in life should be . . ." (I, xii). Eugene's father has determined that Eugene should be a barrister, just as he determined that his other sons should enter the church, the navy, and the commercial world. He has also determined that Eugene should marry a woman with money "down in the parental neighbourhood", and his notion of a proper marriage for his son is coherent with Eric Hobsbawm's analysis of the economic underpinnings of bourgeois marriage arrangements:

> The "family" was not merely the basic social unit of bourgeois society but its basic unit of property and business enterprise, linked with other such units through a system of exchanges of women-plus-property (the 'marriage portion') in which the women were by strict convention deriving from pre-bourgeois tradition *virgines intactae.*[7]

Eugene's refusal to participate in the bourgeois marriage market is another demonstration of Dickens' distaste for certain insidious social customs. In the Lammle marriage, which is nakedly founded upon the commoditisation of bourgeois women, Dickens reveals his moral dislike of this commoditisation by condemning Sophronia and Alfred to the joyless discovery that they have duped each other, and by marching them right out of the novel to France. Eugene's lazy recalcitrance is a less overt demonstration of Dickens' moral distaste. Just as Dickens' transformation of what could well have been a commonplace story of seduction into a myth of spiritual love shows his dislike of the sexual commoditisation of the female lower classes, so Eugene's refusal to marry a woman with money shows Dickens' dislike of the bourgeois marriage market.

Paternal control in *Our Mutual Friend* is, of course, most fully exercised in old Harmon's three wills. A will is a document which conjoins three important themes of *Our Mutual Friend*: it is written down and is an obvious expression of literacy; it is concerned with the distribution of money and property; and it seeks to determine the social existence of its legatees. The common reluctance of John Harmon and Eugene Wrayburn to acquiesce in their fathers' schemes is one expression of the general reluctance of all the characters to accept the destiny which their society determines for them. And, in yet another sense, because a will may be said to constitute, or at least lay down, a plot for its beneficiaries, it may be said to resemble a novel. The powers of the omnipotent novelist are, therefore, similar to the powers of the father and the powers of society. The omnipotent novelist decides the fate of his characters; the father who makes a will decides, or at least may be said to try to decide, the lives of his beneficiaries; and the society that Dickens represents in *Our Mutual Friend* decides the lives of all who live in it. In *Our Mutual Friend*, the novelist, the father, and society are united, in an imaginative conjunction of fictive and actual authority, by their shared power to manipulate, indeed to determine.[8] And at the end of the novel the authority of the father remains unchallenged as Harmon's money is distributed in accordance with the provisions of his first will and his son marries the once discontented little girl maliciously chosen for him by his father as a condition of his inheritance.

Shielded by the mechanisms of civilisation from the sight of pain in others, Eugene Wrayburn is a member of that class which John Stuart Mill described in 1836, enjoying in "their fullness the benefits of civilisation", and separating themselves more and more from "the spectacle, and even the very idea of pain":

> There has crept over the refined classes, over the whole class of gentlemen in England, a moral effeminacy, an inaptitude for every kind of struggle. They shrink from all effort, from everything which is troublesome and disagreeable. The same causes which render them sluggish and unenterprising, make them, it is true, for the most part, stoical under inevitable evils. But heroism is an active, not a passive quality; and when it is necessary not to bear pain but to seek it, little needs be expected from the men of the present day.[9]

Eugene embodies Mill's paradigm of the sluggish modern English gentleman. He shrinks from "all effort, from everything which is troublesome and disagreeable", and the "inevitable evil" which he endures (his severe physical suffering) is a form of inevitable punishment which Dickens inflicts upon him for his life of careless indifference to others. In general, he is a remarkably unsympathetic character. He grabs Charley Hexam under the chin with an overbearing insolence; he ridicules the analogy which Mr Boffin innocently draws between the work of man and the industry of the bees, and thereby scorns the exigency of working which has been Boffin's experience, and from which Eugene has been comfortably immune;

and his dealings with Bradley Headstone are a form of civilised barbarism. Eugene's physical suffering facilitates Dickens' transcendence of social reality which makes marriage to a "female waterman" untenable, but it is also an implicit punishment for his insolence, irresponsibility, and unfeeling exercise of the privilege afforded him by his class position.

Dickens actually presents Eugene with a vision which suggests an imaginative correspondence between his psychological prevarication in regard to Lizzie and a horrifying physical manifestation of indecision. Eugene is not one of the visionary characters in *Our Mutual Friend*, and it is apt that Dickens provide a vision for him. He is "lounging" along the Strand when he sees "Jenny Wren's bad boy trying to make up his mind to cross the road":

> A more ridiculous and feeble spectacle than this tottering wretch making unsteady sallies into the roadway, and as often staggering back again, oppressed by terrors of vehicles that were a long way off or were nowhere, the streets could not have shown. Over and over again, when the course was perfectly clear, he set out, got halfway, described a loop, turned, and went back again, when he might have crossed and re-crossed half-a-dozen times. (III, x)

Eugene doesn't know if he cares for Lizzie, and he doesn't know if he doesn't care for her, and it is as if his indecision is a psychological embodiment, less terrifying for *him* to be sure, of the physical unsteadiness of poor Mr Cleaver which he witnesses in the Strand.

Eugene's exposure to the suffering of Jenny Wren's bad boy is an instance of how *Our Mutual Friend* also insists upon the indissoluble connections between its characters, however unrelated those characters may appear to be. They are joined by the common, if different, experience of psychological and physical suffering. Eugene's psychological irresolution and Mr Cleaver's physical waverings point to a common condition of social dissatisfaction, which, however provocatively different in its manifestations, is determined in the larger sense by society. The more extreme nature of Mr Cleaver's suffering, the final and dreadful fulfilment of *his* destiny, is an implicit indictment of a society which permits, indeed perpetuates, his miserable struggle and Eugene's privileged existence. And just as the image of disease which radiates out from the rotten core of Tom-All-Alone's in *Bleak House* shows the indissoluble connection between Jo and Esther Summerson, Dickens' imaginative identification of Eugene with Mr Cleaver shows their connection and inevitable subjection to the society in which they live. Their identification also implicitly illuminates the disquieting disparity in their different levels of social existence.

Eugene manages to arrive at a point when he realises he is at a crisis, and at this very moment he is attacked by Bradley Headstone and rendered impotent to make a decision whether to seduce, marry, or leave Lizzie Hexam. This sequence of events is crucial in *Our Mutual Friend*'s mediation between the reality of a bourgeois marriage market and the romantic desire for marriage generated only by love. Eugene is walking by the river, and Dickens' description of his thoughts and feelings is a remarkable representation of the conscious and unconscious workings of the mind:

> The rippling of the river seemed to cause a correspondent stir in his uneasy reflections. He would have laid them asleep if he could, but they were in movement, like the stream, and all tending one way with a strong current. As the ripple under the moon broke unexpectedly now and then, and palely flashed in a new shape and with a new sound, so parts of his thoughts started, unbidden, from the rest, and revealed their wickedness. 'Out of the question to marry her,' said Eugene, 'and out of the question to leave her. The crisis!'
> (IV, vi)

The smooth river represents, so to speak, Eugene's conscious mind, and the ripples which break the calm surface of the water represent that suppressed material which, by every means at its disposal, seeks to make itself conscious. The "wicked" thought of seducing Lizzie is what "starts" from Eugene's unconscious. This is not to say that Eugene has never thought of seducing Lizzie; he has suppressed those thoughts but they "start" up again in this scene. However, he does not have to consider the matter any further because his crisis is resolved for him by Bradley's blows. Just before that moment, Eugene looks down into the water, looks, in a sense, into his own mind, and as he is plunged into the river it is as if he is plunged into himself, into the rippling movement which is the composite representation of the workings of his conscious and unconscious mind. But the positive implications of his immersion in the river and in himself are severely ambiguous. He is rendered so physically weak and so psychologically ineffectual that his desire to marry Lizzie is expressed in the context of what seems to be his approaching death:

it does not represent an alteration in the social consciousness decided for him by his upper-middle-class culture.

The problematic nature of these episodes demonstrates how *Our Mutual Friend* tries to mediate between an authentic description of social reality and a desire for its transformation. Dickens mythologises the attraction between Lizzie and Eugene into a love which can only be consummated after months of dramatic prevarication, violence and death – and then only in a marriage where the upper-middle-class husband is less sexual partner than dependent patient for his working-class bride.

In my discussion of *North and South*, I pointed to a passage in *Mary Barton* where Elizabeth Gaskell speaks of the actions of the uneducated as typified in "those of Frankenstein, that monster of many human qualities, ungifted with a soul, a knowledge of the difference between good and evil". In her second industrial novel, Gaskell transforms this monster into a chastened and cooperative partner of the Northern middle class.

In *Our Mutual Friend*, Bradley Headstone has struggled to achieve the education which Gaskell posited as a remedy for class conflict. It is ironic that the price of his transformation from "pauper lad" to lower-middle-class school teacher is his metamorphosis into a monstrous creature of the night. He becomes a "passion-wasted night bird with respectable feathers", tormented by class hatred and sexual jealousy in his pursuit of Eugene Wrayburn, so "seamed with jealousy and anger" that he passes in the dark "like a haggard head suspended in the air". His tormented existence suggests the unexamined nature of Gaskell's well-meant remedies for social tension, and demonstrates Dickens' astute apprehension of man's aggressive impulses which he necessarily renounces as the price for civilisation.[10]

It is interesting that in his description of the forces which bring Bradley Headstone to ruin, Dickens conjoins sexual jealousy and class resentment. In *Civilization and Its Discontents*, Freud draws a connection between the suppression of sexual freedom and the suppression of social groups, and the connection which Dickens draws between the suppression of Bradley's sexual passion and the suppression of his class resentment may be seen as an imaginative and intuitive expression of an idea which was given full and formal expression in Freud's theory. Freud is discussing the expansion of cultural units which is one sign of civilisation, and he writes:

> The tendency on the part of civilization to restrict sexual life is no less clear than its other tendency to expand the cultural unit. Its first, totemic, phase already brings with it the prohibition against an incestuous choice of object, and this is perhaps the most drastic mutilation which man's erotic life has in all time experienced. Taboos, laws and customs impose further restrictions, which affect both men and women. Not all civilizations go equally far in this; and the economic structures of the society also influence the amount of sexual freedom that remains. Here, as we already know, civilization is obeying the laws of economic necessity, since a large amount of the psychical energy which it uses for its own purposes has to be withdrawn from sexuality. In this respect civilization behaves towards sexuality as a people or a stratum of its population does which has subjected another one to its exploitation. Fear of a revolt by the suppressed elements drives it to stricter precautionary measures. A high-water mark in such a development has been reached in our Western European civilization.[11]

"Civilisation" in *Our Mutual Friend* has indeed "behaved" towards Bradley's sexuality and towards his class in the similarity of manner which Freud suggests. For Bradley to transform himself from "pauper lad" to schoolmaster, it has been necessary for him to withdraw "psychical energy" from an expression of his sexuality. But it would seem that once that transformation has been achieved, it is his sexuality which demands expression:

> It seemed to him as if all that he could suppress in himself he had suppressed, as if all that he could restrain in himself he had restrained, and the time had come – in a rush, in a moment – when the power of self-command had departed from him. Love at first sight is a trite expression quite sufficiently discussed; enough that in certain smouldering natures like this man's, that passion leaps into a blaze, and makes such head as fire does in a rage of wind, when other passions, but for its mastery, could be held in chains. (II, xi)

To be sure, Dickens' description of the dynamics of Bradley's psychical energy is formulated in terms of suppression and restraint, rather than in the terms of unconscious economic organisation which is Freud's concept. But Dickens' understanding of the power of Bradley's sexuality is still remarkable.

Bradley's society has also required him to suppress his resentment of the system of class by which he has been confined, and it is remarkable that his resentment of this system is manifested simultaneously with his sexual desire for Lizzie Hexam. His "smouldering nature" is inflamed by passion for Lizzie at almost the same moment he discovers that a gentleman is interested in her. When Bradley and Charley leave Lizzie after the first meeting between the three of them, they encounter Eugene Wrayburn on Vauxhall Bridge as they begin their epic walk back to that jumble of a Kentish suburb which houses their school. Eugene is taking up "twice as much pavement as another would have claimed", and when Bradley learns of his crude impertinence towards Charley, and that Eugene also knows Lizzie, he begins to talk of "some man who had worked his way" (rather, of course, than someone who has had it all handed to him on a plate) coming to admire her. His interest in Lizzie is, in part, kindled by class rivalry.

The encounter on Vauxhall Bridge is followed very shortly by a disastrous interview in Eugene's chambers. The brother and the schoolmaster come to claim their rights to supervise Lizzie's education. Charley is ignored while Bradley and Eugene engage in an explicit battle for Lizzie, and in an implicit confrontation of class with class. The confrontation is fuelled by Eugene's languid scorn of Bradley's graceless manners and by Bradley's furious contempt for Eugene's seeming indifference: "Those two, no matter who spoke, or whom was addressed, looked at each other. There was some secret, sure perception between them, which set them against one another in all ways." Eugene remains calm to the point of insult, his only movement is to blow the ash from his cigar, while Bradley sweats, shakes, and laments his inability to control himself.

When Bradley, incensed by Eugene's insolence and tormented by Lizzie's refusal on that grey and withered evening in the city churchyard, begins to trail his rival about London,[12] Eugene finds a perverse excitement in this pursuit – he turns it into a parody of the hunt, devising ways to increase the pleasure of the chase, and taking Mortimer along for the fun. Bradley becomes the hunted, not the hunter, and in a chilling apprehension of the criminal mind, Dickens describes how Bradley sheds his civilised skin and becomes a monstrous animal, how, once the trappings of respectability are discarded, Bradley begins to relish the enactment of all that is released:

> Tied up all day with his disciplined show upon him, subdued to the performance of his routine of educational tricks, encircled by a gabbling crowd, he broke loose at night like an ill-tamed wild animal. Under his daily restraint, it was his compensation, not his trouble, to give a glance towards his state at night, and to the freedom of its being indulged. If great criminals told the truth – which, being great criminals, they do not – they would very rarely tell of their struggles against the crime. Their struggles are towards it. They buffet with opposing waves to gain the bloody shore, not to recede from it. (III, xi)

This passage is remarkable, too, for what it suggests about the restraints which have been imposed on Bradley Headstone by society. He has been "tied up", made to put on a "disciplined show" of "educational tricks", and he breaks loose under the pressure of all that has been repressed. This is not to suggest some simple and reductive motive for Bradley's murderous impulses. Dickens' extraordinary depiction of Bradley's suffering and violent character is anything but simple. It is notably complex for it displays a remarkable understanding of the renunciation of impulse which is required by civilisation, of the suppression of class resentment which is required by a dominant culture, and of the dreadful and destructive price paid in psychological suffering by a man who, although he is indeed a murdering animal, has become so, in part, by virtue of an inordinate amount of self-suppression so that he may surmount his pauper lad origins.

Bradley's last days are enacted in a cold and snowy landscape. He trudges out to Riderhood's lock past snowy fields and alongside the river into which he had plunged Eugene Wrayburn. The river is now full of floating ice and the cold landscape symbolises Bradley's condition. The blood which he sheds in his act of self-mutilation in the churchyard (he brings his hand down upon the stone coping which he has been wrenching so maniacally) is, as it were, drained out of him in the last stages of his despair. At the very end he is reified into a cold statue:

> Rigid before the fire, as if it were a charmed flame that was turning him old, he sat, with the dark lines deepening in his face, its stare becoming more and more haggard, its surface turning whiter and whiter as if it were being overspread with ashes, and the very texture and colour of his hair degenerating.

> Not until the late daylight made the window transparent did this decaying statue move. Then it slowly rose, and sat in the window looking out. (IV, XV)

He is a "night-bird" turned to ashes, a phoenix for whom there will be no mythical rebirth, and he wipes himself out in the same way that he has erased his signature from his blackboard when he realises that Riderhood is on to him. Bradley Headstone is dilapidated by his self-destructive passion, and by the terrible price which is exacted by society from those who try too hard to elude their social class. The radical meaning of dilapidate is to break down an edifice made of stone, and the broken stones of Bradley Headstone are returned to the primeval earth at the bottom of the river. All his visions of petit-bourgeois respectability go with him.

In Chapter the Last of *Our Mutual Friend*, the Voice of Society makes itself heard on the subject of "whether a young man of very fair family, good appearance, and some talent, makes a fool or a wise man of himself in marrying a female waterman, turned factory girl". Mortimer is greeted as a "long-banished Robinson Crusoe" by a tipsy Lady Tippins: he is a story-teller who navigates the waters surrounding the Veneering mainland of bourgeois self-satisfaction, and he is asked for news of the "savages", the newly-married Lizzie and Eugene. Podsnap enquires whether Lizzie ever *was* a female waterman or a factory girl, and Mortimer's response to this question is connected with Dickens' most positive representations of the river in *Our Mutual Friend*, and with his most self-conscious allusions to reflection and to mimesis.

As to Lizzie being a "female waterman", Mortimer replies, "Never. But she sometimes rowed in a boat with her father I believe." He manages to make Lizzie's employment on the river sound like a Sunday afternoon excursion on the Serpentine. The reader has learned in the first chapter of the novel that Lizzie rows more than sometimes with her father (" . . . with every lithe action of the girl, with every turn of her wrist, perhaps most of all with her look of dread or horror, they were things of usage"), and Mortimer, in his excursion to Limehouse Hole in pursuit of Gaffer, has been informed of the nature of Lizzie's work. Mortimer's answer, while motivated by a desire to protect Eugene, nevertheless distorts a social reality with which he is entirely familiar, and, in a sense, it shows him engaging in a specific censorship of social actuality which parallels the novel's general muting of Lizzie Hexam's working-class background. Mortimer is like Dickens here, as he tries to mediate between Podsnap's morality and Eugene's violation of it. And his firm denial that Lizzie ever was a factory girl, when Podsnap pursues his enquiry, represents a further distortion of social reality, "Never. But she had some employment in a paper mill, I believe." Paper manufacture was not brought under Government control until the Factory Acts Extension Act of 1867, and Lizzie was not therefore technically a "factory girl", but Mortimer's casual reference to "some employment in a paper mill" minimises what has been, in actuality, at least three months steady employment as a mill-worker.

It is probable that in a scale of industrial horrors, Dickens placed a paper mill lower, say, than the cotton mills of Preston – a visit to that city in 1854 to observe the current strike situation provided foundation for the "regulated savagery" of Coketown in *Hard Times*. And, in fact, the Commissioners on the Employment of children and Young Persons reported in 1865 that many paper mill buildings were "airy and commodious", and that they were often located in "healthy situations", and that there was less naked and brutal exploitation of children than in the cotton mills.[13] A paper mill, too, possesses a positive significance in terms of Dickens' pervasive concern with literacy in *Our Mutual Friend.* But his description of the paper mill where Lizzie Hexam is employed presents an image of flawless industrialism – industrialism without dirt, noise or exploitation.

This image forms a startling contrast to Dickens' other representations of industrialised manufacture – to the inferno through which Little Nell and her grandfather wander in *The Old Curiosity Shop*, for example, or to the barbaric monotony of Coketown in *Hard Times*. In these two novels, industrialism is a horror in the context of certain positive, if ambiguous, alternatives. In *The Old Curiosity Shop*, the industrial inferno is one of the trials of modern life through which Little Nell must pass on her journey to secular beatification. In *Hard Times*, Gradgrindery and rationalised manufacture are opposed, among other things, by the childlike anarchy of Sleary's horse-riding and the unself-conscious sweet morality of Sissy Jupe. But in *Our Mutual Friend*, industrialism itself becomes a pastoral alternative; it receives a positive representation in contrast to Dickens' descriptions of urban desolation which permeate the novel.

To be sure, the city is already a foggy, greasy and infectious monster in *Bleak House*, inhabited by stunted creatures like the Smallweeds, but Dickens establishes the abundant pastoralism of Mr Boythorn's rustic retreat and of Esther Summerson's very own Bleak House as an alternative to the wretchedness of London. By the time of *Little Dorrit*, the second of Dickens' three great novels of the city, the pastoral alternative has been abandoned (despite the Plornish "Happy Cottage") and after their marriage Amy and Arthur Clennam come down into the "roaring streets", where the "noisy and the eager, and the arrogant and the forward and the vain, fretted, and chafed, and made their usual uproar". In *Our Mutual Friend*, Dickens combines the pastoral alternative of *Bleak House* with the bittersweet resignation to city life of *Little Dorrit*, and he creates a coherent fusion of benevolent industrialism and benevolent nature in his description of the paper mill:

> The Paper Mill had stopped work for the night, and the paths and roads in its neighbourhood were sprinkled with clusters of people going home from their day's labour in it. There were men, women, and children in the groups, and there was no want of lively colour to flutter in the gentle evening wind. The mingling of various voices and the sound of laughter made a cheerful impression upon the ear, analogous to that of the fluttering colours upon the eye. Into the sheet of water reflecting the flushed sky in the foreground of the living picture, a knot of urchins were casting stones, and watching the expansion of the rippling circles. So, in the rosy evening, one might watch the ever-widening beauty of the landscape – beyond the newly-released workers wending home – beyond the silver river – beyond the deep green fields of corn, so prospering, that the loiterers in their narrow threads of pathway seemed to float immersed breast-high – beyond the hedgerows and the clumps of trees – beyond the windmills on the ridge – away to where the sky appeared to meet the earth, as if there were no immensity of space between mankind and Heaven. (IV, vi)

The gentle evening wind bears no resemblance to that gritty, "sawing" horror which whips through London. Dickens creates a "living picture" of pleasing sounds and pleasing colours, a harmonious synesthesia which is reflected in the river. The pattern of ever-widening circles which is made by stones cast into the water is imposed upon this "living picture". Dickens imposes one agreeable pattern upon another. And the pattern of expanding ripples is repeated in the "ever-widening beauty of the landscape". We move out from the people (and it is important to remember that they are workers from the mill), beyond the river, beyond the fields where loiterers seem "to float immersed breast-high" (which connects the fertile fields with the silver river), beyond trees and windmills to a point where sky meets earth, to where it is "as if" there is no break between man and the universe. The landscape, then, is described in terms of interlocking levels of perception – and what is seen is a topographical affirmation of the cohesive order and connection of the paper mill. The mill itself is run by kindly Jews who treat their employees with justice and respect (despite Mrs Milvey's suspicions, they are not out to convert every Christian they can get their hands on). The work is so untaxing that Lizzie Hexam's hands are made soft and supple, whereas her rowing on the Thames made them coarse and rough, which is an amazing fringe benefit when one considers that in the 1860s female paper mill workers were primarily employed in rag sorting and cutting and in glazing, that they worked something close to a 68-hour week, and that the sorting and cutting rooms were the most unhealthy areas of paper mills. The mill possesses a "sweet" and "fresh" storeroom to which Betty Higden's body is taken after her death, and the noise of its water-wheel even has a "softening influence on the bright wintry scene" of her funeral. The paper mill is a mythical construct and the river Thames which is its source of power is "silver" and benign – the waters here are vastly different from the murky and polluted depths of London, the depths from which dank and sodden bodies are retrieved by those scavengers, Hexam and Riderhood.[14]

There is another moment in the novel when Dickens meditates upon the image of the river and his meditation draws together the meanings of social existence in *Our Mutual Friend* which are suggested by the scene in Miss Abbey's first-floor bedroom as Rogue Riderhood struggles between life and death. Bella Wilfer and John Harmon walk along the river bank after Betty Higden's funeral:

> The trees were bare of leaves, and the river was bare of water-lilies; but the sky was not bare of its beautiful blue, and the water reflected it, and a delicious wind ran with the stream, touching the surface crisply. Perhaps the old mirror was never yet made by human hands, which, if all the images it had in its time reflected could pass across its surface again, would fail to reveal

> some scene of horror or distress. But the great serene mirror of the river seemed as if it might have reproduced all it had ever reflected between those placid banks, and brought nothing to the light save what was peaceful, pastoral, and blooming. (III, ix)

Dickens here talks about two kinds of reflection, that to be perceived in nature and that to be perceived in a mirror made by human hands. In other words, he is talking about nature and mimesis, for the "old mirror made by human hands", is, I think, a metaphor for the novel, and for *Our Mutual Friend* in particular. Nature's reflection is benevolent – the water reflects the beautiful sky, and the images which the "great serene mirror of the river" reflect would seem to be always "peaceful, pastoral, and blooming". But the reflections which "the old mirror made by human hands" deliver would never fail to produce "some scene of horror or distress".

*Our Mutual Friend* reflects scenes of physical and psychological suffering, of social restlessness and dissatisfaction, and of a teeming, yet withered, city plagued by dry winds, dust and detritus. It seems that the comparison which Dickens implicitly draws between the river and a mirror, between nature's reflection and the reflection which is delivered by *Our Mutual Friend*, contains a small, but significant, note of sad resignation to the social reality which he has both described and attempted to transcend.

There is no nature in the mythical kingdom of the mounds. They have been erected as Old Harmon's answer to nature; they are his own "geological formation", and they exist in a new world founded upon profit. The characters who inhabit the mythical kingdom of the mounds are remarkably more alive and sometimes more terrifyingly comic than any who inhabit the world of the ancient river and the East End. They, too, are profoundly dissatisfied. But they struggle with a vitality and a comic energy which is absent from the river world, and they struggle in a landscape far different from the flat reaches of the river. It is imaginatively dominated by the dust-heaps.

NOTES

1. In the context of the wealth of fairy-tale allusion in *Our Mutual Friend*, Rogue Riderhood is a kind of perverted Little Red Ridinghood who would, one imagines, sell his grandmother to the wolf as a means of survival. Mortimer Lightwood calls him "little Rogue Riderhood",

saying, "I am tempted into the paraphrase by remembering the charming wolf who would have rendered society a great service if he had devoured Mr. Riderhood's father and mother in their infancy . . ." (II, xvi). The Red Ridinghood fairy-tale crops up in various places in the novel. When Eugene and Mortimer go down the river in search of Hexam, the Thames, its shipping and its wharves, take on a quality of evil intention, "Not a figurehead but had the menacing look of bursting forward to run them down. Not a sluice-gate, or a painted scale upon a post or wall, showing the depth of water, but seemed to hint, like the dreadfully facetious Wolf in bed in Grandmamma's cottage, 'That's to drown *you* in My dears!'" (I, xiv). Riderhood is, of course, devoured by this "dreadfully facetious Wolf", the river. And Riah becomes the wolf when he acquiesces in Fledgeby's charade of Christian benevolence and Jewish greed. Jenny Wren cries, "You are not the godmother at all! . . . You are the Wolf in the Forest, the wicked Wolf" (III, xiii). For an interpretation and a history of the Red Ridinghood fairy-tale, see Bruno Bettelheim, *The Uses of Enchantment* (London, 1976), pp. 166–83.

2. *Ragged London in 1861* (London, 1861), a collection of journalistic essays by John Hollingshead, offers some harrowing descriptions of working-class life in the East End. It also offers a contemporary confirmation of how the world appears to Pleasant Riderhood.
3. That monumental record of the sexual relationship between an upper-middle-class man and the female English working class, *My Secret Life*, includes instances far too numerous to mention of the dispiriting availability of servant girls, shop girls, and out-of-work girls. It is easy to concede the exaggeration of male sexual performance and a mythologising of female sexual response in *My Secret Life*, but it is not so easy to disregard all the small and exact details of how much it cost its prolific author to get all those working-class girls to pull up their skirts. One servant girl is given a brooch and ten sovereigns in return for the unrestricted use of her body: for her, ten sovereigns represents one year's wages. In another exchange, which is so rich in meaning one hardly knows what to do with it, the author stuffs eighty-four shillings up a prostitute's vagina. Instead of receiving payment for the insertion of a penis, she is inserted with the payment itself. Sexual relationships in *My Secret Life* are so determined by money that there is an alarming fitness in a woman being stuffed with shillings rather than with the genitals of the person who dispenses the shillings.

   "A Study of Victorian Prostitution and Venereal Disease", by E. M. Sigsworth and T. J. Wyke in *Suffer and Be Still*, edited by Martha Vicinus, (Bloomington, 1972), documents the alarming number of prostitutes in mid-Victorian England.
4. *Munby man of Two Worlds, The Life and Diaries of Arthur J. Munby*, edited by Derek Hudson (Boston, 1972), pp. 198–9.
5. *The Other Victorians* (London, 1971), pp. 105–6.
6. *The Condition of the Working Class in England* (Berkeley, 1958), pp. 30–1.

   In his study of the casual labour market in Victorian London, Gareth Stedman Jones points to the increase in the absence of direct contact between classes in London during the course of the nineteenth century:

> ... the social distance between the rich and poor expressed itself in an ever sharper geographical segregation of the city. Merchants and employers no longer lived above their places of work. The old methods of social control based on the model of the squire, and parson, face to face relations, deference, and paternalism, found less and less reflection in the urban reality. Vast tracts of working-class housing were left to themselves, virtually bereft of any contact with authority except in the form of the policeman or bailiff.

*Outcast London* (London, 1971) pp. 13–14. I think that Dickens' myth of the Fellowships is some sort of counter to the absence of social authority which Jones describes: he creates authority and control in the shape of Miss Abbey, and Boffin, too, may be seen as a benevolent urban squire – dispensing largesse derived from the collection of city rubbish.

7. *The Age of Capital 1848–1875* (New York, 1975), p. 236.
8. Boffin's innate generosity is demonstrated by his instructions to Mortimer Lightwood regarding *his* will. He wants a "tight" one. Mortimer responds, "'Exactly so. And nothing can be more laudable. But is the tightness to bind Mrs. Boffin to any and what conditions?' 'Bind Mrs. Boffin?' interposed her husband. 'No! What are you thinking of? What I want is, to make it all hers so tight as that her hold of it can't be loosed'" (I, viii).

   The notion of manipulation is alien to Boffin's nature. The meaning of his manipulation of Bella Wilfer is discussed in Chapter 6.
9. "Civilization", *Mill's Essays on Literature and Society*, ed. J. B. Schneewind (New York, 1965), p. 163.
10. It was Dickens' own painful experience to struggle with debilitating social restraints. He transformed himself from the lonely child at Warren's Blacking, who budgeted his pennies for a pudding and lived alone in lodgings while the rest of his family was ensconced with his insolvent father in the Marshalsea, to the celebrated novelist of Gads Hill. (See Forster's *Life*, Vol. I, Ch. II, for Dickens' autobiographical fragment.) If, for a moment, one can overlook the obvious difference in class origin, and one can compare Dickens' experience with the fictive experience of a character which bears some correspondence to his own, Bradley's tragedy is that he possesses none of the genius which enabled Dickens to transform some of the pain and humiliation of his childhood into fiction. Bradley Headstone has a rather dull intelligence, and has pulled himself out of working-class ignorance by dogged application. His fictions destroy, rather than console him, and his class resentment is not channelled into an altruistic attitude towards the education of children with similar histories to his own: he promotes Charley Hexam as an "undeniable boy to do credit to the master who would bring him on", rather than from an unselfish desire for Charley's advancement. Bradley sublimates nothing.

11. Translated by James Strachey (New York, 1962), p. 51.
12. The amount of walking which is done in *Our Mutual Friend* is phenomenal. Bradley Headstone and Charley Hexam make the trek from Kent to Millbank with an amazing endurance and regularity quite simply because there was no means of cheap transportation available to them. Cheap mass travel to the suburbs did not exist until the 1880s, and even if they had wanted to take the railway, workmen's tickets were not introduced on the London, Chatham and Dover until 1865.

    Riah's walk from St Mary Axe to see Jenny Wren in Westminster follows a route prescribed by the exigencies of the work going on along the northern embankment of the Thames. He crosses to the south bank over London Bridge, proceeds along this side of the river and recrosses the Thames over Westminster Bridge. Because of the completed southern embankment of the river, this was a faster route than coming through Fleet Street, the Strand and Whitehall.
13. Fourth Report of the Commissioner on the Employment of children and Young Persons in Trades and Manufactures not already regulated by the Law, British Parliamentary Papers, 1865, vol. xx.
14. Perhaps Dickens was influenced in his creation of the paper mill in *Our Mutual Friend* by an article which appeared in *Household Words* on 31 August 1850, written by Harriet Martineau. It presents an unwaveringly happy picture of such industrialisation: "... as I turn down the hawthorn hedge into the valley, a sound comes in my ears – like the murmuring and throbbing of a mighty giant, labouring hand .... It is the noise of the Steam Engine. And now, before me, white and clean without, and radiant in the sun, with the sweet clear river tumbling merrily down to kiss it, and help in the work it does, is the Paper-Mill I have come to see!" (Vol. I, p. 529).

    In *Victorian Working Women* (New York, 1929), Wanda Neff has something rather different to say about conditions in paper mills. She uses the Parliamentary Papers of 1844, Vol. XXVII, as her evidence, and writes, "In the rag rooms, where the dust and foul atmosphere were especially annoying, and in the glazing and sorting departments, women earned from 2/- to 4/- weekly for a working day from 6 to 6 either day or night." (p. 101)

    For a description of working conditions in the paper mills in the 1860s, see D. C. Coleman, *The British Paper Industry* (Oxford, 1958), p. 294.

    Until the late 1860s rag fibres were the mainstay of paper-making. Rags were collected, sorted into grades according to whether they were cotton or linen and placed into rotary boilers where they were heated in a caustic solution. This boiling and tumbling loosened the dirt and destroyed the dyes, and the rags were then placed into something called a "breaking engine" where they were thrashed to pieces and the dirt removed by virtue of the fresh water which was continuously fed into the engine. Paper was made by filtering these fibres through a screen held in water suspension, and by drying the fibres left on the screen. Paper thus came into being through a process which mixed rags with water. *Our Mutual Friend* is about two mythical kingdoms, rubbish and the river, and it is fitting that the paper itself on which the novel was written came into being by virtue of the combination of rags (rubbish) and water (the river). See Edwin Sutermeister, *The Story of Papermaking* (Boston, 1954), Ch. II, and *Handbook of Pulp and Paper Technology* (New York, 1970), edited by K. W. Brut.

# 6 The Mounds

When Mr and Mrs Boffin decide to adopt an orphan, they take themselves in their makeshift equipage to the home of the Rev. Frank Milvey. The Rev. Milvey, burdened by the mundane imperative of caring for six children and the flock of a less than prosperous parish, remarks that the Boffins are like the "Kings and Queens in the Fairy Tales" who always wish for children to complete their kingdom. The Boffins, by virtue of their inheritance of the mounds, have become the rulers of the mythical kingdom of dust. The benevolence which is given a fairy-tale meaning by the Rev. Milvey, is interpreted by incipient orphan-suppliers as the opening of an official market, and a fierce competition ensues for the Boffin custom:

> The suddenness of an orphan's rise in the market was not to be paralleled by the maddest records of the Stock Exchange. He would be at five thousand per cent. discount out at nurse making a mud pie at nine in the morning, and (being enquired for) would go up to five thousand per cent. premium before noon. The market was 'rigged' in various artful ways. Counterfeit stock got into circulation. Parents boldly represented themselves as dead, and brought their orphans with them. Genuine orphan-stock was surreptitiously withdrawn from the market. It being announced, by emissaries posted for the purpose, that Mr. and Mrs. Milvey were coming down the court, orphan scrip would be instantly concealed, and production refused, save on a condition usually stated by the brokers as a 'gallon of beer.' Likewise, fluctuations of a wild and South Sea nature were occasioned by orphan-holders keeping back, and then rushing into the market a dozen together. But the uniform principle at the root of all these various operations was bargain and sale . . . (I, xvi)

In the society which *Our Mutual Friend* describes, children are a marketable commodity; Silas Wegg is quite wrong when he declares to Venus, "You can't buy human flesh and blood in this country, sir; not alive, you can't." Absolutely everything may be turned to profit in this world. And indeed everything is. Wegg's amputated leg has been sold by a hospital porter to Venus as part of a parcel of "human warious"; Jenny Wren buys Pubsey's waste for her dolls' millinery; Gaffer Hexam profits, however minimally, from the retrieval of the dead; and old Harmon has accumulated mountains of rubbish which he has sorted and sifted for resale.

The "uniform principle" at the root of the orphan market is "bargain and sale", that is to say, exchange for profit, and Dickens shows that this "uniform principle" is at the root of almost every transaction in the novel. Dickens does this by using the same language, by repeating certain phrases, to describe different operations. For example, the profit extracted from the dust heaps is described in a way which links it with the profit extracted from the orphan market. When the mounds are eventually levelled under the gleeful and vigilant eye of Sloppy, Silas Wegg is driven almost round the bend in his efforts to keep a watch on their disintegration:

> Over the whole slow process of levelling the Mounds, Silas Wegg had kept watch with rapacious eyes. But eyes no less rapacious had watched the growth of the Mounds in years bygone, and had vigilantly sifted the dust of which they were composed. No valuables turned up. How should there be any, seeing that the old hard jailer of Harmony Jail had coined every waif and stray into money long ago? (IV, xiv)

Orphans are transformed into marketable commodities by the Boffin request, and the marketable commodities which old Harmon has found in the dust are described by Dickens as "waifs and strays" which have been coined into money. Despite the fact that one can make a technical distinction between an orphan and a waif, and that all the children offered to the Milveys are not strictly orphans, Dickens, by showing that orphans represent profit and that profit can be imaginatively represented as waifs and strays, points to the abstraction of all values into the principle of profit which is the underlying "uniform principle" of the society which *Our Mutual Friend* describes.

The language of waifs and strays also appears in Dickens' description of London on that grey and withered evening when Bradley Headstone comes to pay his gloomy court to Lizzie Hexam:

> . . . melancholy waifs and strays of housekeepers and porters sweep melancholy waifs and strays of papers and pins into the

> kennels, and other more melancholy waifs and strays explore them, searching and stooping and poking for anything to sell. (II, XV)

The linguistic process whereby Dickens makes his language work all ways (orphans are marketable commodities, marketable commodities are waifs and strays, waifs and strays are housekeepers and porters, scraps of paper are waifs and strays, and, finally, waifs and strays are literally waifs and strays) is analogous to the economic process, in which all values are abstracted into an occasion for profit, which works all ways to determine the social being of most of the characters in *Our Mutual Friend*. And the creative power of language to make a particular phrase do several things at once, with both literal and metaphorical meanings, with the intention of describing a process in which the value of all things is subsumed under the heading of marketable commodities, is similar to the creative power of money to subsume all things under the heading of profit. The creative power of language and the creative power of money come together in Dickens' imaginative conjunction of orphans, waifs, and strays, and the "uniform principle" of "bargain and sale".[1]

In the context of the theme of social discontent in *Our Mutual Friend*, the mounds represent a possible means of change for many of the characters who seek to improve their lot. The way to change is frequently perceived in terms of the possession of a secret. For Boffin, his inheritance means that he will have the power to penetrate the secrets of the written word; he purchases Wegg's literacy so that a new world may be opened up to him, the world of Print. Through the utilisation of money which has been accumulated in dusty secrecy, Boffin hopes to unravel this secret world of Print. And as Boffin becomes more involved with Wegg, with Fashion, and with all that his possession of the mounds affords him, an interesting difference between the imaginative meaning of the mounds and the river in the novel is revealed.

If the river represents an immersion in the self, as in the case of Eugene Wrayburn's mythical rebirth, then the mounds represent an alienation from the self. To own them, as Boffin does, means that he becomes a prey for all those people who latch on to him, those "crawling, creeping, fluttering and buzzing" parasites in the Dismal Swamp of his Fashionable life. Boffin retreats into isolation, he becomes alienated, suspicious, and seems to lose touch with that innate "moral straightness" which is the actual reason for his wealth.

(It is this quality which has somehow impelled old Harmon to include the Boffins in his will.) Boffin undergoes an actual change of being as he plays the role of miser. To be sure, it is all performance, but it is not just performance designed by Dickens to test Bella Wilfer. After Venus confesses his part in Wegg's schemes, Boffin becomes suspicious of Venus:

> 'Now I wonder,' he meditated as he went along, nursing his stick, 'whether it can be, that Venus is setting himself to get the better of Wegg? Whether it can be, that he means, when I have bought Wegg out, to have me all to himself, and pick me clean to the bones?'
>
> It was a cunning and suspicious idea, quite in the way of his school of Misers, and he looked very cunning and suspicious as he went jogging through the streets. (III, xiv)

Boffin has no audience here, he is alone in the street and this is a "cunning and suspicious" idea in his consciousness, quite different from his imitation of cunning and suspicious behaviour. I don't think Dickens is engaged at this point in a manipulation of the reader so that the re-emergence of good old Boffin is that much more effective: Dickens wants us to see how Boffin's inheritance of the mounds has actually made him "cunning and suspicious", how the mounds have the power to effect essential, if temporary, alteration in those characters who come in contact with them.

Old Harmon has had "serpentining" walks laid out to ascend to the top of his dust heaps – from that spot, literally on the top of his wealth, and figuratively at the peak of his financial power, the empire of dust may be perceived. Boffin, at the very lowest point in his dealings with Silas Wegg, is placed on a chair on a table while the "dockyment" (Harmon's second will which Wegg has discovered in a pump in the yard) is shown to him; the inheritor of Harmon's wealth and the inheritor of all those who covet that wealth, he is placed in a solitary and elevated isolation which repeats the solitary and elevated isolation afforded old Harmon at the top of his dust heaps.

Wegg's most favoured position is not an elevated one – he is fascinated with the mechanics of sifting, sorting, prodding and scooping – and he searches, stoops and pokes like the melancholy waifs and strays who search the London streets for anything to sell. His belief that there are secrets buried in the mounds is not unfounded, but, ironically, the one thing which is buried in the mounds affords him no profit; it is Harmon's *third* will which Boffin has secreted in a gin bottle and buried in his own little mound.[2]

Until Wegg takes up residence in the Bower we have no idea where he sleeps, nor indeed where he comes from: his domain is the street.[3] He arrives every morning at eight o'clock to set up his stall outside the great dingy house which is the feudal manor to which he owes allegiance; Wegg labours under the delusion that he is "one of the house's retainers and owed vassalage to it and was bound to leal and loyal interest in it" (I, v). At the end of *Our Mutual Friend*, Wegg is shot into a scavenger's cart; he is back on the street, back, in fact, in the very spot where Boffin found him. He is fired from the window by Sloppy, and he is fired from his jobs as caretaker of the Bower and resident reader for Mr Boffin. He is worse off than when he started, for his arid stock and stall have been given up, and, like Riderhood, he ends up in the scummy elements. But, unlike Riderhood, he is alive, and the instinct for survival of this "ligneous sharper", this wooden rascal, has been so effectively suggested that one imagines Wegg is resilient enough to stay afloat and to embark on further voyages of "Weggery".

Wegg possesses one secret which he uses in an attempt to gain possession of another; through his literacy, his access to the secrets encoded in Print, he hopes to get hold of the mounds and all the precious items which he imagines are stashed away inside them. He is employed by Boffin as an "official expounder of mysteries", an employment which gives an official seal to the activity in which he is most often engaged, namely observing and interpreting: "Mr. Wegg was an observant person, or as he himself said, 'took a powerful sight of notice'" (I, v). He has interpreted the house on the corner with the "same imaginary power as over its inhabitants and their affairs . . . and it cost his mind a world of trouble to lay it out as to account for everything in its external appearance" (I, v). He is, in fact, very much like a novelist. He is always on the watch and is the only character in the novel to wear spectacles. He declares that Venus has a "speaking countenance", whereas he, Wegg, lays no claim to such a gift – he speaks in words. And does he speak in words! He drops into the most extraordinary and execrable poetry, and his conversations with Venus have a demented rationality which reminds one of twentieth-century absurdist drama.[4]

Albert Guerard has suggested that the playfulness of Wegg's language serves to "screen the reader from a too realistic contemplation of villainy". Guerard makes no essential distinction between

Riderhood, Venus and Wegg and says that one of Dickens' "finer strategies is to endow such repulsive beings . . . with their own brands of forensic nonsense; all three enjoy playing with language and logic".[5] Guerard is partly right about Wegg, but wrong, I think, about Riderhood and Venus. Riderhood does not enjoy playing with language and logic, he is an entirely unselfconscious villain; Venus is only mildly villainous, and then only up to a point and for a very short time. And in the case of Wegg, the master of language as spell, as charm, his linguistic play does anything *but* screen the reader from a contemplation of villainy – it is through his manipulation of language that we know he is a villain. Wegg belongs with Pecksniff and Chadband in Dickens' group of comic villains who play with lanaguage both as the expression and as the mode of their villainy.

Wegg decides to engage Venus as his partner in the enterprise to displace Boffin, and the reasons he requires Venus are important in a consideration of why Dickens dispatches Wegg in such ignominy from *Our Mutual Friend*:

> Mr. Wegg then goes on to enlarge upon what throughout has been uppermost in his crafty mind: – the qualifications of Mr. Venus for such a search. He expatiates on Mr. Venus's patient habits and delicate manipulations; on his skill in piecing little things together; on his knowledge of various tissues and textures; on the likelihood of small indications leading him on to the discovery of great concealments. (II, vii)

Wegg hopes to discover an actual treasure in the mounds.[6] But it seems to me that the mounds may also be considered as more than an actual source of wealth, that their meaning may be extended to give them a larger, more complex, and even symbolic significance. By virtue of the power which lies in their possession to so effectively determine the social situation of so many characters in the novel, they bear an imaginative correspondence to *all* of the actual economic situations which play so large a part in determining the dissatisfaction of these characters. The mounds, in other words, may be read as a unifying symbol of economic situation in *Our Mutual Friend*. Wegg, by wanting Venus to lead them on "to the discovery of great concealments", by wanting to discover the secret of the mounds, may be said implicitly to want to discover the economic secrets of his society. This is not to suggest that Wegg is an incipient political economist, or detective, but rather to show one of the possible reasons why Dickens eventually disposes of him as rubbish.

In *Capital*, Marx examines the mysterious character, the secret nature, of the process whereby products of labour are mysteriously transformed into commodities. Capitalists necessarily conceal the amount of labour-time which has gone into the production of a commodity, and "the determination of the magnitude of labour-time is . . . a secret, hidden under the apparent fluctuations in the relative value of commodities". Marx theorises that the abstraction of value which takes place in capitalist societies "converts every product into a social hieroglyphic. Later on we try to decipher the hieroglyphic, to get behind the secret of our own social products; for to stamp an object of utility as a value, is just as much a social product as language."[7]

Wegg, as the paramount "reader" in *Our Mutual Friend*, uses one "social product", language, as a means of trying to discover the secrets of another, the mounds. The mounds themselves are a "social hieroglyphic", and Wegg, in trying to explicitly discover what is actually buried *within* them, may be said implicitly to want to demystify them, that is to say, to penetrate the economic secrets of his society.

Wegg fails at demystification. His one discovery affords him no profit, and he is banished from the mythical kingdom, literally thrown out of the fairy-tale palace. I think we have to ask ourselves what it is about Wegg which makes it imperative that Dickens dispatch him in such mucky disgrace. He is a crafty rascal, but that really tells us nothing, for crafty rascals in fairy-tales, and in novels which resemble fairy-tales, always get their desserts.

Silas Wegg symbolically displays a dangerous curiosity about the economic workings of his society and the price of Dickens' admittance of Wegg's curiosity into *Our Mutual Friend* seems to be his confinement to a condition of obsession and delusion. Wegg is a grotesque, confined by his actual social situation, and confined by Dickens to exile from his fable of regenerated bourgeois culture. Wegg becomes madder and madder in the course of *Our Mutual Friend*, and, ironically, in the course of the realisation of his fantasies. His delusions about having been "passed over" in his rights to the Harmon property reach a frenzied pitch in the actualisation of his desire for attachment to a wealthy family. "Our House" becomes occupied by Wegg's *real* patron, and it is as if the realisation of his wish to be a "retainer", to be "bound to leal and loyal interest" in the house, intensifies his social paranoia. He has lived so long in a sealed world of delusion, in a world destitute of human attachment, that the transformation of his fantasies into actuality seems literally to send him off his rocker. And Wegg's obsessive transformation of reality into fiction, and the intensification of his madness by the transformation of some of those fictions into reality, suggest, perhaps, Dickens' conscious or unconscious uneasiness about the ambivalent position of the fiction-maker; that is to say, the position of the novelist who inhabits a world of reality, and also a world where that reality is transformed into fiction.

Through Wegg's curiosity about the mounds, Dickens imaginatively represents a curiosity about the mystification of capitalist profit, but Wegg is punished for this curiosity by his eventual banishment from the mythical kingdom of the dust heaps. I think that Dickens thereby admits into his novel a lively interest in the (by definition) secret workings of capitalism, but at the same time, by punishing Wegg for his inquisitiveness, Dickens may be said to alleviate the anxiety of his readers, who perhaps shared Wegg's nosiness, that such inquisitiveness could reach the stage of being actually disruptive of established social structures. Wegg's interest in discovering secrets remains just that, an interest which is allowed expression to a certain point, and then is halted before it gets out of hand.[8]

Mrs Wilfer, too, is punished by permanent exile from the kingdom of the mounds and by isolation from family and friends. Where Wegg is punished for his dangerous curiosity, she is punished for her exaggerated consciousness of class and for the manner in which her expression of this class consciousness affects her family.

In a novel about assumed identities and role-playing, she undertakes the part of a lower-middle-class Lady Macbeth. The adjective which Dickens most frequently employs to describe her is "majestic", and the source of her comic presence is the disjunction between her lofty manner and the seedy reality of the Wilfer household. Her regal behaviour is entirely misplaced, and it is one of the implicit reasons for her final exile. A comparison of her behaviour and that of the other female regal character in the novel, Miss Abbey Potterson, suggests the inappropriateness of Mrs Wilfer's manner. Miss Abbey "reigns supreme" over the kingdom of the Fellowships – a kingdom composed of the riverside working class. While Dickens' creation of an orderly working class ruled by a female publican is a myth generated out of urban alienation and desolation, Miss Abbey's assumption of regal authority does not seem out of line, for her charges, so to speak, are not intimately related to her. But Mrs Wilfer tries to rule her *family*. Her efforts in this direction are an expression of the aggressive resentment she feels by virtue of her imagined social humiliation in marriage to R. W. Unable to rule from the social position she thinks she deserves, she tries to rule her family instead. Ma is an English joke, a figure on the picture postcards sent from the seaside which George Orwell analyses in his essay on Donald McGill: she is the henpecking wife, the large and domineering woman, and the impossible mother-in-law. When Dickens writes that she washes her hands of the Boffins and takes herself to bed "after the manner of Lady Macbeth", this is a wonderfully comic perception. But implicit in this perception is an allusion to the aggressive ambition of Lady Macbeth and to the destruction which it causes.

Mrs Wilfer's paramount interest, the English class structure, is the locus of her comic personality. By making her concern with class a source of comedy Dickens defuses the explosive possibilities inherent in the class consciousness which he so effectively describes everywhere in *Our Mutual Friend*. Bradley Headstone's class consciousness transforms him into a feral creature of the night, and the dangerous potential of his class feeling is realised in the destruction and self-destruction which he wreaks. Dickens' representation of Mrs Wilfer's class consciousness works in a somewhat similar, if clearly less violent, manner. By making her dotty and malevolent pronouncements comic, Dickens defuses the resentment which is their energising source, a resentment which, in social actuality, was not necessarily confined to such deranged personalities as Mrs Wilfer. By turning Ma into a joke, by exaggerating her class consciousness to a point of absurdity and comic obsession, Dickens mitigates his representation of a social dissatisfaction which is perhaps the most deeply-felt in the novel. As Dickens admits Wegg's curiosity about the workings of society into the novel and then summarily dispatches it before it can become dangerous, so he admits Mrs Wilfer's class resentment into *Our Mutual Friend*, and then undermines it by turning her into something like a music-hall turn.

If Mrs Wilfer is compared with some of Dickens' other lower-middle-class female characters, one has a sense of the degree to which *Our Mutual Friend* is concerned with social dissatisfaction, and with its debilitating effect upon family life. The Kenwigses in

*Nicholas Nickleby*, for example, are lower-middle-class like the Wilfers, and, also like them, they live on the shabby margins of London poverty. Mrs Kenwigs is "of a very genteel family" and has an uncle who is a water-rate collector, one Lillyvick: like Mrs Wilfer she has family connections which mark her as slightly superior to her neighbours. But her wedding anniversary celebration is conducted in a far different fashion from the annual feast of the Wilfers, which is the occasion for Ma "to hold a sombre, darkling state". The Kenwigses are surrounded by family and friends; they have a jolly supper and enjoy a small programme of entertainment put on by their guests. The Wilfer celebration is conducted in an atmosphere of severe gloom, and is devoted to Mrs Wilfer's annual oration on the disaster which befell her in marriage to a man smaller than herself.

Mrs Kenwigs utilises her children to gain Uncle Lillyvick's approbation, but she is not estranged from them. The Kenwigses form a cohesive family unit, partly bound together by their class feeling, but when Dickens arrives at the Wilfers all that seems to be left of lower-middle-class family life *is* class feeling. The alliance which the Kenwigses form in the face of making-do is exploded in *Our Mutual Friend* into Ma's social paranoia, Lavinia's caustic jealousy of Bella, Pa's resignation to his lot ("Ah me! . . . what might have been is not what is!" is his strongest admission of a disappointed life), and Bella's desire to get away from Holloway as soon as she is able. In effect, the lower-middle-class family whose members were allied in a struggle for improvement in *Nicholas Nickleby* is blown apart in *Our Mutual Friend*. The Wilfer family is effectively broken up at the end of the novel. Pa is absorbed into the fairy-tale kingdom (he is taken on as secretary); Lavinia will presumably settle down to tyrannise George Sampson in the way in which Ma has tyrannised Pa, and Ma herself is left out in the cold, which is where she has always been anyway.

Dickens replaces that lower-middle-class family with a mythical family composed of a childless King and Queen, a wealthy Grand Prince and a tried and true Princess. By the time of his last completed novel, it seems as if Dickens' creation of a mythical family, under which are subsumed the smaller family units of Lizzie and Eugene, and Jenny Wren and Sloppy, reveals a diminished faith in the viability of cohesive family life as a means of dealing with depressing social actuality.

The breakdown of family life is primarily registered through Ma and her coldness. She is a "frozen article on display in a Russian market", and her cheek is as welcome as the back of a soup spoon, a "cold slate for visitors to enrol themselves upon". She repels by her glaring as the Veneering furniture repels by its veneer. And just as the Veneerings and their furniture give off nothing but a reflection of themselves, so Mrs Wilfer's animosity is registered in the countenances of those she glares at:

> A magnetic result of such glaring was, that the person glared at could not by any means successfully pretend to be ignorant of the fact: so that a bystander, without beholding Mrs. Wilfer at all, must have known at whom she was glaring, by seeing her refracted from the countenance of the beglared one. (III, xvi)

When Ma visits the "new abode of Mendicancy" at the end of *Our Mutual Friend*, she bears herself as a suspicious "Savage Chief" in the world of fairy-tale civilisation:

> She regarded every servant who approached her as her sworn enemy, expressly intending to offer her affronts with the dishes, and to pour forth outrages on her moral feelings from the decanters. She sat erect at table, on the right hand of her son-in-law, as half-suspecting poison in the viands, and as bearing up with native force of character against other deadly ambushes. (IV, xvi)

Mrs Wilfer is dispatched by Dickens into native country, to the world of the uncivilised and suspicious. Through her, Dickens demonstrates that an exaggerated consciousness of class is the road to social Siberia; she is fierce, "savage" in her bearing, and unrelentingly cold to her daughter to the very end. I think it is significant that perhaps the most severely discontented character in a novel about social discontent, ends up entirely isolated. In some sense, her experience in *Our Mutual Friend* is as chilling and tragic as that of Bradley Headstone, even though her class resentment never generates the physical destruction which is the direct consequence of Bradley's feelings of social inferiority.

Although Fascination Fledgeby is not directly connected with the mythical kingdom of the mounds, he knows a great deal about the "uniform principle" of bargain and sale which has determined the accumulation of the dust heaps. He operates in the secret world of money-lending.[9] He is an "outlaw" roaming the "merry greenwood of Jobbery Forest", and as a cover for his less than jolly operations, he invents the fiction that he is employed by Riah. He appropriates the myth of Jewish greed, and he profits from what Dickens calls a "very convenient fiction".

Fledgeby has inherited Riah from his money-lending father to whom Riah owed "principal and interest", and so Riah represents a return upon Fledgeby senior's investment. And Fledgeby, too, represents a return upon an investment made by his father. He is the son of a money-lender and a minor member of the aristocracy – a child of usury, the progeny born of his mother's settlement of bills when she marries the man who has lent her money. If we consider Fledgeby for the moment as a dividend, returned, so to speak, from his father's investment, we can perceive yet another instance in *Our Mutual Friend* of how the father determines the lives of his children. Old Harmon determines, through his "will", the destiny of John Harmon and the plot of *Our Mutual Friend*, and the elder Wrayburn determines the professions of his children. A money-lender is the progenitor of Fascination Fledgeby and he, in his turn, is a money-lender. But Dickens, in a wonderfully ironic twist, suggests that Fledgeby can be the progenitor of nothing but money. Dickens shows that money "makes" the world in *Our Mutual Friend*, but he also shows that there are some transformations which money cannot effect.

Fledgeby has a secret which presents a greater problem for concealment than his bill-broking operations: he is not sexually mature. Pubsey & Co., is, I think, a play on pubes, and while Fledgeby is a fully fledged financial hawk, he is an immature sexual fledgling. He is a Victorian version of Chaucer's Pardoner, avaricious and sexless, and making a pilgrimage through the financial alleys of the City in search of profit. The Pardoner's sandy hair and lack of beard suggest that he is a eunuch:

> This Pardoner hadde heer as yelow as wex,
> But smothe it heeng as dooth a strike of flex;
> By ounces henge his lokkes that he hadde,
> And therwith he his shuldres overspradde;
> But thynne it lay, by colpons oon and oon.
> . . . No berd hadde he, ne nevere shoulde have;
> As smothe it was as if it were late shave.

I trowe he were a gelding or a mare.
(General Prologue, ll. 675–91)

Fledgeby is an "awkward, sandy-haired, small-eyed youth, exceedingly slim (his enemies would have said lanky) and prone to self-examination in the articles of whisker and moustache" (II, iv). Like Chaucer's Pardoner, Fledgeby has absolutely no whiskers and he loathes the "gingerous bush" which is one of the signs of Lammle's sexual vitality: he consoles himself with the fact that "money can't produce them". But if he can be said to want anything more than he wants money, it is to possess such a gingerous bush. Fledgeby is a grotesque, sexless and prematurely old by virtue of his avarice, and he is altogether an unnatural phenomenon.

His unnatural being is suggested by his self-secretion behind the façade of Jewish greed; Riah is the front for Pubsey & Co. and Fledgeby is the solid and sordid reality. Dickens creates a spatial arrangement of façade and reality in the relationship between Fledgeby and Riah; it is interesting that he deliberately upsets this arrangement in Riah's actual physical position at Pubsey & Co. Riah lives on the top storey of the counting house premises, which was a common practice for city caretakers in mid-nineteenth-century London, and the reality behind Fledgeby's fiction is brought out by Riah's occupation of the top storey of the house. Fledgeby's unnatural fiction is that Riah *is* Pubsey & Co., but in actuality Riah lives a kind of natural life on the roof. He has a garden which represents the only bit of nature on the whole premises: the counting house office is adorned with "strings of mock beads", samples of cheap clocks and cheap vases of artificial flowers. Riah has real flowers in his roof garden. But, paradoxically, he creates his own kind of fiction in this creation of nature among the chimney tops. In Riah, however, fiction-making is given a positive significance; he makes his own world on the roof as an alternative to the squalid business conducted on the premises below.

Dickens' complex juxtaposition of façade and content, of unnatural fiction and natural actuality in the relationship between Fledgeby and Riah shows how money has the power to create fictions, and effective fictions, too, for Fledgeby manages a good deal of profitable manipulation in *Our Mutual Friend* before he is finally rooted out. The murkiness surrounding Fledegeby's transactions and his relationship with Riah is suggested by the fantastic aspects of Riah himself. As he walks through the fog in his long gaberdine coat, "more than one head, turning to look back at his venerable figure already lost in the mist, supposed it to be some ordinary figure indistinctly seen, which fancy and the fog had worked into that passing likeness" (II, i). His actual fantastic appearance is rejected as totally implausible, and he is therefore thought to have been transformed by the fog. The confusion, the phenomenological disorientation generated by his actuality, affirms the confusion generated by Fledgeby's appropriation of fact for profit.

Fledgeby is clearly as villainous as Silas Wegg, and maybe more so because he deliberately, and even rationally, sets out to deceive, whereas Wegg is a victim of his own social paranoia. Fledgeby is alarmingly sane. But his punishment in *Our Mutual Friend*, even though parallel to that of Wegg, is not as severe as the one dished out to that sharper. Fledgeby is not an aggressive character in the sense that he tries to change his place in society. And indeed why should he? The one thing needful in his life is a beard: he is discontented, to be sure, but his discontent is with his sexlessness and not with society. He is not deluded by fantasies of majestic grandeur like Wegg and Mrs Wilfer, nor destroyed by obsession with self-advancement like Bradley Headstone. He comfortably inhabits his social situation, indeed embraces it, and it would seem that to do that makes him immune from exile and death. He is certainly not enfolded within the golden circle of domesticity at the end of the novel, but he really gets off very lightly. His punishment is to be thrashed by Lammle, to have salt and snuff stuffed into his nose and mouth so that he crows with the pain of someone who seems to be "contending with every mortal disease incidental to poultry". And the last we hear of him is that Mortimer Lightwood applies himself with "infinite zest to attacking and harassing Mr Fledgeby who, discovering himself in danger of being blown into the air by certain explosive transactions in which he had been engaged, and having been sufficiently flayed under his beating, came to a parley and asked for quarter" (IV, xvi). He is given quarter by Mortimer and, indeed, by Dickens. Fledgeby is odious, to be sure, but at the end of *Our Mutual Friend* he is relatively unregenerate and unchanged, as the social structures which the novel has described are not regenerated or changed by Dickens.

The Lammles, too, know all too well about the ins and outs of finance and they also escape fairly lightly when their career in duplicity is examined in the light of that of other characters in the novel. They are literally exiled from the kingdom of the mounds when the fiction of their mutuality and solvency is unmasked, and they take up residence abroad. The Lammle union is a parody of the bourgeois marriage market which Eugene Wrayburn rejects; it is a "fiction" arranged by the Veneerings, and the Lammles maintain it as a fiction of mutual adoration and financial security. It is the marriage of a gingerous devil (Lammle trails his stick behind him as he walks on the Shanklin sands so that it is "as if he were of the Mephistopheles family indeed and had walked with a dropping tail") and a mature young lady with too much powder and too few marital prospects. The implicit meaning of their marriage is accurately assessed by Lady Tippins as she evaluates the wedding in terms of how much it cost:

> Bride; five-and-forty if a day, thirty shillings a yard, veil fifteen pounds, pocket-handkerchief a present. Bridesmaids, kept down for fear of out-shining bride, consequently not girls, twelve and sixpence a yard, Veneering's flowers, snub-nosed one rather pretty but too conscious of her stockings, bonnets three pounds ten . . . Mrs. Veneering: never saw such velvet, say two thousand pounds as she stands, absolute jeweller's window, father must have been a pawnbroker, or how could these people do it? Attendant unknowns: pokey. (I, x)

The marriage is assessed in monetary terms, but the irony of the situation is, of course, that neither of the principals has a bean. It is Sophronia, the wife, and not Alfred, the husband, who articulates the reality behind the fiction of mutual adoration and solvency, and considered in general for the moment and compared with the male characters, the female characters in *Our Mutual Friend* seem to be the more astute assessors of social reality, however distressing that social reality may be to *them*. Lizzie Hexam is uncomfortably conscious of her class and of the social gulf which yawns between her and Eugene. Bella Wilfer is fully aware of the economic nature of her society, and she is not reluctant to voice her resentment of the ways in which this fundamental structure has determined the Wilfer family life. Even though Lady Tippins participates in the Veneering fictions and has created some pretty dreadful ones of her own (her skeletal body and ravaged face are masked by cosmetic artifice, and she maintains a fictive list of lovers), she understands the reality behind these fictions. Sophronia Lammle staggers poor Twemlow with a depressing, but accurate, evaluation of her marriage:

> We must eat and drink, and dress, and have a roof over our heads . . . what can a woman at my age do? My husband and I deceived one another when we married; we must bear the consequences of that deception – that is to say, bear one another, and bear the burden of scheming together for to-day's dinner and tomorrow's breakfast – till death divorces us. (III, xvii)

Sophronia intuitively understands that Riah is the mask for Fledgeby's avarice, and in the scene where she tries to warn Twemlow about Fledgeby, she insists upon the reluctance of men to face such realities:

> Men are very wise in their way . . . but they have wisdom to learn. My husband, who is not over-confiding, ingenuous, or inexperienced, sees this plain thing no more than Mr. Twemlow does – because there is no proof. Yet I believe five women out of six in my place, would see it as clearly as I do. (III, xvii)

The Lammles discover their mutual deception on their honeymoon. When they start their walk on the Shanklin sands, the brown cliffs seem to have a "golden surface", emblematic of the surface of their marriage, and when they finish their walk they discover that the cliffs are only composed of "damp earth". They discover the damp and heavy substance of their deception. They agree to keep their discovery a secret and to work together in the furtherance of their own schemes. They only manage to get two schemes going, and neither of them comes off. One is to procure Georgiana Podsnap for Fledgeby, and the other is to supplant Rokesmith in Boffin's employment and esteem. It is interesting that in the formal implementation of these schemes the procedure is identical; Sophronia and Alfred do all the talking while the other people remain silent.

In the first, they get Georgiana and Fledgeby together for dinner and the opera. The scene is farcical as the Lammles display a quite extraordinary amount of linguistic energy and conduct a surrogate conversation for the sexually petrified Georgiana and the graceless Fledgeby. The Lammles have trapped Georgiana through Sophronia's initially feigned, and then quite genuine, sympathy for the oppression she has suffered under Podsnappery, and through Alfred's sexual vitality. Even though Georgiana is terrified of the power of her own sexual feelings, her fascinated horror of sexuality is implicitly expressed in her fear of dancing; she imagines that she will kill her partner if she ever gets up to dance. She is fascinated by Alfred's sinuous attractions. Dickens gives Lammle a sexual past (he admits to Fledgeby that women "were pleased to like him"), and he also gives him a distinctly sexual presence. Just as Carker's teeth in *Dombey & Son* signify his animal sexuality, so a palpitating nose and the abundant whiskers which are the envy of the incomplete Fledgeby, signify Alfred's devilish vigour.

In the scene with the Boffins, the Lammles come to breakfast to ingratiate themselves with the "Golden Dustman". They do all the talking, calling each other "precious" and "My dear love" and generally carrying on like love birds. They get nowhere and discover that they are "discoursing at once affectingly, and effectively, but discoursing alone". Driven to elaborate artifice, they invent a conceit that the Boffins are a "court" and they throw themselves open to it for judgment as to whether they over-praise each other or not. Boffin finally opens his mouth, and it is to shatter their conceit, to deflate their figurative language and to speak directly to the matter in hand: the "court" and "Mrs. Court" have had enough and he asks them "which of you two is Cashier?" He pays them off, and they exit from the novel and from the mythical kingdom of the mounds:

> They walked arm in arm, showily enough, but without appearing to interchange a syllable. It might have been fanciful to suppose that under their outer bearing there was something of the shamed air of two cheats who were linked together by concealed handcuffs; but not so, to suppose that they were haggardly weary of one another, of themselves, and of all this world. In turning the street corner they might have turned out of this world, for anything Mr. and Mrs. Boffin ever saw of them to the contrary; for they set eyes on the Lammles never more. (IV, ii)

It is important here that "this world" *is* the world of the Boffins, and the punishment Dickens measures out to the Lammles is that they are banished from the one world which finally matters in *Our Mutual Friend*.

Veneering's explicit relationship to the mythical kingdom of the mounds in *Our Mutual Friend* lies in his unquestioned acceptance of the "Golden Dustman" as a desirable member of Society once Mr and Mrs Boffin go headlong into fashion: his implicit association with the dustheaps lies in his status as a *nouveau-riche* businessman who thoroughly understands the "uniform principle" of bargain and sale which is the source of their power.

Dickens not only excludes Veneering from the resolutions of social tension which come into being at the end of *Our Mutual Friend*; he also keeps him at a formal distance from all the significant action in the novel. The Voice of Society chapters, which have the Veneering dinner table as their centre, form an accumulative chorus which comments upon the action, but essentially has nothing to do with it. These chapters are concerned with anecdote, with comment upon the doings of the world outside the *nouveau-riche*, and their formal and rhetorical significance is analogous to the attitude towards the world of the characters who constitute the Voice of Society chorus.

Mortimer Lightwood, a gifted story-teller, is the link between the artifice of the Society world and the substantial reality that exists outside that world and which is the material of its entertainment. Reality intrudes upon artifice when Mortimer's narrative of the "Man from Somewhere" is interrupted by the news of the drowning of the hero of that story. Mortimer leaves to inspect that reality, and subsequently returns with further material for anecdote. It is interesting that his story-telling receives none of the satiric volleys that Dickens directs at Messrs Veneering and Podsnap's appropriation of these same events. The Veneerings' prime fiction is that they are surrounded by a circle of old and dear friends. It is a compelling and poisonous illusion, and Twemlow notices "how soon the Veneering guests become infected with the Veneering fiction". The Veneerings acquire some more "bran-new" bosom friends through their relation of the Harmon story. Dickens' description of their forays into narrative is an imaginative affirmation of the profit to be exacted from telling stories and from retrieving bodies from the river:

> So, addressing himself to the most desirable of his neighbours, while Mrs. Veneering secured the next most desirable, he [Veneering] plunged into the case, and emerged from it twenty minutes afterwards with a Bank Director in his arms. In the meantime, Mrs. Veneering had dived into the same waters for a wealthy Ship-Broker, and had brought him up, safe and sound, by the hair. Then Mrs. Veneering had to relate, to a larger circle, how she had been to see the girl, and how she was really pretty, and (considering her station) presentable. And this she did with such a

> successful display of her eight aquiline fingers and their encircling jewels, that she happily laid hold of a drifting General Officer, his wife and daughter, and not only restored their animation, which had become suspended, but made them lively friends within an hour. (I, xi)

Mortimer Lightwood's narrative talent is represented uncritically in *Our Mutual Friend* because he is, despite and because of his amoral detachment from all events, an ally for Dickens. He facilitates the connections between the mythical kingdom of the dust heaps and the mythical kingdom of the river: he articulates the diffused restlessness in both these kingdoms when he raises his eyebrows and says to his new client, "Is Anything satisfactory, Mr. Boffin?" (I, viii). And in an analogue to the work of the novelist, he "reduces" Rogue Riderhood to writing when that honest fellow comes to give his "Alfred David". He is a literary-minded solicitor who tells stories in ironic fashion with playful references to fairy-tales, and to the expectations of his listeners which are founded upon reading second-rate novels. He continually demonstrates a critical and selfconscious awareness of self and society in his detached presence. Veneering and his wife tell their stories with none of this critical awareness: Veneering is a bourgeois businessman, and Dickens' description of his narrative efforts is coherent with *Our Mutual Friend*'s satire of bourgeois culture.

Veneering is the head of a drug-house in Mincing Lane, and this is an appropriate occupation for a man who seeks to veil his travelling salesman past under the veneer of a "bran-new" life. There are several significant references to drugs in *Our Mutual Friend* which serve to draw attention to the pain and stress of social existence described in the novel. Discontent is so pervasive in *Our Mutual Friend* that even the houses seem to be under the influence of quieting narcotics. Smith Square, where Jenny Wren lives, is described as being in a state of unnatural quietude; there is a "deadly kind of repose on it, more as though it had taken laudanum than fallen into a natural rest". These houses lie in an unnatural and deadly repose, far different, say, from the relaxed calm with which Wordsworth invests early morning London in his Westminster Bridge sonnet. There "the very houses seem asleep"; they seem to be lying in a natural rest soon to be broken by the bustle of the morning: in *Our Mutual Friend*, the houses seem to have given up on the world, to have sedated themselves in the face of its dreariness and misery.

Eugene Wrayburn floats through the novel in a haze of cigar smoke; he uses tobacco as a relaxing narcotic and as a screen. He cloaks himself in smoke as he tries to cloak himself from the disturbing effects of Lizzie Hexam, and he tells Mortimer that a cigar can dispel unpleasant sights, in particular the picture of ruin presented by Mr Dolls. "Take a cigar. Look at this of mine. I light it – draw one puff – breathe the smoke out – there, it goes – it's Dolls! It's gone, and being gone, you are a man again!" (III, x). Bella Wilfer, a vision of ripe sexuality on her wedding morning, is perceived through a narcotic haze by old Gruff and Glum. And Bella herself tells Pa of a wish-fulfilling fantasy in which he comes back to England with enough opium to cut Chicksey, Veneering and Stobbles out of the market – in effect, with enough opium to cut Ma out of the family picture, and to leave Bella and her father living in the lap of luxury.

The importing of opium was a profitable business in the mid-nineteenth century, profitable enough to deck Mrs Veneering out in two thousand pounds worth of velvet and jewels at the Lammle wedding. The profit to be had in this trade is indicated in an article which appeared in *All The Year Round* on 8 October 1864. The article is a discussion of the 1864 Report of the Medical Officer to the Privy Council, and points to the reliance of the English working class upon drugs:

> A retail druggist in the Fens will regard opium as his leading article, and sell as much as two hundred pounds of it in a year, serving three or four hundred customers on a Saturday night with penny sticks or pills. A man in South Lincolnshire complained that his wife had spent a hundred pounds in opium since she married him. A man setting about a hand job takes his pill to set him a-going, and many never take their beer without dropping a piece of opium into it. With the opium believed in by the parents and nurses, children are quieted and quieted to death.

Here it is the working class which dopes itself up to face its work and indeed its recreation.[10] But the middle class in *Our Mutual Friend* is addicted, too; it is enslaved to another variety of narcotic – to Shares:

> As is well known to the wise in their generation, traffic in Shares is the one thing to have to do with in this world. Have no

> antecedents, no established character, no cultivation, no ideas, no manners; have Shares. Have Shares enough to be on Boards of Direction in capital letters, oscillate on mysterious business between London and Paris, and be great. Where does he come from? Shares. Where is he going to? Shares. What squeezes him into Parliament? Shares. Perhaps he never of himself achieved success in anything, never originated anything, never produced anything! Sufficient answer to all; Shares. O mighty Shares! To set these blaring images so high, and to cause us smaller vermin, as under the influence of henbane or opium, to cry out night and day, 'Relieve us of our money, scatter it for us, buy us and sell us, ruin us, only we beseech ye take rank among the powers of the earth, and fatten on us!' (I, X)

The imperative, "Have no antecedents, no established character, no cultivation, no ideas, no manners; have Shares," suggests the imperative of an addiction – nothing matters but to have Shares. The passage takes on biblical resonances and becomes a prayer to Shares themselves – those blaring images which enslave us like "henbane or opium" – Shares are elevated to the status of a deity. Henbane, incidentally, is a narcotic plant especially destructive to domestic fowls, and it is fitting that Fledgeby, truly one of the addicted, should crow like a barnyard animal afflicted with poultry disease.

Veneering is "sly, mysterious, filmy – a kind of sufficiently well-looking prophet – not prophesying", and he tries to improve his social position by consorting with parasitic nonentities and giving dinners in an arid atmosphere where a caravan of silver camels trudges across the desert of the dining table. He also tries to transform himself by paying "two thousand five hundred per letter" to put M. P. after his name. His friends rally round and he is brought in for Pocket Breaches – a pocket borough which one imagines would be destined for extinction under the provisions of the 1867 Reform Bill. Lady Tippins tools around town in the Veneering equipage, "rattling on" about the suitability of her candidate for the House, and rattling is an appropriate verb for this grotesque bag of bones. In her electioneering activities, she gives voice to the reality behind the fiction as she does in her smart account of the Lammle wedding. Why is she "pretending" to be an electioneering agent? Because Veneering has "bought" Pocket Breaches. And why are we carrying on this "little farce"? – "to keep up appearances." The election itself is a political fiction; Pocket Breaches is a pocket borough already firmly deposited in the pocket of Veneering's breeches by virtue of *his* deposit of five thousand pounds in the pocket of the Party.

The Veneerings are destined in the "Books of the Insolvent Fates" to make a resounding smash. The ex-M.P., ex-W.M.P., and Baby, retire to Calais to live on Mrs Veneering's diamonds, and it is significant that while Dickens dispatches them to France, he keeps the Podsnaps firmly in their bourgeois place in English society. Veneering is a kind of filmy illusionist, a *nouveau-riche* conjuror who creates the illusion of bourgeois solidity. But Podsnap performs no conjuring tricks; he doesn't need to because he is the all too solid embodiment of the bourgeois power which Veneering has tried to conjure up.[11]

The Podsnaps live in a house full of massive furniture and "swarthy giants of looking glasses". Podsnap, who is large like his furniture, can tolerate glitter "in a mushroom man", but he goes in for "hideous solidity", and he remains firmly in his solid place at the end of *Our Mutual Friend*.[12] Dickens does not make him disappear in a fictive conjuring trick which is an appropriate end for the illusionist Veneering, and he does not have him stroll out of the novel like the Lammles. I think that Dickens makes Podsnap immovable because he stands for an immovable structure of society. Where Veneering is "filmy, sly, mysterious", almost on the point of disappearance, Podsnap is always, quite simply, immovably present. He exists in *Our Mutual Friend* as a pure representation of the bourgeois culture which Dickens seeks to regenerate. He has prudently married his own "good inheritance" to an equally good one, and he has "thriven exceedingly in the Marine Insurance way" (I, xi). To remove Podsnap would, in a sense, be to remove the economic foundation of society, which was formed by such solid commercial enterprises as shipbuilding, transportation, and insurance. Dickens, in his idiosyncratic selection of characters for escape from their debilitating social situations, transcends those situations, which is something quite different from making them disappear. Dickens can blow Veneering away in a puff because Veneering is a sham, a genii who gives dinners out of the Arabian nights, a conjuror who conjures up the illusion of bourgeois solidity. Podsnap is no illusion. He remains in place at the end of the novel because he represents what is, in effect, unyielding, and which must therefore be transcended. He remains prosperous and dominant as a register of the complexity of the society which Dickens describes. *Our Mutual Friend* is no fable where good is simply and satisfyingly triumphant over evil; it does not gratify the reader with the neat dispatch of every villain. The fact that Podsnap does not get his desserts intensifies the effectiveness both of Dickens' representation of a society founded upon bourgeois power, and his transcendence of that representation.

Where Podsnap relishes the weight of his furniture and his financial solidity, John Harmon is almost buried under the weight of the mounds. While Podsnap sits enormous and complacent on his mounds of money and household furnishings, Harmon is oppressed by the dust heaps. At the end of the novel, the dust heaps are demolished, but Harmon still remains Harmon, still subject to the mounds and their history. To be sure, all the rusty old money is shined up and Harmon replaces Harmony Jail, with its denuded bannisters and air of desuetude, by a new menage, teeming with life and replete with painted rainbows. However, the manner in which Harmon's mythical rebirth is described suggests that even though Harmon may call himself Julius Handford/John Rokesmith, he can never be anything other than John Harmon, son of the man who made the mounds.

About half way through *Our Mutual Friend*, Harmon embarks on a first-person narrative of self-examination. In October 1865 an anonymous reviewer found this part of the novel "objectionable", because it served "no other purpose than to inform the reader of the complicated events".[13] While Harmon's narrative certainly does serve this purpose, it does something else as well. It demonstrates how Harmon attempts to define himself through narrative, through language, in a manner which is similar, say, to the way Pip defines himself in the one long narrative of self-examination which is *Great Expectations*. Pip becomes Pip in the process of the novel, and Harmon becomes Harmon in the process of his soliloquy.

He begins with the recognition that he came back to England, "shrinking from my father's money, shrinking from my father's memory, mistrustful of being forced on a mercenary wife, mistrustful of my father's intention in thrusting that marriage on me, mistrustful that I was already growing avaricious" (II, xii). He recalls that when he was drugged he "could not have said my name was John Harmon". He is disturbed because there is no way he can express this experience to himself "without using the word I. But it was not I. There was no such thing as I, within my knowledge." Drugs, which in other places in *Our Mutual Friend* appear as a form of self-obfuscation, work upon him to obliterate his sense of self. At this moment, he recalls, he was plunged into the river:

> It was only after a downward slide through something like a tube, and then a great noise and a sparkling and a crackling as of fires, that the consciousness came upon me, "This is John Harmon drowning! John Harmon, struggle for your life. John Harmon, call on Heaven and save yourself". I think I cried it out aloud in a great agony, and then a heavy horrid unintelligible something vanished, and it was I who was struggling there alone in the water. (II, xiii)

His "downward slide through something like a tube" suggests the natal journey through the birth canal, and Harmon is mythically reborn from the river; the "heavy horrid unintelligible something" vanishes and it is an I, a self, who struggles in the water. But he is not reborn as anything other than John Harmon; his rebirth leads to an intensified consciousness of what it means to be the son of the jailer of Harmony Jail. Dickens' description of Harmon's struggle in the river suggests that he cannot escape the destiny which has been prescribed for him by his father and by his society.

He makes an actual and mythical journey across the river. This is not the river of death, of forgetfulness, on which Betty Higden sees a barge bearing all her dead children and dead grandchildren; it is the river of consciousness and he undertakes a journey which brings him to a living and painful awareness of his allotted place in society. At the close of his narrative, his self-examination as a "living-dead man", he decides to see if Bella will have him as Rokesmith. She will not, for she is resentful, confused, and ambivalent about her posh life at the Boffins and about the power of money in her society. He interprets Bella's refusal as a sign that he has no future as John Harmon, and he feels that even if he were pressed to reveal himself, his dispossession of the Boffins would be untenable in the light of their kindness. He decides to finish off John Harmon:

> He went down to his room, and buried John Harmon many additional fathoms deep. He took his hat, and walked out, and as he went to Holloway or anywhere else – not at all minding where – he heaped mounds upon mounds of earth over John Harmon's grave. (II, xi)

Mortimer Lightwood has told the Voice of Society that old Harmon gave directions for his burial "with certain eccentric ceremonies and precautions against his coming to life", and it is as if Harmon's son repeats, in symbolic fashion, his father's desire to ensure an irreversible burial. Harmon becomes his own sexton, admonishing himself to "cover him, crush him, keep him down!"

When Harmon first accosts Boffin in the street to propose himself as secretary, he says, "I am nobody . . . and I may say that I have now to begin life." He assumes a second pseudonym and presents himself as Rokesmith, a name which has an especially appropriate meaning. An archaic usage of the verb "to roke" is to give off smoke, mists and fogs; Harmon, with his disguises and manipulative obfuscations, becomes a kind of "smith" of "roking", a master of mystification. But what he does not realise when he becomes Rokesmith and does not fully understand as he "buries" himself, is that he is, indeed, somebody and that he cannot choose to "begin life" at any given moment. He comes to realise that no one can recreate himself, and it is for that reason that Dickens has him cry out, at the moment of his mythical rebirth, "John Harmon, struggle for your life."

If the elder Harmon may be said to be the last of Dickens' patriarchal misers, then Reginald Wilfer is the last of Dickens' sweet, but fatally passive, fathers. The elder Harmon descends from Anthony Chuzzlewit, and Reginald Wilfer descends from Mr Jellyby. Bella Wilfer's principal consolation for the shabby reality of her lower-middle-class life is the loving relationship she maintains with her Pa. The main thing we know about Bella's childhood is that she was once seen by old Harmon stamping her little feet, screaming with her little voice, and laying into her Pa with her little bonnet. She did not like the direction of her Sunday morning walk, and she was not reluctant to express her dissatisfaction. She was a wilful child and she is a wilful young woman. Bella, grown-up, is a fully blossomed, delectable version of that expressive child who ventilated her discontent. She bites the curls which are a major prop in the incestuous play with Pa, and she laments the lack of money which she came so close to having. She is the daughter of an impossible mother, the sister of a mean-spirited girl, and the victim of the economic inequality dished out to her class: her dissatisfaction with her family and with her society are not unfounded.

All we ever really need to know about Bella Wilfer is given to us when Dickens first describes her in Chapter iv of Book II: she is aggressive, very pretty, acutely conscious of the economic nature of her society, and does not hide her dissatisfaction. She is very quickly sprung from her lower-middle-class deprivations by Mrs Boffin's desire to improve the lot of John Harmon's maliciously "intended", and Bella becomes an ornament in the Boffin mansion. After a few months she makes a disastrous visit to Holloway – her mother is decked out in devastating gloom, and her sister parades her appropriation of the cast-off George Sampson. When Ma begins to talk of the Boffins being proud, Bella's realistic awareness of their disinterested generosity propels her out of the house and in search of Pa. Father and daughter elope, "innocently" to be sure, to Greenwich for the day. It is there that Bella makes her confession of mercenary wretchedness, but her view of money and what money makes of life, is more astute than wretched:

> When I was at home, and only knew what it was to be poor, I grumbled, but didn't so much mind. When I was at home expecting to be rich, I thought vaguely of all the great things I would do. But when I had been disappointed of my splendid fortune, and came to see it from day to day in other hands, and to have before my eyes what it could really do, then I became the mercenary wretch I am. (II, viii)

When she was poor she was resentful, but she accepted the social destiny determined for her: she knew that if she did not marry George Sampson, then she would end up with someone else of his class. When the conditions of Harmon's will are revealed, and when she moves in with the Boffins and begins to witness the power of money, what it can really do, her resentment is translated into aggressive scheming. She has been the subject of old Harmon's schemes, of his plot to marry his son to that wilful little girl, and she, in her turn, becomes a schemer, a plotter of strategies to marry money:

> If ever there was a mercenary plotter whose thoughts and designs were always in her mean occupation, I am the amiable creature. But I don't care. I hate and detest being poor, and I won't be poor if I can marry money.

Even though this confession scene with Pa is very arch and is conducted on a teasing and playful level, I think one of its meanings is to show how Bella's quite rational desire for money is exacerbated by coming into contact with real wealth. And this contact also exacerbates her fine sense of the economic and social inequality which is a function of the prevailing class structure: when she returns from Greenwich to the West End and sees her "poor dear struggling shabby little Pa" set off for Holloway, she weeps. She weeps when she compares the Boffins' brilliant furniture with the dingy parlour in Holloway. She weeps for her class, and she weeps with resentment of a society which can contain such splendour and such shabbiness. She weeps for her contradictory wishes, for her wish that "the deceased old John Harmon had never made a will about her", and for her wish that "the deceased young John Harmon had lived to marry her". Her contradictory feelings constitute a psychological analogue to the social contradictions which she has experienced so fully and in so short a time.

Her refusal of Harmon is not prompted by some silly sense of disparity in their social position, but rather because of the resentment she feels at being controlled. She has been made the subject of a debilitating system of class, and she sees what that experience has done to her family; she has been made the subject of a malicious will; and she now feels that she lives subject to the generosity of her patrons, however kind and disinterested they may be. She feels as trapped in the West End as she did in Holloway, and she expresses herself in terms which suggest her resentment of the reification of her being into a negotiable piece of property:

> . . . was it not enough that I should have been willed away, like a house, or a dog, or a bird; but must you too begin to dispose of me in your mind and speculate in me, as soon as I had ceased to be the talk and laugh of the town? Am I forever to be made the property of strangers? (II, xiii)

She has been "willed away"; she is now being "disposed of" and "speculated in"; she is the "property of strangers"; her language, which is the language of the novel, reveals her understanding of the economic nature of her society.

Bella declares to Pa that "the whole life I place before myself is money, money, money, and what money can make of life". She articulates the power of money as a transforming agent, it "makes" things out of life, and in *Our Mutual Friend* money does, in great part, make the world. It is money which enables Boffin to play the role of miser, to transform himself from a kindly old chap into a rambunctious old devil. It is money which enables John to play the role of humble secretary. Because these two men have money, because in effect they possess the mounds, with all their actual and symbolic meaning, they are enabled to transform themselves into what they are not. They can play roles and it works, for they possess the financial support for their "acting" to be effective. Ma can play Lady Macbeth to the hilt and it gets her nowhere and Sophronia and Alfred Lammle can play the roles of devoted husband and wife and achieve nothing. There is nothing to back Ma but her fierce resentment and there is nothing to back the Lammles but a fiction of mutuality and solvency.

Money is the means whereby a benevolent and patriarchal figure such as Boffin can perform and manipulate, and it is interesting that his performance in some ways resembles that of Jarndyce in *Bleak House*; Jarndyce is an eccentric, benevolent, childless and paternal figure. In *Bleak House*, it is Esther Summerson's desire for Alan Woodcourt which is tested, but the parallel to the testing of Bella Wilfer's desire for money is clear. It seems as if by accepting Jarndyce's proposal of marriage, by suppressing her sexual, but always lady-like, desire Esther is permitted to give it full expression in marriage to the man she really wants. By running away from Mr Boffin (and who would not? he becomes positively demonic), by momentarily denying her desire for money (and who would not, when *having* money is represented in such alarming negative terms?), Bella is allowed to be rich.

In a discussion of the power of money in Dickens' novels, and in particular of the power exercised by Jarndyce and Boffin, Grahame Smith has this to say:

> . . . one of the biggest disappointments in literature occurs in *Our Mutual Friend* at the moment we discover that Boffin's moral degeneration has been nothing but a well-intentioned sham . . . he [Dickens] seems here to have reverted to that almost contemptuous dealing in deception at the expense of human feeling which was so evident in Mr Jarndyce's trifling with Esther on the subject of their marriage. Such manipulation of people, in life or in art, is at once arrogant and frivolous.[14]

It is certain that Boffin and John Harmon are arrogant, but they are certainly not frivolous. And Dickens is neither arrogant nor frivolous in *Our Mutual Friend*: the manipulations of Boffin and Harmon have a deeply serious meaning which connects them to the overall concerns of the novel. The manipulation of Bella comprises an affirmative analogue to the determinative nature of the structures of her society. The Boffin/Harmon manipulation, which is licensed by their financial security, is an imaginative parallel to the manipulation which society effects upon the individual.

Dickens sustains Bella Wilfer's awareness of social actuality almost to the end. When asked by John if she would like to be rich and to use her riches to benefit others, she replies that it is easier to hope that one would use money benevolently when one doesn't have any than when one does. She declares that John's wishes for her to have new dresses and a carriage are "as real to me as the wishes in the Fairy Story, that were all fulfilled as soon as spoken". It is John who thinks in terms of fairy-tales, who has constructed the fabulous plot whose resolution is Bella's elevation to fabulous wealth.

Bella is in the "state of a dreamer" when she, Mr Inspector, and Harmon set off for Limehouse where her husband is to be identified by Job Potterson, Miss Abbey's brother and a steward on the ship which brought Harmon back to England. Now Bella has never been a dreamer: the play with her father is fanciful, but they both know it *is* play, and she has never entered the fantasy world of class superiority inhabited by her mother and her sister. But her sharp grasp of reality is slowly eroded as the Boffin/Harmon plot is revealed to her. Mrs Boffin tells her the story of deception which began with a "confabulation" between John and his old friends; they joined together to confabulate, to make a fable. The revelation alarms Bella, as indeed it should, and the scene takes on an atmosphere of mounting hysteria. Mrs Boffin starts to scream with rapture, she beats her feet on the floor, claps her hands, and bobs herself "backwards and forwards like a demented member of some Mandarin's family". Grahame Smith remarks that "behind the hysteria of the character [Mrs Boffin] there lies the unsure creator's lack of control. We find in this the direct expression of a tiredness that runs throughout a great deal of the novel."[15]

First of all, I am not at all sure that we necessarily have to assume that a novelist's last completed novel is tired, and, second, it would seem that Mrs Boffin goes off into her demented and oriental rocking because the strain has clearly become too much for her. Rather than her hysteria showing "the unsure creator's lack of control", it makes us wonder how on earth she has borne her husband for so long. Bella, too, becomes hysterical and subsides into alternating fits of laughter and tears. She manages to recover long enough to declare that she was becoming "grasping, calculating, insolent, insufferable", but these adjectives seem rather strong and self-lacerating for the confused responses of a lower-middle-class girl transported to the West End world of shops and parties.

Bella Wilfer's subjection to the Harmon/Boffin plot undermines her own sense of herself and her class, and it is difficult to understand all of Dickens' meaning in this manipulation of one of his most interesting and complex heroines. Her aggressive, and certainly not misplaced, desire for material comfort hardly requires moral correction after her marriage: she lives in cosy serenity for almost two years in Blackheath with John, Baby Bella, and a "fluttering little servant", her problems easily solved by reference to *The Complete British Family Housewife*.

Through Bella, Dickens articulates some of the meaning and effect of the economic foundation of the society he describes in the novel. She consistently affirms this meaning and effect, and her reward for such realism is the mythical release from all that has confined her. Until her final transportation to the West End she remains notably astute about herself and her society, but it would seem that the price of Bella's transcendence of social actuality is the paradoxical attrition of the qualities that have permitted that transcendence, qualities which have, in fact, made her an attractive and lively figure for John Harmon. She loses her self-possession, her aggression, and her class-consciousness (and I think one can safely call it that – she understands the meaning of class in her society) as she enters the fairyland founded upon the dust heaps.

It seems to me that Dickens, in his fabulous social transformation of Bella, actually affirms the power of social determinants upon the individual, while he is engaged at the same time in transcending them. I have already suggested that Bella's extended testing by her husband and Boffin creates an imaginative parallel to the manipulations that society effects upon the individual. Dickens, in his desire that things not be the way they are in Holloway, chooses to release Bella from her social misery through marriage to a fairy-tale prince about to inherit a kingdom founded upon dust. The combination of social realism and fantasy in Bella's experience suggests the impossibility in the bourgeois world that Dickens seeks to regenerate in *Our Mutual Friend* of Bella ever getting to the West End – she can, in fact, only do it in fantasy. And because this is fantasy, Bella undergoes a Victorian version of fantastic, medieval testing. Where a medieval princess might be imprisoned in a tower, Bella is imprisoned by

Harmon and Boffin in ignorance of her husband's identity and wealth. And as she enters the fabulous kingdom of the fairy prince, as all released princesses do, she, too, becomes fabulous – no more the canny lower-middle-class girl who riles against the landlord and the necessity of having to take in lodgers, no more the energetic Blackheath wife and mother – she is transformed into a fairy-tale character on whose "exquisite toilette table was an ivory casket, and in the casket were jewels the like of which she had never dreamed of . . ." (IV, xiii).

Mr and Mrs Boffin are the king and queen of Bella's fairyland. By virtue of their actual contact with the mounds, by virtue of the years spent sorting and sifting under the malevolent eye of old Harmon, they understand the economy of the dust-yard. The economic history of the mounds may be seen as a history of the culture which has produced them: the Boffins, by explicitly understanding the history of one, implicitly understand the history of the other.

Dust heaps such as Harmon's were amassed principally through the emptying of dust bins, and the mounds of dust were sorted for resale. Soil or fine dust was sold to brickmakers; rags, bones and old metals were sold to marine store dealers; old tin and iron was sold for trunk ends; old bricks and oyster shells were sold to builders for sinking foundations and forming roads; and jewellery was either kept or sold to dealers. Everything in the dust heaps had some sort of marketable value, and all these marketable objects had a previous history of usage in the culture which had discarded them. The Boffins may be said to understand the component qualities of their culture through their familiarity with all the different things which have gone into the dust heaps. In other words, they understand the principle of component parts and a whole; and beyond this they understand a principle of mutuality which comes from an understanding of component parts.

Their living room in the Bower reveals this acceptance and understanding of mutuality. On either side of the fire are Noddy's two wooden settles, and facing the fire is a "centrepiece" devoted to Mrs Boffin and to "Fashion". Her centrepiece sports a collection of garish, but expensive, drawing-room furniture, and a flowery carpet stops short at a footstool and gives way to a region of sand and sawdust. Mrs Boffin's area is decorated with such "hollow ornamentation" as stuffed birds and wax edible solids of cold joints and pies. Mrs Boffin's area is devoted, so to speak, to mimesis and Mr Boffin's to substantial actuality.

"Do you understand it, Wegg?" asks Boffin, and of course Wegg does not understand it. The notion of convivial adjustment to another's requirements, and an understanding of the separate components of a whole which the mounds symbolise, are alien to Wegg's consciousness. To him, the mounds represent one great whole in which treasure is buried. He has no sense of the history of his culture, of its defining and component parts, because he perceives it entirely in terms of opposition to himself. "Sociability, Fashion, and Comfort" are harmoniously and simultaneously present in the Bower by "mutual consent" and this concept of mutuality is foreign to Wegg's social isolation.

It is the Boffins' "moral straightness" which old Harmon has respected and which sustains them in their journey through the "dismal swamp" when they go headlong in for Fashion. Fashionable life almost buries them, but they survive and keep their common-sensible heads above the slime. A good deal has been said by critics and readers of *Our Mutual Friend* about the deceptive plausibility of Boffin's mimesis of a miser; it is so utterly convincing that the reader feels cheated when he discovers that Boffin has been faking it all along. For Grahame Smith, as I have already noted, it is "one of the greatest disappointments in literature", but I don't think this is what Dickens had in mind. Inasmuch as one can speculate in these matters, I think Dickens means us to see that Mr Boffin, in playing a miser, almost *does* become the thing he mimics.

When Boffin hides behind the alligator in Venus' shop to overhear Wegg expound on the "friendly move", Venus remarks to Boffin that the alligator is "very much like you in tone". It is as if at this moment, when Boffin is playing his miser part to the hilt, he becomes like one of the creatures in the Dismal Swamp of fashionable life. Where he was once a charging rhinoceros, blundering his innocent way around the London streets, he is now a creeping and cunning amphibian – half in the world of the slimy swamp and half in the world of decency and common sense. Boffin is saved from becoming the thing he imitates because he retains a firm grasp on the meaning of his experience. When Mortimer Lightwood declares, "My dear Mr. Boffin, everything wears to rags," Boffin responds, "I won't go so far as to say everything because there's some things I never found among the dust." Mrs Boffin's sympathy for the seven-year-old boy sent away to a foreign school never leaves her; it gently diminishes, but it is never "worn to rags", and it is this imperishable tenderness which enables her to recognise the twenty-eight-year-old man. When Boffin is asked for his word of honour by Venus he says, "I've sorted a lot of dust in my time, but I never knew the two things go into separate heaps." The Boffins' experience with the mounds is the measure of *all* their experience; by knowing what can and what cannot be found in the dust heaps they survive their journey through Fashion, through greed and corruption, and they reign triumphant at the end of *Our Mutual Friend.*

In the young Henry James' less than enthusiastic review of Dickens' last completed novel, he declares that characters such as Boffin are "a mere bundle of eccentricities, animated by no principle of nature whatever . . . among the grotesque creatures who occupy the pages before us, there is not one whom we can refer to as an existing type". And James considered Jenny Wren "a little monster; she is deformed, unearthly, unnatural; she belongs to the troop of hunchbacks, imbeciles, and precocious children who have carried on the sentimental business in all Mr. Dickens's novels".[16] James is obviously correct in describing Jenny Wren's physical deformity, but I think she does everything but carry on the sentimental business: she is far more like Daniel Quilp than Little Nell. She is, among many other things, a fully-developed sadist, and she is a million fictive miles away from the passive suffering embodied in Dickens' other diminutive female creatures such as Little Nell and Little Dorrit. One of the first things we hear her say in *Our Mutual Friend* is that she would like to cram all the neighbourhood children into the black vaults of that petrified monster of a church in Smith Square and blow pepper on them.

Her connection with the mythical kingdom of the mounds is formed by her relationship with Lizzie, and she is included in the new social order at the end of the novel because of Lizzie's connection with Bella. But, in one way or another, Jenny Wren is everywhere in *Our Mutual Friend.* She is *the* visionary of the novel. She embodies a recognition of dispiriting reality and a transformation of that recognition into a new vision of the world. In other words, she is very much like Charles Dickens.

She is a conundrum, a riddle, and her unfathomable peculiarity is best exemplified when Charley Hexam and Bradley Headstone first arrive at her house in search of Lizzie. The opened door discloses "a child – a dwarf – a girl – a something". The riddle she presents to the world, and to the reader of *Our Mutual Friend*, is compounded by her ability to translate her experience into vision, and yet at the same time to remain almost supernaturally conscious of the reality of her society. One of her consolatory visions is remarkable for the perception it reveals of the impossibility of this vision ever being actualised.

> I dare say my birds sing better than other birds, and my flowers smell better than other flowers. For when I was a little child . . . the children that I used to see early in the morning were very different from any others that I saw. They were not like me: they were not chilled, anxious, ragged, or beaten; they were never in pain. They were not like the children of the neighbours; they never made me tremble all over, by setting up shrill noises, and they never mocked me. Such numbers of them too! All in white dresses, and with something shining on the borders, and on their heads, that I have never been able to imitate with my work, though I know it so well. (II, ii)

Her admission that she cannot imitate the workmanship on the dresses of these visionary children implies a recognition, an acceptance, of the fact that they *are* visionary. And yet at the same time, she keeps trying to reproduce this vision with the artist's tenacious drive to bridge the gap between perfect vision and imperfect representation.

In her dolls' dressmaking, she expresses her resentment of a society which comforts her so little for her back being so bad and her legs being so queer. Jenny Wren dresses the dolls of fine ladies, and she does it with a sharp professionalism. When she and Riah are walking through London on their way to Miss Abbey's, they stop in front of a toy shop window: "All my work!" she declares proudly:

> This referred to a dazzling semi-circle of dolls in all the colours of the rainbow, who were dressed for presentation at court, for going to balls, for going out driving, for going out on horseback, for going out walking, for going to get married, for going to help other dolls get married, for all the gay events of life. (III, ii)

It is ironic, to say the least, that Jenny dresses these dolls for events in which she, because of her class and her deformity, can never participate. The ironical meaning which Dickens gives to her work is intensified by her smallness, by her deformity, by her youthfulness, and by the fact that she dresses dolls. It would be conventionally ironic if Jenny were a seamstress making dresses for upper-class women to go to court, to go to balls, to attend "all the gay events of life" from which she is excluded.

In *Ruth*, Elizabeth Gaskell illuminates the ironical meaning of a situation in which a troop of exhausted working-class women sew all night in a cold and badly lit room to finish dresses to be worn by their upper-class superiors to a county assembly. Dickens intensifies the ironical meaning of this situation by miniaturising it. But he also does something else; by reducing the scale of the social situation, he mitigates his criticism of it. Jenny Wren says that she makes her great ladies suffer, but because this is not the full grown-up relationship of seamstresses and upper-class women the force of Dickens' social criticism is reduced. Jenny Wren enacts a desire for revenge on behalf of all the milliners and seamstresses of Victorian England, but by making her a dolls' dressmaker rather than a ladies' one, Dickens mediates between his mimesis of a distressing social actuality and a desire for it to be different. He takes the actual social situation of exploited working-class women and alters it to become a situation where a deformed adolescent girl makes dresses for dolls. And at the same time, he also manages to convey the fierceness of Jenny's class resentment, and the strange, displaced means by which she satisfies her desire for class revenge.

As Jenny and Riah stand in front of the toy-shop window, Jenny describes how she hobbles around town to see fashionable women parade in the park; if their clothing can be transformed into a doll's dress, she hobbles home to "cut her out and baste her". She says this with such glee, hitching up her chin and darting glances from her sharp grey eyes, that one senses she wishes she could take a pair of scissors to that particular lady's flesh and use the sharp little needle which she is forever jabbing in the air to stab that particular lady's pink and pampered body. She says that she makes a "perfect slave" of her models, dogging them for imaginary fittings, and making one society beauty, Lady Belinda Whiterose, take particular pains about it. She concludes this exposition of her trade by pointing, with some satisfaction, to Lady Belinda hanging up by her waist with her toes turned in, "much too near the gaslight" for the good of her waxed presence. Dickens suggests that Jenny Wren would like to see all those society women she sees around town hanging up by their waists and being roasted by gaslight; in her exposition of her trade he conveys a fine sense of her suffering and of the sadistic impulses which are her response to it. He does it in a manner which is as sharp and clever as Jenny's intelligence itself.

Jenny's relationship with her father is a grotesque perversion of family life. He is her "bad child" and she is his scolding parent, the real "person of the house". Mr Cleaver is an alcoholic, given over to self-destruction. When he comes home drunk, Jenny sends him into the corner like a naughty boy. Dickens calls the Cleaver family experience "a dire reversal of the places of parent and child", but it is actually much more than this, for even if there were no reversal and Mr Cleaver were the scolding, sadistic father rather than the masochistic "indecorous threadbare ruin" who grovels before his daughter, what a family this would be! Jenny says she wishes Mr Cleaver had been "poked into cells and black holes", and run over by "rats and spiders and beetles". She threatens him with being transported for life, and says that she wishes all his chattering teeth would "drop down your throat and play at dice in your stomach". She declares that he is fit for nothing but to be "preserved in the liquor that destroys him, and put in a great glass bottle as a sight for other swipey children of his own pattern" (III, x). It is inconceivable to imagine any of Dickens' other suffering female children speaking in this manner. Dickens seems to explode all the sentimental father/daughter relationships of his previous novels into this picture of an almost surreal sadism, just as he explodes the united lower-middle-class family into fragments in his descriptions of the Wilfers.

Mr Dolls meets a horrible end after wandering through Covent Garden and having convulsions in the Temple as he tries to importune Eugene for threepennyworth of rum. Dickens describes the vegetable detritus of the market in terms which suggest its horrible fitness as a hang-out for the drunks and derelicts of London:

> Such specimens there are as can be seen nowhere else in London, such stale vapid rejected cabbage-leaf and cabbage-stalk dresses, such damaged-orange countenance, such squashed pulp of humanity, are open to the day nowhere else. (IV, ix)

Mr Dolls is the squashed, left over, spoilt, and decaying matter of his society. He is in a severe state of decomposition, drunk and illiterate, and he dies in a doctor's shop with "a ghastly light" shining upon him from the coloured bottles which fill the windows. This is not the heavenly light which Jenny sees in her visions of consolation, nor is it the light which shines from the fires into which Lizzie Hexam gazes for her pictures of the future: it is the light of bottled medicines and drugs. Mr Dolls dies with "a strange mysterious writing on his face, reflected from one of the great bottles, as if death had marked him mine!" Illiterate, he dies with a strange indecipherable writing impressed upon his face and drunk, he dies with the light reflected from bottled drugs.

Jenny accepts his death as she has accepted all her other misery, with a combination of realistic acceptance of necessity and an impulse to turn her suffering into art. She works furiously to earn some money for her father's funeral, "many flaunting dolls had to be gaily dressed for the occasion", and she transforms her experience of this occasion into the creation of a clergyman doll to officiate at dolls' weddings.

The psychological ambivalence experienced by Rogue Riderhood after his rescue from near-drowning, which I have suggested is an epitome of the nature of social consciousness in *Our Mutual Friend*, is given its most beautiful and chilling form in the scene where Jenny Wren and Lizzie Hexam sit on Pubsey's roof. Jenny tells Fledgeby that they come there for the quiet and the air, and that "you can see the clouds rushing on above the narrow streets, not minding them, and you see the golden arrows pointing at the mountains in the sky from which the wind comes, and you feel as if you were dead" (II, V). Fledgeby, who possesses an imagination strictly concerned with the things of this world, asks her how it feels to be dead:

> 'Oh, so tranquil!' cried the little creature, smiling. 'Oh, so peaceful and so thankful! and you hear the people who are alive, crying and working and calling to one another down in the close dark streets, and you seem to pity them so! And such a chain has fallen from you, and such a strange good sorrowful happiness comes upon you!'

For Jenny Wren, to feel as if one were dead is to be removed from a social misery in which people live in "close dark streets, crying and working". The paradoxical nature of this feeling (she is very much alive as she sits with Lizzie on the roof) is affirmed by her feeling "a sorrowful happiness". Her cry to "Come back, and be dead" comes from her as she is engaged in living, and it exists in an affirmative relationship to the paradoxical and contradictory society which can include poor, ruined creatures like her father and dandies like Fascination Fledgeby. I think the fact that Dickens so clearly relates Jenny's enraptured state as she imagines what it would be like to be dead with her social misery affirms the relationship which he draws between Riderhood's reluctance to return to life and the nature of consciousness in *Our Mutual Friend.* That is to say, Jenny's description of how it feels to be dead and to be peaceful is simultaneous with her consciousness of how it feels to be alive and to suffer.

At the end of the novel Jenny joins forces with Sloppy and they form a sub-unit of the new family structure presided over by the Boffins and John and Bella. Sloppy comes to get a doll for the Inexhaustible, and the doll is folded in silver paper "as if she were wrapped from head to foot in new bank notes". Baby Bella's doll is symbolically wrapped in the money which has comes out from its long rust in the dark. Sloppy, who once used to sing comic songs with "spoken" in them for Betty Higden, says he would love to hear Jenny sing, and Jenny and Sloppy form a true mutuality composed of opposites. He appears to tiny Jenny like a giant with his enormous mouth and extraordinary laugh, and she fears that she will be swallowed up by him. But while he is enormous, he is gentle, and his gentleness offsets her sadism, as her sharpness complements his slowness.

Perhaps the most moving moment in the novel comes when he says he would like to make a stick for the crutch he sees standing against the wall of Jenny's room. He does not know it is hers for she is sitting down, and when she insists he watch her use it, he says, with "an instinctive delicacy behind his buttons", "I am very glad it's yours, because I'd rather ornament it for you than for any one else." Here there is no mediation, no struggle against society; it is as if Dickens transcends his own efforts to transcend social actuality and Sloppy speaks with an instinctive delicacy that is really inexplicable. Sloppy was discarded on a "sloppy" night, cast out by society and taken in by Betty Higden, but he represents something which cannot be found in the dust heaps. He understands nothing of the economic foundation of society and he is, perhaps, the only truly contented character in the novel. By including Sloppy in the mythical kingdom founded upon dust at the end of *Our Mutual Friend*, Dickens suggests that there are some things which cannot be categorised, cannot be sorted or sifted, given labels, sold for profit, and whose source cannot be identified. Sloppy is instinctively and inexplicably sweet and it is for that reason alone that he is enfolded within the new social order. He is there, in a sense, because he represents the things which cannot be found among the dust.

NOTES

1. The creative power of money which Marx describes in his essay "The Power of Money in Bourgeois Society" is similar to the creative power of language in Dickens' novel. Marx writes:

   > That which I am unable to do as a *man*, and of which therefore all my individual powers are incapable, I am able to do by means of *money*. Money thus turns each of these powers into something which in itself it is not – turns it, that is, into its contrary. If I long for a particular dish or want to take the mail-coach because I am not strong enough to go on foot, money fetches me the dish and the mail-coach: that is, it converts my wishes from something in the imagination, translates them from their meditated, imagined or willed existence into their *sensuous, actual* existence – from imagination to life, from imagined being into real being. In effecting this mediation, money is the *truly creative* power.
   > *Economic and Philosophic Manuscripts of 1844*, translated by Martin Milligan (New York, 1964), p. 168.

   In *Our Mutual Friend*, language is the creative power which converts orphans into marketable commodities and marketable commodities into waifs and strays. And money is indeed the power which converts "wishes from something in the imagination" into their "*sensuous, actual* existence".
2. A will, incidentally, is a form of secreted information which will be revealed to the legatees, and the secret of John Harmon's identity (no secret, to be sure, from the reader, but that is exactly as Dickens wished things to be) is metaphorically buried in the mounds of dust accumulated by his father.

   Harmon becomes Rokesmith, the secretary. In the story of Daniel Dancer which Wegg reads aloud to Boffin, one of Dancer's "richest escretoires" is a dung heap. "Escretoire" is a version of "escritoire" (a writing desk or secretary) and Dancer's dung heap is a metaphoric secretary in which secrets are stashed away. Harmon is a secretary buried in the dust heaps of his father, and he himself is a secret by virtue of his concealed identity. Dickens' idiosyncratic spelling of "escritoire" reinforces the manifold associations of the novel's concern with secrecy and secretion.

   J. Hillis Miller suggests that there are "no real secrets in *Our Mutual Friend.* The characters are immediately available to one another, primarily, perhaps, through language, but also through gestures and mute body-language which are perfectly comprehensible . . . even when the full truth about one character is hidden from another, an intuitive understanding of the other's genéral nature and situation is available at a glance." *Charles Dickens The World of His Novels* (Indiana, 1958), pp. 288–9.

This is certainly sometimes true, but I think the fact that the characters *are* always trying to "read" each other, to interpret the meaning of gestures, and to get behind what is overtly stated in language, is a sign that the society in which they live is one permeated by secrets. And it is not true that the characters in *Our Mutual Friend* always read each other correctly. For example, Mrs Wilfer entirely misreads Mrs Boffin. She announces that "the craft, the secrecy, the dark deep underhanded plotting written in Mrs. Boffin's countenance, makes me shudder". And when Mr Boffin is at the demonic height of his miser performance, Bella Wilfer tries in vain to read Mrs Boffin's face for some "comment on, or explanation of, this stormy humour in her husband, but none was there. An anxious and a distressed observation of her own face was all she could read in it."

J. Hillis Miller's observation of the degree to which characters try to interpret each other is astute, but I think it is important to note that they do not always interpret each other correctly.

3. Wegg does appear to have had a father, one Thomas, a waterman. The occupation of Wegg's father is a small illustration of how almost everyone in *Our Mutual Friend* has connections both with the mythical kingdom of the river and with the mythical kingdom of the mounds.
4. I am thinking especially of Harold Pinter's *The Dumb Waiter* (1960). Two gunmen wait in a basement to do a job, and spend all their time trying to satisfy demands for such things as "Two braised steak and chips. Two sago puddings. Two teas without sugar." which come down to them on the dumbwaiter. In a wonderfully absurd, yet horrifyingly accurate, working-class fashion they discuss football, hobbies, and whether they should send up an eccles cake as a substitute for soup of the day and jam tart.
5. *The Triumph of the Novel: Dickens, Dostoevsky, Faulkner* (New York, 1976), p. 151. Guerard also suggests that Gaffer Hexam's rhetorical questioning of Riderhood in the first chapter of *Our Mutual Friend* ("Has a dead man any use for money? Is it possible for a dead man to have money? What world does a dead man belong to? T'other world. What world does money belong to? This world. How can money be a corpse's? Can a corpse own it, want it, spend it, claim it, miss it?") constitutes an early establishment in the novel of the right "of the poorest outcasts and eccentrics to engage in forensic and verbal play" (p. 154). It seems to me that Gaffer is notable for his taciturn and close-mouthed disposition, and while his questioning is important because it introduces a central question of the novel, I don't think Gaffer ever engages in play, forensic, verbal, or otherwise.
6. Wegg is not deluded in this department. In Anthony Trollope's *Can You Forgive Her?* George Vavasour throws the engagement ring he has bought for his cousin Alice in the fire. She finds it but discovers that one of the diamonds is missing: "She searched even for this, scorching her face and eyes, but in vain. Then she made up her mind that the

diamond should be lost forever, and that it should go out among the cinders into the huge dust-heaps of the metropolis." The Oxford Trollope, Vol. II, Ch. XLVI. *Can You forgive Her*? appeared in monthly parts from January 1864 to August 1865.

7. Part I, Ch. I, Sec. 4. "The Fetishism of Commodities and the Secret thereof." (Moscow, n.d., English edition of 1887, edited by Friedrich Engels).
8. Grahame Smith calls Wegg "a stereotyped comic figure" and says that "his tiresomeness is only increased when we compare him with Wemmick, the perfect representative of the alienated modern man". *Dickens, Money and Society* (California, 1968), p. 191. I think this is an untenable comparison. Wegg is a street character, without family and friends, and existing at the lowest level of the working class. Wemmick is a lawyer's clerk, a member of the lower middle class, and he owns a little cottage in Walworth. To be sure, he is alienated from his work when he is at home; he has built a drawbridge and fortified his cottage so that it resembles a miniature gothic castle. But Wemmick lives in a small world of human warmth and connection in his castle. He conducts a decorous romance with Miss Skiffins and maintains an affectionate and reciprocal relationship with his Aged Parent.
9. In 1865, *All The Year Round* carried three pieces dealing with the rapaciousness of the bill-broking market. "Wanted to Borrow, One Hundred Pounds" (March 11) describes the experiences of a gentleman very much like Twemlow who is driven into bankruptcy after backing a bill for a friend.

   "Accommodation" (8 April) is a confession of a tout for money-lenders. This tout earns 5 per cent commission by directing his financially embarrassed friends to West End money-lenders who charge 120 per cent per annum. This piece is full of the ornithological imagery associated with Fledgeby: touts are "pigeons" who were "plucked" and they help the "hawks" to pluck the pigeons. "How I Discounted my Bill" (8 July) is an account of the practices of one Mr Steinmetz who frequents city coffee-houses.
10. Frank Kermode makes a felicitous observation when he says that opium was the opium of the people in Victorian England. *New York Review of Books*, Vol. XXI, No. 9, 30 May 1974.
11. Dickens is not the only Victorian novelist to look askance at the *nouveau-riche* businessman. In Trollope's *Phineas Finn*, for example, Phineas strolls on the estate of Robert Kennedy, son of a Glasgow manufacturer, and now an enormously well-off M. P. Phineas remarks to his companion, the Treasury Secretary, on the magnificence of the park, who responds, "Very grand; – but the young trees show the new man. A new man may buy a forest; but he can't get park trees." The Oxford Trollope, Ch. XIV. Veneering, so to speak, tries to hide his new wood under his veneer.
12. Eric Hobsbawm remarks that the objects which filled the Victorian bourgeois household were most often, and most effectively, praised as being "*solid*, a term used characteristically as the highest praise for a business enterprise". *Age of Capital*, p. 231.

13. *Dickens: The Critical Heritage*, ed. Philip Collins (New York, 1971), pp. 467–8.
14. *Dickens, Money and Society*, pp. 182–3.
15. Ibid., p. 191.
16. "The Nation", 21 December 1865, in *Views and Reviews* (London, 1908).

# PART III
# DANIEL DERONDA

# 7 Social Realism and Moral Correction

> . . . the happiest women, like the happiest nations, have no history.
>
> George Eliot, *The Mill on the Floss*, Book VI, Chapter 3.

If one looks back at this point, and considers how *North and South* and *Our Mutual Friend* create fictions of resolution, then the former may be said to reconcile and the latter to mediate. But *Daniel Deronda* seems to collapse. However different their formal and thematic structures, *North and South* and *Our Mutual Friend* hold together as novels; Elizabeth Gaskell's optimistic faith in fiction as an agent of teleological social change and Dickens' belief in the innate and inexplicable goodness of at least some members of society enable them to present gratifying, if problematic, resolutions of the social tensions which these novels describe. But *Daniel Deronda*, which was published in monthly parts from February to September 1876, falls apart under the pressure of offering a moral alternative to its representations of a corrupt upper-class society; Eliot leaves Gwendolen Harleth high and dry with her moral enlightenment and no place to exercise it and sends Deronda off on a Zionist mission whose didactic function is to show the absence of any worthwhile moral life to be had in England. The novel is fatally, if seductively, split, for Eliot is unable to reconcile her fine study in psychological and social realism with the strange, difficult, and sometimes virtually unreadable Deronda narrative of Jewish identity.[1]

Eliot was appalled and disappointed by the instant critical bifurcation of her last novel. She maintained that she "meant everything in the book to be related to everything else there", and she was annoyed by the "laudation of readers who cut the book into scraps and talk of nothing but Gwendolen".[2] What readers didn't talk about, at least in any encouraging way, was a lengthy examination of Jewish alienation and the respective merits of its resolution in assimilation or nationalism, a consumptive visionary named Mordecai, whose fervent rhetoric almost unmercifully taxes the reader's sympathy, an exemplar of Jewish maidenhood who turns out to be his long-lost sister, and Deronda himself, a strangely passive hero whose dark handsomeness is a sign of Jewishness rather than romantic virility, and whose sensitivity dampens rather than enlivens the reader's enjoyment of upper-class doings. Allowing for those who anticipated the modern critical evaluation of *Daniel Deronda* as provocatively flawed, it is probable that many readers only talked of Gwendolen and discarded the "scraps" because she, and the arena of her experience which is the country-house world of hunting, shooting, and fishing, were the engaging and recognisable stuff of a certain kind of popular Victorian fiction, exemplified, say, in Trollope's Palliser novels which were published between 1864 and 1880. The Jews in *Daniel Deronda* were peculiar. Mordecai's visionary flights and the saga of an upper-class English gentleman who discovers he was born an Italian Jew required the reader to see Jews in a different way from that in which they had been conventionally imagined in English nineteenth-century fiction.

The ending of *Daniel Deronda* is also peculiar. *North and South* and *Our Mutual Friend* conclude with affirmation of the family, of bourgeois domesticity as the positive radius of social change; *Daniel Deronda* ends not with the marriage of hero and heroine, not with the family as a metaphor for social unification, but with the hero taking off for foreign parts with someone other than the heroine for his bride.[3] And where *North and South* and *Our Mutual Friend* close with images of generation, *Daniel Deronda* ends with images of physical exile and psychological isolation. Gaskell's exposition of the political tension between masters and men and the sexual tension between men and women, and Dickens' representation of a society marked by manifold dissatisfaction, conclude with descriptions of the generation of family, and with the implicit regeneration of moral values extending *from* the family to society. In *Daniel Deronda* there is no such positive connection between the family and moral regeneration, and George Eliot denies her reader the gratifying "closure" which is common to much of nineteenth-century fiction.

To be sure, Deronda's exile takes the form of a Zionist quest, and his mission may be associated with the idea of national generation. But it is a mission significantly removed from English life, and it represents a withdrawal from society rather than an engagement with it. And even though *Daniel Deronda does* end in marriage, Eliot realises the relationship between Deronda and Mirah Lapidoth in such an unrelentingly non-physical manner that it suggests another kind of withdrawal rather than a union.

Deronda's choice of Mirah and rejection of Gwendolen has several related meanings. For example, he chooses a relationship founded upon religious affinity rather than upon sexual attraction. And because Gwendolen Harleth may be read, in part, as a metaphor for her class and for her culture, Deronda's final rejection of a sexual relationship with her (obviously not some kind of clandestine affair, but a properly sexual marriage) is an implicit reinforcement of his final rejection of the class and the culture which he has criticised, in one way or another, throughout the novel. At the end of *Daniel Deronda* an essentially worldly engagement with English society is put aside in favour of spiritual exile in the East.

Rejection does not make for the most conventional, nor indeed the most gratifying, of endings. But *Daniel Deronda* does not begin in the most familiar or reassuring way either. George Eliot starts off with a provocative and self-conscious epigraph about the arbitrariness of beginnings ("No retrospect will take us to the true beginning"), and she launches into her first paragraph, *in medias res*, with a series of questions raised in Deronda's mind as he watches Gwendolen Harleth at the gaming table:

> Was she beautiful or not beautiful? And what was the secret of form or expression which gave the dynamic quality to her glance? Was the good or the evil genius dominant in those beams? Probably the evil; else why was the effect that of unrest rather than of undisturbed charm? Why was the wish to look again felt as coercion and not as a longing in which the whole being consents.[4]

This prefigures many of the explicit and implicit meanings of the relationship between Gwendolen and Deronda as it is to develop in the novel. She is active and he is passive; she gambles and he watches; what he thinks of her is to be the more powerful agent of psychological change for both of them than what she thinks of him; she suggests a disjunction between surface and substance, whereas his fine physical presence is shown to be complemented by his rare qualities of sympathetic identification and delicate self-examination. Her physical attractions are coercive, and he ultimately resists them as he resists the attractions of an active role in English political life.

Despite her admission that no retrospect will give us a true beginning, Eliot sets out to trace the psychological, social, and racial origins of identity for Gwendolen and Deronda. She explores that "unmapped country within us", which, she says, has "to be taken into account in an explanation of our gusts and storms" (Ch. 24). She brings Gwendolen Harleth to the recognition and acceptance of her own psychological history, and of the inseparable and determinative connections between that history and her society. She brings Deronda to a discovery and acceptance of himself as a Jew with a special mission as Mordecai's "executive self". And having done all that, Eliot sends her enlightened characters off in different directions. She puts aside the conventional, happy ending (to want Gwendolen to marry Deronda is, I suspect, the spontaneous desire of every reader in a first encounter with the novel) in favour of something which suggests another kind of arbitrary beginning: the beginning of a kind of privileged Jewish settler existence for Deronda, and the beginning of a new life for Gwendolen where she will have to confront her psychological dread and live in a society which Eliot has shown to be in a state of severe moral rot.

Throughout the novel, Gwendolen performs as an upper-middle-class girl with an imperial will to control her experience, her environment, and everyone around her. She fails miserably, and through such failure comes to understand the moral stupidity entailed in assertion of the will against that complex blend of history and nature which Eliot sees as the great determinant of social existence. She also comes to understand the smallness of her "petty empire" of manipulation and exploitation in relation to the grand sweep of public events; she is made to experience that "terrible moment to many souls when the great movements of the world, the larger destinies of mankind, which have lain aloof in newspapers and other neglected reading, enter like an earthquake into their own lives" (Ch. 69).

The smallness of Gwendolen's egoism in the context of "the great movements of the world", the futility of her will in the face of Grandcourt's insidious psychological tyranny and in the face of Deronda's racial destiny, are related to the pervasive failure of the human will everywhere in *Daniel Deronda*. Grandcourt is actually imprisoned in a complacent ignorance by his rampant egoism; he cannot see how he is loathed by Lydia Glasher and by Gwendolen; to him, they are merely recalcitrant female objects which need breaking like wilful horses. And in a decisive sense, his human will is powerless in the face of indifferent nature as he drowns in the Bay of

Genoa. The will of Deronda's mother to escape the determinants of religious and patriarchal control is thwarted by what Daniel calls a stronger "Something", essentially a kind of natural, racial inheritance which has its way despite man's efforts to deny it. What was determined by society in *Our Mutual Friend* is often determined by nature in *Daniel Deronda* and a crucial and axial polarity is apparent in Eliot's novel, that of the human will and nature; represented, respectively, in Gwendolen by an ultimately ineffective psychological imperialism, and in Deronda by his innate, natural, and inescapable racial heritage. This polarity is the central one to which all others, social and psychological, are related. And these polarities are, for the most part, also represented by Gwendolen and Deronda. For example, the materialism of Gwendolen's class and the class into which she marries, a materialism which is manifested in the first case, let's say, by social advancement through advantageous marriage, and in the second, by political office as a means of financial gain, is opposed by Deronda's dissatisfaction with the Arnoldian Philistines and Barbarians of his acquaintance.

Gwendolen's marriage to Grandcourt is very much a class marriage, and *Daniel Deronda* is as much a novel of class relationships as *North and South* and *Our Mutual Friend*. Indeed, if one considers the genre's persistent examinations of the tension between self and society, how can any Victorian novel not be a novel of class? The difference here is that while Gaskell and Dickens are concerned mainly with the relationship between working, lower-middle and middle classes, Eliot concerns herself with the fine distinctions between upper-middle-class manners and morals and those of the upper class.

Women in the society which *Daniel Deronda* describes are expected to marry for money or for a title, or both if they can manage it. Catherine Arrowpoint's parents find Klesmer a distinctly unsuitable candidate for her wealthy hand (he is "a gypsy, a Jew, a mere bubble of the earth"), and she asks, "Why is it to be expected of an heiress that she should carry the property gained in trade into the hands of a certain class?" (Ch. 22). She asks this question to deflate her mother's social aggressiveness and artistic pretensions, and she clearly knows why, but the question is cogent for it describes the meaning of marriage for a social group which has risen from trade and is on its way to the minor aristocracy. Gwendolen's marriage is also a metonymy of class movement: she represents a financially embarrassed upper-middle class which came to social power and prominence in the eighteenth century (in the case of Gwendolen's family through the ownership of West Indian plantations), and whose destiny in the nineteenth century lies in its absorption by the class just above it, i.e. the land-owing English gentry.

Gwendolen lives in "that border-territory of rank where annexation is a burning topic" (Ch. 3). In describing the events which propel Gwendolen into Grandcourt's reptilian embraces, Eliot opposes the financial insecurity of Gwendolen's family to the freedom from financial worry enjoyed by Deronda and his class. Gwendolen marries Grandcourt for a number of complex reasons, which I shall discuss and which have a great deal to do with her mother, but the most explicit and alarming reason is the thought of becoming a governess to the Misses Mompert. Eliot opposes such necessity to Deronda's "unproductive questioning" in regard to his career, a questioning which is "sustained by three or five percent on capital which somebody else has battled for" (Ch. 17). Deronda may worry about the meaning of his existence but he never has to worry about money, and I think it is clear that he couldn't do the former without having the latter.

I realise that thematic oppositions are hardly anything new in the Victorian novel. As I have already shown, Elizabeth Gaskell sets up a series of polarities in *North and South* and then proceeds to reconcile them. What is interesting is that such reconciliation is not available to George Eliot and that she seems subject to yet another opposition – on the one hand, her commitment to writing socially realistic novels, and, on the other, her commitment to moral correction. It would seem that her rigorous intelligence and her deeply pessimistic assessment of the condition of English culture would not permit a fabulous resolution of social tension, and reconciliation, therefore, is ruled out. Because she cannot reconcile, I think she is compelled, either consciously or unconsciously, to displace.

*Daniel Deronda* is remarkable for its formal and thematic displacements. Novel is displaced into epic; history is displaced into nature; Gwendolen Harleth's neurotic conflict is displaced into hysterical symptom; and Deronda himself is displaced right out of English society, out of the novel, as it were, into exile and into textual interpretation. Consider for a moment how Eliot's myth of the Jews in *Daniel Deronda* may be seen to represent the displacement of novel into epic and how Deronda becomes an epic hero rather than a novelistic one.

Eliot's overt intention in writing about the Jews was spelled out in a letter she wrote to Harriet Beecher Stowe in October 1876: she wanted to correct a lamentable distaste among the English ruling class for anything not exactly English:

> . . . because I felt that the usual attitude of Christians towards Jews is – I hardly know whether to say more impious or more stupid when viewed in the light of their professed principles, I therefore felt urged to treat Jews with such sympathy and understanding as my nature and knowledge could attain to . . . towards the Hebrews we western people who have been reared in Christianity, have a peculiar debt and, whether we acknowledge it or not, a peculiar thoroughness of fellowship in religious and moral sentiment. Can anything be more disgusting than to hear people called "educated" making small jokes about eating ham, and showing themselves empty of any real knowledge as to the relation of their own social and religious life to the history of the people they think themselves witty in insulting? They hardly know that Christ was a Jew. And I find men educated at Rugby supposing that Christ spoke Greek. To my feeling, this deadness to the history which has prepared half our world for us, this inability to find interest in any form of life that is not clad in the same coat-tails and flounces as our own lies very close to the worst kind of irreligion. The best that can be said of it is, that it is a sign of the intellectual narrowness – in plain English, the stupidity, which is still the average mark of our culture.[5]

She begins by saying that Christian attitudes towards the Jews are either impious or stupid, but the bulk of what she goes on to say is less concerned with the plight of the insulted than it is with the wretched state of English culture. The closest she ever really comes to directly representing anti-semitism in *Daniel Deronda* is to have the Davilow sisters regard Jews as some kind of "zoological" specimens, and to have Klesmer's ideas regarded as "Polish" by the quintessential political materialist, Mr Bult (the Jewish anti-semitism of Deronda's mother is another matter). The self-serving political crassness of people like Bult and the Anglican worldliness of the Rev. Gascoigne are attitudes which exemplify a dismal deadness to history, a deadness which, Eliot means to show, "lies very close to the worst kind of irreligion".

The Jews in *Daniel Deronda* are definitely not dead to history, and they are obviously a moral foil for all that Eliot criticises in English life. But they are alive to a racial history, rather than to a social or political-historical life. As exemplified in the working-men's club at the "Hand and Banner", and as exemplified in Mordecai and Mirah (and eventually in Deronda), they are imbued with a consciousness of ancestral inheritance and with a joyful, if self-examining, acceptance of themselves as Jews. Above all else, they are aware of themselves as a race, as inescapably linked by ties of blood to the past, and in this sense their consciousness is profoundly ahistorical. In some ways, they represent that epic acceptance of themselves and their destiny which Lukacs describes in *The Theory of the Novel*. They struggle with no fracture of self and substance, no imperative to dominate experience and to recreate a lost order which is the mark of so much novelistic experience.

It is true that they examine what it means to be Jews living an immediate social and political existence, but there is a part of them which is eternal, apolitical, and which seems to transcend history, rather than to be a part of it. And the fact that Eliot offers this eternal and apolitical experience as the alternative to the moral decadence which she has so effectively described is, of course, why the novel collapses. It collapses from social realism into pseudo-epic, with Deronda as a Jewish Aeneas who has tarried long enough on England's Gentile and enervating shores, and who is compelled by his Jewish destiny to rebuild Zion in Palestine. While the Jews display a fine consciousness of history and a worthy commitment to their religious heritage, that consciousness and that commitment never connect with English culture because they are idealised representations of historical and religious awareness – there is no possibility in *Daniel Deronda* as a novel of social realism for the fulfilment of such idealism and spiritual yearning. Eliot offers Jewish historical consciousness as an alternative to English Philistinism, as a cure for moral malaise, but in the process she creates a myth of epic rather than novelistic experience.

Gwendolen Harleth is firmly rooted in history. At the beginning of *Daniel Deronda* she doesn't quite know it, and it is part of her painful experience in the rest of the novel to make this discovery. At the end of Chapter II, Eliot interrupts the story of Grandcourt's first languid advances to ask a couple of questions about the relationship between Gwendolen's self-enclosed consciousness and historical experience:

Could there be a slenderer, more insignificant thread in human history than this consciousness of a girl, busy with her small inferences of the way in which she could make her life pleasant? – in a time, too, when ideas were with fresh vigour making armies of themselves, and the universal kinship was declaring itself fiercely: when women on the other side of the world would not mourn for the husbands and sons who died bravely in a common cause, and men stinted of bread on our side of the world heard of that willing loss and were patient: a time when the soul of man was waking to pulses which had for centuries been beating in him unheard, until their full sum made a new life of terror or of joy.

What in the midst of that mighty drama are girls and their blind visions? They are the Yea or Nay of that good for which men are enduring and fighting. In these delicate vessels is borne onward through the ages the treasure of human affections.

Good questions. The time is summer, 1865, and in the previous few years men have died in the American Civil War, and Lancashire cotton workers were "stinted of bread" because of the North American blockade of Southern cotton ports. Gwendolen is untouched by these devastating events. She is busy with "her small inferences of the way in which she could make her life pleasant", and it is Eliot's intention to bring her out of this world into a consciousness of a larger, more challenging, and more frightening one where men die and women mourn. Gwendolen learns that she must renounce her efforts to control her experience. Deronda, as Eliot's ally, is the person who directs her to this discovery, and in so doing, he helps her to understand herself, and to see that she must relinquish her efforts to assert that self upon the world. He initiates her into two forms of historical life, two forms of history, so to speak: one is that of her own psychological history, and the other has to do with the world outside the self, a world filled with such momentous events as the American Civil War and Lancashire unemployment.

Gwendolen Harleth is a remarkable study in neurosis. To read her only as an hysteric, as a case, to analyse her symptoms and to extrapolate some kind of diagnosis and cure for her malaise, would be a reductive exercise in psychoanalytic criticism. But to connect her phobias, her "petty empire" of manipulation and exploitation, her extraordinarily realised psychological life, with politics and history is to do, in essence, what Eliot herself does when she wonders whether there could be a "slenderer, more insignificant thread in human history" than the consciousness of a profoundly egotistical girl. And to understand Deronda's role in the life of this girl is to understand some of the reasons why his role as moral alternative to the English upper-class culture which Eliot finds virtually incapable of regeneration is so problematic.

In awakening Gwendolen to her psychological history, Deronda becomes a nascent psychoanalyst, a vocation perfectly suited to his disposition. He has a "plenteous, flexible sympathy"; "strong partisanship" is an "insincerity" for him, and he has "a meditative interest in learning how human miseries are wrought". Deronda's problem, of course, is that he is too sympathetic, too meditative – in other words, too passive – and when he is finally released from social paralysis into action by the discovery of his racial heritage, he abandons one meditative passive role, sympathetic confessor to women, for another, Jewish epic hero with a destiny to be fulfilled rather than a career to be chosen.

When he becomes Mordecai's "executive self" he accepts the Judaic inheritance of textual exegesis. Interpretation of the text is passed from one generation of Jewish men to another, and Deronda, having interpreted Gwendolen Harleth in all her knotty psychological syntax, becomes an interpreter of Jewish writings. His first action as a Jew is to claim his grandfather's chest which is full of manuscripts and family records, and he declares to Mordecai that this will give them a "sort of communion" with the line of Spanish Jews from which he is descended. Having spent most of the novel interpreting his own history, analysing his own experience, he now becomes an interpreter of the history of his people.

At thirteen (not an insignificant age for a Jewish boy) he has "a passion for history"; he is eager to know "how time has been filled up since the Flood", and as he lies on the grass one July afternoon studying Italian history, he asks his tutor why the Popes had so many nephews. When he learns that nephew is a euphemism for illegitimate offspring, he begins to imagine that Sir Hugo is his father:

> The first shock of suggestion past, he could remember that he had no certainty how things really had been, and that he had been making conjectures about his own history, as he had often made stories about Pericles or Columbus, just to fill up the blanks before they became famous. (Ch. 16)

The impulse to fill in the blanks of his own life is consistent with his impulse to fill them in for others. He fills in the blanks for Gwendolen when he brings her to a consciousness of her psychological being, and he fills them in for Mirah and Mordecai Lapidoth as he acts as detective of their lost histories, and as coordinator of their reunion. In fact he becomes like Eliot herself – the novelist, the critic, the analyst, the interpreter of experience. Just as Eliot stands outside her own narrative, questioning, answering, meditating, and moralising, and finally being compelled to escape from her irreconcilable oppositions into displacement, so Deronda stands outside his own life, and the lives of other characters in the novel, and outside his own culture. He is external until he is, himself, displaced from the novel of English upper-class life into the epic of Zionism. As preparation for his discovery of racial heritage, he becomes a kind of gentleman social enquirer into lower-class Jewish life. It is to the relationship between Deronda and the Jews that I should first like to turn.

NOTES

1. From the time of its first appearance, Eliot's last novel has been criticised for its fatal unevenness. A representative collection of contemporary reviews of *Daniel Deronda* is to be found in *A Century of George Eliot Criticism*, edited by Gordon S. Haight (Boston, 1965).

   The critical acceptance of one part of *Daniel Deronda* and rejection of the other finds its most emphatic modern spokesman in F. R. Leavis. Eliot's hero is a "self-indulgence", doomed to boring sloppiness because he is created by a "determining drive from within, a triumphant pressure of emotion". This view coincides with Leavis's overall assessment of Eliot's novels. When her intellect is in the ascendency her work is very fine, but when what Leavis calls "an alliance of immaturity and fervent emotionalism" gets hold of her, "a woman's creation" such as Deronda is the lamentable result. See *The Great Tradition*, Ch. II, iii, "*Daniel Deronda* and *The Portrait of a Lady*" (New York, 1969).

   Many critics since Leavis have addressed themselves to the split structure of *Daniel Deronda*. See especially, R. T. Jones, *George Eliot* (Cambridge, 1970), Calvin Bedient, *Architects of the Self* (California, 1972), Neil Roberts, *George Eliot: Her Beliefs and Her Art* (London, 1975). This is by no means a representation of Eliot criticism. I have isolated here what seem to me to be the most interesting treatments of the split novel problematic.

   *Daniel Deronda* has, of course, been put into another perspective and seen as an integrated, successful expression of Eliot's analytic social realism and her long readings in Jewish history, philosophy and religion. The novel is seen as effectively unified by, among others, Barbara Hardy,

William Baker and E. S. Shaffer. In her introduction to the Penguin edition, Hardy pays special attention to the relatedness of everything to everything else (for which Eliot would have been grateful), and to the form of the novel, which she sees as breaking new ground in Victorian fiction. Baker, in *George Eliot and Judaism* (Salzburg, 1975), sees Eliot's last novel as the moving and learned culmination of her studies in Jewish thought. For Shaffer, Deronda is a redemptive, Christ-like figure who unifies all parts of the novel. See *"Kubla Khan" and The Fall of Jerusalem: The Mytholological School in Biblical Criticism and Secular Literature, 1770–1880* (Cambridge, England, 1975).

2. Letter to Madame Eugène Bodichon, 2 October 1876. *The George Eliot Letters*, edited by Gordon S. Haight (New Haven, 1955), Vol. VI, p. 290. All further references in the text to George Eliot's letters will be to this edition.
3. Raymond Williams sees George Eliot's novels as "transitional between that form which could end in a series of settlements, in which the social and economic solutions and the personal achievements were in a single dimension, and that new form which extending and complicating and then finally collapsing this dimension ends with a single person going away on his own, having achieved his moral growth by distancing or by extrication". *The English Novel from Dickens to Lawrence* (London, 1973), pp. 86–7.

   I think this is especially true of *Daniel Deronda*. Gwendolen Harleth's moral rehabilitation is connected with the old form, her psychological change may be said to represent a hope, however ephemeral, for social change. Deronda's emigration is connected with the new form, even though he doesn't extricate himself from English life entirely alone.
4. *Daniel Deronda* (Penguin Books, Harmondsworth, 1967), edited and with an introduction by Barbara Hardy. All further references in the text to *Daniel Deronda* will be to this edition. There is no complete, standard, or critical edition of George Eliot's works. The Penguin edition is based on the Cabinet edition of 1878 which was the last to be corrected by George Eliot.
5. *Letters*, Vol. VI, pp. 301–2.

# 8 Deronda and the Jews

When Deronda, at the age of thirteen, discovers the correct familial relationship between Renaissance popes and their nephews, he begins his adult life of interpretation and criticism. His interpretation is initially faulty: contrary to his wishful thinking, Sir Hugo is not his father, and his mother, rather than being the injured figure of his fantasy, has wilfully and deliberately given him away. But at the end of *Daniel Deronda* there are no more secrets – Deronda meets his Jewish mother, discovers his Jewish origins, and, in an ironic twist, undoes all that she has exerted her will to effect. Although he remains, in every way, the English gentleman that she wished him to become, he implicitly renounces his mother by committing himself to Mordecai's philosophy of separateness with communication. His new identity does not exactly assume the form of the "Jewish tatters and gibberish" that his mother says "make people nudge each other at the sight of us" (Ch. 51) (the Eastern travelling outfits provided by Sir Hugo for the newly-married Zionists are anything but tatters, Jewish or otherwise), but by accepting his male Jewish inheritance, by relinking himself to the grandfather whose will was a form of bondage for his mother, Deronda effectively nullifies her rebellion against that bondage. From the significant age of thirteen, Eliot readies him for the assumption of his Jewish destiny by endowing him with a prevailing interest in interpretation, which finds its full and proper expression in interpretation of records at the end of the novel, and, from the moment he rescues Mirah Lapidoth, by exposing him to Jewish life.

As a boy, Deronda has read Shakespeare and a good deal of history, and, if it were demanded of him, "he could have talked with the wisdom of the bookish child about men who were born out of wedlock, and were held unfortunate in consequence" (Ch. 16). But he has never made a connection between such knowledge and his own life. He has assumed that Sir Hugo is his uncle as he has assumed the authority of his writings, writings which are, to the thirteen-year-old Deronda, "alike in having an unquestionable rightness by which other people's information could be tested" (Ch. 16). After he discovers the disjunction between reality and fiction, the reality of being a son and the fiction of being a nephew, Deronda begins to question the values embodied in *his* uncle's writings as he begins to question the assumption that Sir Hugo is, indeed, his uncle. When it is time for Deronda to leave Eton and go to Cambridge, Sir Hugo suggests that he might eventually go into the House, where his Latin and Greek will constitute "a little disinterested culture to make head against cotton and capital". Deronda keeps a respectful silence, scornful of this Philistine appropriation of a classical education for "his enthusiastic belief in Sir Hugo's writings as a standard, and in the Whigs as the chosen race among politicians, had gradually vanished along with the seraphic boy's face" (Ch. 16).

As Deronda matures, his critical examination of his culture and his self-consciousness in regard to his origins is associated by Eliot, in one way or another, with writing and with texts, and it is interesting that *Daniel Deronda*, in general, is self-consciously concerned with interpretation of social and psychological actuality by language. As Deronda stands outside his own life, meditating upon it as if it were a text, and eventually dissociating himself from English society, so Eliot seems to stand outside her own narrative, meditating upon the novelist's work of representation and eventually dissociating herself from a fictive regeneration of all that has been criticised in that representation. Deronda's self-reflexiveness is matched by that of Eliot, and in a novel that is remarkable for its split structure, it is notable that the hero himself is split, unable to integrate himself into his society and only made whole in radical separation from it, just as Eliot is unable to integrate her novel of social realism with her work of moral correction, and can only resolve the dilemma by radical withdrawal into myth.

Examination of the self is likened to examination of a text as Deronda realises that he may be in love with Mirah Lapidoth:

> . . . reasons both definite and vague made him shut away that question as he might have shut up a half-opened writing that would have carried his imagination too far and given too much shape to presentiments. Might there not come a disclosure which would hold the missing determination of his course? What did he really know about his origin? . . . The disclosure might bring its pain, indeed the likelihood seemed to him to be all on that side; but if it helped him to make his life a sequence which would take

> the form of duty . . . he wanted to escape standing as a critic outside the activities of men, stiffened into the ridiculous attitude of self-assigned superiority. (Ch. 37)

Shutting up an examination of his feelings is likened to shutting up a half-opened text and the self is something to be read. Deronda cannot read himself too closely or too finely for fear of the powerful interaction of text and reader in which the text gives shape to the associations which it engenders. A reading of the self might reveal the "missing determination" of Deronda's existence. But he is ambivalent, for while he is reluctant to read himself too closely, he also wants to make his life a "sequence", to give it chronological and narrative order, so to speak, to save himself from fixation at one stage of moral development and knowledge of the self. To be a reader or a critic like Deronda, then, is to have no knowledge of the "missing determination", no knowledge of one's origins; it is to search for them and, paradoxically, once they are discovered one ceases to be a reader of oneself, and, implicitly, a critic. When Deronda discovers his Jewish ancestry, his critical examination of himself and of English society is terminated. It seems as if Eliot equates being Jewish, or rather *knowing* that one is Jewish, with a dissolution of critical externality: if one thinks of, say, Freud and Marx, one a critic of the self and the other a critic of society, and both Jews, then Eliot's equation becomes ambiguous, to say the least.

An admission that language is ultimately insufficient in an effective transmission of social and psychological actuality is hardly anything new in literature. But *Daniel Deronda* is remarkable for Eliot's insistence on this admission. As she introduces Grandcourt into the novel, contrasting him with the "correct Englishman" who always seems "to be in a state of internal drill", she stops short after this felicitous phrase, and announces:

> Attempts at description are stupid: who can all at once describe a human being? even when he is presented to us we only begin that knowledge of his appearance which must be completed by innumerable impressions under differing circumstances. We recognize the alphabet; we are not sure of the language.(Ch. 11)

To the modern reader, the metaphor of alphabet and language suggests the methodology of anthropological linguistics in which speech acts are recorded in different contexts, an alphabet established, and a language reconstructed. In Eliot's metaphor, the novelist reconstructs a character for the reader from "innumerable impressions under differing circumstances" which are transformed by the literary imagination; an alphabet composed of, among other things, gestures, modes of thought and verbal expressions is established, and the reader is presented with a language of character, however unsure Eliot may be about the language she reconstructs.

Eliot never lets her reader forget that there is something inaccessible to language and to interpretation. In describing how Gwendolen's eyes attract Grandcourt's lazy and malevolent stare, she says this occurs "mysteriously" because the "subtly-varied drama between man and woman is often such as can hardly be rendered in words put together like dominoes, according to obvious fixed marks" (Ch. 27). Syntactical arrangement is performed like a game of dominoes in which three white dots on one piece, say, must match three white dots on another. In linguistic terms, for random words to be arranged into sentences, a system of word order is established (at least in English) and syntactical function becomes like the domination in a game of dominoes. Whoever wins the game dominates by creating a chain of meaning, and whoever makes a sentence dominates words by creating a chain of meaning through syntactical arrangement.

Now Deronda is essentially one who interprets, however faultily, rather than one who dominates, a discoverer of meaning rather than a maker of it. He is passively made aware of his origins, for while his quasi-sociological investigation of the East End Jews becomes inseparable in his mind from a search for the "missing determination" of his life, that investigation does not lead him to his mother. He does not discover *her* existence, she sends for *him* when she decides the time is right, and when he first encounters the Jewish girl whose lost family becomes the object of his search, he is indulging himself in what Eliot describes as "that solemn passivity which easily comes with the lengthening shadows and mellowing light". He is stretched out in his rowboat, his hands propped behind his head:

> He was forgetting everything else in a half-speculative, half-involuntary identification of himself with the objects he was looking at, thinking how far it might be possible habitually to shift his centre till his own personality would be no less outside him than the landscape. (Ch. 17)

He is engaged in a kind of Wordsworthian interfusion with the landscape, down in the boat, almost one with the river, and he is attempting another kind of interfusion, trying to dissolve a consciousness of self so that his personality will be "no less outside him" than the landscape into which he has tried to merge himself. He is floating to his destiny, just as Grandcourt and Gwendolen float to theirs as they cruise the Mediterranean. But on that boat there is no attempt to fuse the observing self with what is observed. The Grandcourt yacht is firmly *on* the water, luxuriously detached from its environment, as the two people on board are irrevocably detached from themselves and their environment, condemned to aimless cruising as a defence against dissatisfaction and boredom.

Deronda is compelled to one of his rare moments of physical action by the sight of Mirah Lapidoth dipping her cloak in the Thames to make it a more effective drowning shroud.[1] The impression she makes upon him stirs "a fibre that lay close to his deepest interest in the fates of women – 'perhaps my mother was like this one' " (Ch. 17). But Mirah is totally unlike Deronda's mother. In a strongly matrifocal novel, she becomes, for Deronda, the positive image of Jewish womanhood, and, implicitly, of Jewish motherhood. Mirah submits to patriarchal Jewish dominance, whereas Deronda's mother has rebelled against it; she is obedient to the teachings of a religion which Deronda's mother has found oppressive and has renounced. Mirah accepts her history where Deronda's mother has consistently sought to deny hers.

After Deronda deposits Mirah with the incurably romantic Meyrick women (he knows they will associate "a lovely Jewess with Rebecca in 'Ivanhoe' "), he undertakes "a less fashionable form of exercise than riding in Rotten Row", and goes "rambling in those parts of London which are most inhabited by common Jews" (Ch. 33). In a sentence remarkable for its convoluted syntax, Eliot describes how Deronda is forced to face the actuality of working-class Jewish life:

> The fact was, not withstanding all his sense of poetry in common things, Deronda, where a keen personal interest was aroused, could not, more than the rest of us, continuously escape suffering from the pressure of that hard unaccommodating Actual, which has never consulted our taste and is entirely unselect. (Ch. 33)

The "hard unaccommodating Actual" is cemented in the sentence surrounded by clauses, as if Eliot is forced by its hardness, its unaccommodating actuality, to place it there. Deronda must suffer the pressure of this "Actual" as Eliot, I think, felt she must suffer it to write those parts of *Daniel Deronda* which deal with the "common Jews". Like her hero, she has a fine "sense of poetry in common things" (one thinks of the Poyser kitchen in *Adam Bede*), but when it comes to a representation of lower-class city life she tends to idealise rather than to suffer the pressure which she declares is inescapable.

In describing Deronda's forays into the East End she goes on to say:

> ... if the scenery of St. Mary Axe and Whitechapel were imaginatively transported to the borders of the Rhine at the end of the eleventh century, when in the ears listening for the signals of the Messiah, the Hep! Hep! Hep! of the Crusaders came like the bay of blood hounds; and in the presence of those devilish missionaries with sword and firebrand the crouching figure of the reviled Jew turned round erect, heroic, flashing with sublime constancy in the face of torture and death – what would the dingy shops and unbeautiful faces signify to the thrill of contemplative emotion? But the fervour of sympathy with which we contemplate a grandiose martyrdom is feeble compared with the enthusiasm that keeps unslacked where there is no danger, no challenge – nothing but impartial mid-day falling on commonplace perhaps half-repulsive objects which are really the beloved ideas made flesh. Here undoubtedly lies the chief poetic energy: – in the force of imagination that pierces or exalts the solid fact, instead of floating among cloud pictures. (Ch. 33)

Eliot is, of course, talking about Deronda but one senses that Eliot wishes *she* had the "poetic energy", that she could pierce and exalt "the solid fact, instead of floating among cloud pictures". Deronda is very much a projection of Eliot's artistic and interpretive consciousness, both here, as she describes his poetic energies, and in other places in the novel, as he becomes the link between the two social worlds which she represents, and as he becomes an omniscient coordinator of Mordecai and Mirah's reunion. Deronda really fails to have that "unslacked enthusiasm" in the face of common things, as Eliot herself fails to have it when it comes to representing the common Jews in *Daniel Deronda*. Rather than giving them to us with their "garlic breath", "dingy shops and unbeautiful faces", she paints a rosy portrait of working-class urban Jews who eat nothing more offensive than challah, have nice clean shops and look handsome and robust.

The most obvious and most fully discussed meaning of the Jews in *Daniel Deronda* is their function as a positive alternative to upper-class materialism and irreligion, but it seems to me that in addition to their significance as a moral foil for all that Eliot criticises, they also offer her a way of mediating between two irreconcilable ideals – one to do with her ideas about class and the other to do with her ideas about the duties of the novelist. Deronda is her agent in this mediation.

From a reading of Eliot's letters and essays, it is clear that, on the one hand, she puts forward certain ideals of class cooperation which, for her, must be struggled for so that a decent moral life might be achieved, and, on the other, that she is committed to the faithful mimesis of the working man in fiction. (Eliot is consistently articulate about the faithful mimesis of *all* social actuality, but I am especially concerned here with what she says about one particular social class.) It seems to me that in *Daniel Deronda* she displaces her ideal of English working-class conduct into the myth of an orderly, conservative and morally admirable people, the Jews (while at the same time rehearsing a few popular and prejudiced notions about them), for she is confronted by a social reality which she finds reprehensible, by a working class which in her view cared more for anarchy than for culture, and by her quite clearly stated commitment to the accurate representation of the lower orders in fiction. To see how Eliot mediates between these two ideals, it is necessary first to examine her ideas about the English working class.

In 1848, a year in which it was virtually impossible not to be conscious of working-class agitation, George Eliot wrote to her friend, the Rev. John Sibree, and made the following comparison between French and English manifestations of class struggle:

> Our working classes are eminently inferior to the mass of the French people. In France, the *mind* of the people is highly electrified – they are full of ideas on social subjects – they really desire social *reform* .... Here there is so much larger a proportion of selfish radicalism and unsatisfied brute sensuality (in the agricultural and mining districts especially) than of perception of

> desire of justice, that revolutionary movement would be simply destructive – not constructive.[2]

It would seem that Laurence Sterne was right; even in matters of political agitation, they do, indeed, order these things better in France. The French worker is concerned with reform, the English with selfish radicalism. English "brute sensuality" is unfavourably compared with the "highly electrified" French mind.

Eliot never abandoned this negative assessment of the possibilities for English working-class self-improvement. To be sure, she is hardly the first person who springs to mind when one thinks of nineteenth-century novelists who concerned themselves with working-class social and political experience. While Eliot is celebrated for the analytic intelligence which she brought to an examination of the mutual responsibilities of the individual and society, and to the mutually determinative relationship between public and private historical experience, she did not address herself to any specific problematic social situation, as, say, the industrial novelists did. Although the Reform Bill of 1832 is certainly an important aspect of the social change described in *Middlemarch* and *Felix Holt the Radical*, and *Adam Bede* is partly about the place of the artisan in a newly industrialised society, these novels are not strictly industrial or "social question" novels and it is a confirmation of Eliot's expansive intellect that they cannot be categorised in this way.

But *Felix Holt* does deal with the complex consequences of political action, and Eliot examines the place of such action in a society which she perceived (or at least wanted to perceive) as an organic whole, where the private experience is determined and sustained by social structures, and where these structures are, in turn, determined and nourished by the individual. After a reading of *Felix Holt* (published in June 1866), one has to conclude that Eliot still believed the English worker was bent on "selfish radicalism" and on satisfying his "brute sensuality".

In a crucial scene in the novel, Felix finds himself caught in the sway of an inflamed mob. Dissatisfied with the brand new Reform Bill of 1832, which did not provide for universal suffrage, the vote by ballot or election districts, the mob begins to carry on in a fashion remarkably similar to that of Matthew Arnold's Populace. Eliot describes the majority of the crowd as "excited with drink", and says that "their action could hardly be calculated on more than those of oxen and pigs congregated amidst hootings and pushings" (Ch. 33).

This barnyard crew ignores a reading of the Riot Act, starts throwing turnips at the special constables brought in to control the crowd, and sets about pummelling the manager of the local colliery. Felix, finding it "intolerable . . . to be witnessing the blind outrages of this mad crowd, and yet be doing nothing to counteract them", manages to deflect the fury of the working men by sending them off in the wrong direction. They all end up at the local manor house where resentment of political inequality finds expression in looting silver plate and in forcing the butler to open the cellars, and Felix is charged with leading a riot and with manslaughter. He is convicted, but given mercy because of a plea from the heroine, Esther Lyon, and he emerges from the novel as a mediating figure between working-class resentment and ruling-class conservatism, his barely discernible radicalism subsumed under his rational patriotism, and ready to be properly civilised with French lessons from Esther.

The fictive Felix Holt was a voice of rational moderation, and in late 1867 John Blackwood suggested that Eliot use him as a spokesman for a polemical essay designed to counter the social disorder thought to be incipient with the passing of the second Reform Bill in August of that year. In the mind of Eliot's readers, Felix Holt was associated with the events of 1832, and it seemed appropriate to Blackwood that Felix have his conservative say in the events of 1867. The essay, "Address to Working Men by Felix Holt," pleads for the preservation of a treasure-house of culture, and for the elimination of the class conflict which Eliot, in concert with many of her conservative contemporaries, feared would precipitate wholesale vandalism.[3]

"Society stands before us," says Felix, "like that wonderful piece of life, the human body, with all its various parts depending on one another, and with a terrible liability to get wrong because of that delicate dependence."[4] Society likened to the human body is a familiar metaphor, but in the context of social unrest in 1867, it takes on an especially gratifying meaning for every member of society except those who constitute those parts of the "human body" that cause the "getting wrong" of the whole. If we say that society is like the human body, then we never have to take responsibility for the creation of that society/body, except in the most literal, biological sense. It is an organism whose genesis lies beyond our comprehension, and this tacit refusal of responsibility for the social mechanisms which, in part, determine the "getting wrong" of society by some of its members is the implicit comfort of metaphors that convert what is a complex process of historical and social relationships into what is natural and therefore ultimately inexplicable.

The way to steady improvement of the working-class lot is not to "do away with the actually existing class distinctions and advantages, as if everybody could have the same sort of work, or lead the same sort of life . . . but by the turning of Class Interests into Class Functions or duties".[5] The cultivation of Duty, by which I think Eliot means something close to Arnoldian Hebraism, will preserve and disseminate Culture, Arnoldian Hellenism.[6] And the working classes are shut out from culture, from the "precious benefits" of the "common estate of society". The common estate cannot be measured in monetary terms; it has a value over and above all the material measurements of Britain's domestic wealth and imperial power. As Felix describes it, it is:

> . . . the treasure of knowledge, science, poetry, refinement of thought, feeling, and manners, great memories and the interpretation of great records, which is carried on from the minds of one generation to the other. This is something distinct from the indulgences of luxury and the pursuit of vain finery; and one of the hardships in the lot of working men is that they have been for the most part shut out from sharing this treasure. . . .[7]

Eliot is clearly not setting up some simplistic choice for the working class between hot dinners and good housing on the one hand or poetry readings and musical evenings on the other, but Felix Holt displays so little awareness of working-class deprivation, and so much fierce contempt for the vices of "a too craving body", and for the "fading delusions of drugged beer and gin", that even while one respects the seriousness of Eliot's political opinions, it is difficult not to wonder what has happened to her analytic intelligence. It is true that when Felix speaks of "Class Functions or duties", the privileged classes are not exempt. Nevertheless, Eliot has him declaim:

> . . . in this matter of the wealth that is carried in men's minds, we have to reflect that the too absolute predominance of a class whose wants have been of a common sort, who are chiefly struggling to get better and more food, clothing, shelter and bodily recreation, may lead to hasty measures for the sake of having things more fairly shared, which, even if they did not fail of their object, would at last debase the life of the nation.[8]

It seems that her abhorrence of any change in society which would unbalance the delicate, interdependent mechanisms of its metaphoric body blind her to the fact that England was *already* ruled by the "too absolute predominance" of one class. This was a class whose needs were definitely not of "a common sort", needs which ran to country houses, to seats in the House, and to Mediterranean yachts – a class which, is, of course, the principal butt of her social satire in *Daniel Deronda*.[9]

It is not my intention to charge Eliot with an indifference to working-class misery, or to dismiss Felix Holt's political prescriptions as the product of some dotty conservatism, but rather to show that an understanding of Eliot's political opinions, as articulated here through her spokesman, Felix Holt, is necessary to an examination of the conflict in her novelist's consciousness between two ideals. Felix's stern pronouncements are important in this regard, and his alarming attentiveness to ruling-class interests and his devotion to "culture" have to be considered in the light of what Eliot says about representing *his* class in fiction and the collision of ideals which leads her, I believe, to mythologise the Jews in *Daniel Deronda*.

A little more than a year after Eliot wrote the first of her *Scenes of Clerical Life*, she made a fairly long entry in her journal under the heading "How I Came to Write Fiction". As she describes it, "a new era" in her life began, and this new era turned out to be a highly self-conscious one in which she was constantly mindful of the moral responsibilities of the novelist. Two of her most important essays in this connection are "Authorship", which was published four years after her death, and "The Natural History of German Life", which first appeared in the *Westminster Review* in 1856.

In "Authorship" she adopts the language of commercial capitalism. "The author's capital is his brain power"; he performs "social activity", and he "can no more escape influencing the moral taste, and with it the action of the intelligence, than a setter of fashions in furniture and dress can fill the shops with his designs and leave the garniture of persons and houses unaffected by his industry".[10] The author who writes to make a "money-profit" is likened to an irresponsible calico manufacturer who uses a poisonous dye to achieve an attractive and marketable effect. Eliot's use of commercial language leads her into some very knotty and contradictory implications. She suggests on the one hand that the author sells his books as a manufacturer sells cotton (and therefore, one assumes, earns money) but, on the other, that he must not be motivated by a desire for making money. And it is worth bearing in mind here that Eliot's literary earnings were not inconsiderable; for example, she notes in her book of "Personal Expenses" that by the end of 1873 she was receiving an annual income of £1,500 from the money invested from these earnings.[11]

But the more important aspect of the essay is Eliot's assertion that the novelist performs a social activity and that he must bear the same moral burden which she wishfully ascribes to the civic-minded capitalist. And when the middle-class novelist sets out to represent the lower orders, the moral responsibilities entailed in authorship become even more onerous.

In "The Natural History of German Life", Eliot attacks English artists for sentimentalising working-class experience. Her particular target is William Holman Hunt who, she declares, paints shepherds and their sweethearts who are "not much more real than the idyllic swains and damsels of our chimney ornaments".[12] Ornamental chimney art has its place, which is on the mantelpiece, but when it comes to "the life of the People" something more exacting is required from the artist than dainty china work:

> Art is the nearest thing to life; it is a mode of amplifying experience and extending our contact with our fellow-men beyond the bounds of our personal lot. All the more sacred is the task of the artist when he undertakes to paint the life of the People. Falsification here is far more pernicious than in the more artificial aspects of life. It is not so very serious that we should have false ideas about evanescent fashions – about the manners and conversation of beaux and duchesses; but it *is* serious that our sympathy with the perennial joys and struggles, the toil, the tragedy, and the humour in the life of our more heavily-laden fellow-men, should be perverted, and turned towards a false object instead of the true one.[13]

Eliot implies that working-class life is less "artificial" than that of "beaux and duchesses", and if by this she means it is less made by art, then she is correct, for the working class in Victorian England could rarely afford to "make" its life in any sense, artistic or otherwise: it was already largely being made for it by a complex set of forces, primarily economic, outside its control. But Eliot is clearly saying something more, or something else, here, and it seems that she articulates a familiar bourgeois myth in this plea for faithful mimesis of life among the lower orders. It is the myth of the noble savage transposed to the English village and the English streets, a myth which implies that in the life of the "more heavily-laden worker" the "perennial joys and struggles" of human existence are experienced more deeply than in the false and decadent life of his social superior. To be fair, Eliot's intention is to awaken a sympathy for those less fortunate than ourselves, to show a universality of suffering and of struggle, but while making a plea for the faithful mimesis of lower-class life in place of "pernicious" falsification, she seems to imply a differing degree of feeling that is dependent on class position.

Eliot, then, experienced a conflict in her artistic consciousness between an ideal of working-class conduct, expressed most clearly in the "Address to Working Men by Felix Holt", and a commitment to represent faithfully the working class in all its heavily laden actuality. Her ideal working class is to be bound to the conservation of the treasure-house of culture, the best that has been thought and said in the Arnoldian sense. But Eliot is a profoundly self-conscious novelist, always concerned with the moral responsibilities entailed in the social action of writing novels and always alert to the necessity of representing as truthfully as she is able the manners and mores of her society. In this sense, she is both novelist and sociologist, but she cannot be both at once when it comes to the English working class, for if she were to remain faithful to her own strict edicts, she could never have written a novel in which the working class behaved in accordance with her idealised prescriptions.

By the time of *Daniel Deronda* all possibility of writing about class relationships as she would like to see them, with conflict dissolved by a shared conservation of culture, and by a joyful assumption of class duties and functions, seems to find its only expression in displacement. Deronda, as the interpreter of lower-class Jewish life, becomes the fictive agent of this displacement.

When Deronda abandons Rotten Row for Whitechapel, he undertakes the expedition "very much as if, Mirah being related to Welsh miners, he had gone to look more closely at the ways of those people, not without wishing at the same time to get a little light of detail on the history of Strikes" (Ch. 33). The Jews are a social group about whom Deronda is mildly curious; he wants "to look more closely" at their ways, yet desires no more than "a little light of detail" on the history of their struggles.

In 1879, some three years after the publication of *Daniel Deronda*, Eliot herself undertook an enquiry into the Jews in an essay on anti-semitism entitled "The Modern Hep! Hep! Hep!" While her intentions are far different from Deronda's, the essay is remarkable for its explicit expression of what is implied in his forays into the East End. It is an attempt to widen the English vision by excoriating medieval Christian notions about Jews (Hep! Hep! Hep! was the war cry of the Crusaders), and by celebrating Hebrew culture. For all her laudable intentions, Eliot comes up with some startling ideas about the place of the Jews in English society, and despite her stirring praise of the "humanizing and elevating habits" of the Jewish mind which inspire "sacrifices of individual comfort, gain, or other selfish ambition" for the sake of a national ideal, she finally announces that the English *must* deal with the Jews because they will not go away:

> They are amongst us everywhere; it is useless to say we are not fond of them. Perhaps we are not fond of proletaries and their tendency to form Unions, but the world is not therefore to be rid of them. If we wish to free ourselves from the inconvenience that we have to complain of, whether in proletaries or in Jews, our best course is to encourage all means of improving these neighbours who elbow us in a thickening crowd, and of sending their incommodious energies into beneficient channels.[14]

In a circular pattern of similitude, the Jews are like the proletaries, who are like the Welsh in their tendency to form Unions, and the Welsh are like the Jews whose ways Deronda sets out to investigate. The Jews, the proletaries and the Welsh miners may be seen as one grand inconvenience, for which I think one may substitute the term English working class. And the way to deal with this inconvenience is to improve it, which is the remedy put forward by Felix Holt in his "Address to Working Men", and to send its "incommodious energies into beneficent channels", which it seems to me is the answer put forward by *Daniel Deronda* when Eliot imaginatively "sends" that incommodious energy into her ideal representation of Jewish national consciousness.

She explicitly channels the dispersed energies of the Jews into Deronda's project to put an end to the *diaspora*. This channelling has a disguised gratification for those people for whom the Jews are an inconvenience in a thickening crowd: the Jews will not proliferate and prosper on English soil. (In the 1860s and 1870s there was an increase in Jewish immigration from Russia and Poland to England.) And at the same time, Eliot implicitly channels, displaces as it were, her negative views of the English working class from the novel of class without conflict which she clearly could never write if she were to remain faithful to her own prescriptions for authorship, into a novel which endows the Jews with all the cultural and historical awareness missing from the English working class.

The Cohen family in *Daniel Deronda* is of the elbowing variety, and Deronda's initial response to the East End and its racy inhabitants is as class-bound as Eliot's. Mrs Cohen, for Deronda, has "the look of having made her toilet with little water, and by twilight, which is common to unyouthful people of her class, and of having presumably slept in her large earrings, if not in her rings and necklace" (Ch. 33). And the Cohen children look "more Semitic than their parents as the puppy-lions show the spots of far-off progenitors", a distinctly Darwinian observation which turns them into interesting zoological items, caged in Whitechapel, and confined by race and class from breaking out and behaving like the piggy villagers in *Felix Holt*. Yet Eliot also endows the Cohens with a warmth and political conservatism distinctly attributable to a stable religious life.

Deronda visits the Cohen shop on a Friday and is invited to observe what is for him, and what must have been for contemporary readers of *Daniel Deronda*, the exotic rituals of the Sabbath. Eliot's description of the family scene is highly visual. The smoky walls throw into relief the "human figures" (a phrase suggestive of art criticism, rather than novelistic description), giving the family "a Venetian glow of colouring" (Ch. 34). The mother is in yellowish brown and looks as handsome as is "necessary for picturesque effect". Young Mrs Cohen is in red and black, the baby reposes under a scarlet counterpane, Adelaide is in braided amber, and Jacob in black velveteen with scarlet stockings. This family portrait is set against some nice old oak furniture and filled out with such pleasing details as blue and yellow dishes and old silver vessels. It is all richly mellow, and Deronda stands outside it as if he were in the National Gallery, enjoying it in all its colourful and picturesque externality, so that the reader remains at a double remove from the felt actuality of Jewish East End life. We never enter into this life; it is rendered for us in rich textures which do not seem to invite an understanding of Jewish lower-class experience except in visual terms. But the Cohen family, despite and because of its externality to the reader, united by its religion and untroubled by matters of inheritance, advantageous marriage and political advancement, stands in marked contrast to the decadent upper-class English society which Eliot describes in the other part of *Daniel Deronda*.

The Cohens constitute a united family, given to us as an ornamental delight and as a moral contrast. They also leave nothing to be desired in matters of political opinion. Mr Cohen keeps up his conversation with Deronda "with much liveliness, introducing as subjects always in taste (the Jew is proud of his loyalty), the Queen and the Royal Family, the Emperor and Empress of the French" (Ch. 34). Eliot's patronising parenthesis about Jewish loyalty is an apt stylistic indication of her social and novelistic distance from the Jews, and one begins to wonder why she has the Cohens in the novel at all. They are the wrong Jews as far as Deronda is concerned for they are not related to Mirah. Yet if they play no significant part in the plot, then presumably they have a different and perhaps more complex function in the novel which goes beyond adding a spot of local East End colour.

The Cohens allow Deronda, and the reader, to experience both positive and negative elements of Jewish culture as Eliot perceived them, to appreciate the familial stability in contrast to the sado-masochistic domesticity of Gwendolen and Grandcourt, to appreciate the political and religious conservatism which Eliot found to be missing from English working-class life, *and* to be repulsed by the vulgarity and greed which are conventionally associated with Jews, and which Eliot, in her description of them as an elbowing inconvenience, was not hesitant to make explicit in her essay on anti-semitism. The positive values of Jewish family life function as a displaced ideal image of working-class life, and the negative characteristics function as an expression of Eliot's own anti-semitic attitudes, and as an implicit gratification for those of her readers who shared these attitudes. The Cohens are admitted into the novel and then felicitously dispatched because they are the wrong Jews; Deronda will never have to cope with Mrs Cohen, in all her unwashed and bejewelled splendour, as a mother-in-law, and it is therefore ultimately of no matter that the Cohens are vulgar and greedy. But by making them vulgar and greedy Eliot propagates one of the more popular myths about Jewish culture.

The negative side of the Cohen family is represented by a prevailing interest in money. From the pawnbroker father down to the precocious Jacob who gleefully executes a profitable trade of penknives with Deronda, they inhabit a world of small commerce.

When Deronda informs Mr Cohen that Mordecai is to undergo a great change in his life (the reunion with his sister which Deronda is in the process of coordinating), Mr Cohen's response is the hopeful question, "Relations with money, sir?" (Ch. 46). And Mr Cohen employs the language and metaphors of money to assess the meaning for his family of Mordecai's departure. Their lodger has been "a property bearing interest" (an unpaid resident tutor for Jacob), and he declares rather ruefully that after they "cast up their accounts" and see where they are, they will doubtless be glad for Mordecai's sake.

To be sure, almost everyone in *Daniel Deronda* is interested in money; the Cohens merely express such an interest in their own Jewish, ingenuous and outright fashion. The Arrowpoints, for example, want to get the best that money can buy in musical instruction and in husbands for their daughter. Their misfortune, so to speak, is not to foresee that she will combine these two commodities, rather than understanding, as they do, that musical instructors and husbands are separate items to be purchased in different metaphorical shops. And Sir Hugo is anxious to get his hands on the Diplow property which has been left to his nephew, Grandcourt, as a means of securing a comfortable inheritance for his wife and daughters. And, as a third example of the importance of money (or the lack of it) in all strata of English social life in *Daniel Deronda*, Gwendolen's marriage is precipitated by the failure of the Davilow investments.

Eliot rejects materialism at both ends of the social scale; she finds it as reprehensible at Quetcham as she does in St Mary Axe. The only place in *Daniel Deronda* where people do not think about money is in Chelsea, that is to say in the Meyrick household. The embroidering and sketching Meyrick women live in a world "spotlessly free from vulgarity, because poverty had rendered everything like display an impersonal question, and all the grand shows of the world simply a spectacle which rouses no petty rivalry or vain effort after possession" (Ch. 18). They inhabit Matthew Arnold's ideal world of culture without anarchy, or, in their case, without envy. They live "a wide-glancing, nicely-select life, open to the highest things in music, painting and poetry . . . united by a triple bond – family love, admiration for the finest work, the best action, and habitual industry" (Ch. 18). Were they not rigorously middle class, it would be possible to suggest that the Meyrick family also functions as a displacement of Eliot's ideals for working-class conduct. They are certainly ideal women, however, and they are united by a fourth bond, that of female self-sacrifice to the male artist. They adore Hans because he is an artist like their father was: their miniscule Chelsea house is a veritable museum devoted to the work of the men of the family. They are also devoted to learning. Where Greek was useful to Sir Hugo because "it formed his taste and his English is the better for it", the study of foreign languages is undertaken by the Meyrick women for and in itself. And they are literally bowled over by genius. When the magnificent Klesmer comes to hear Mirah sing, their small feminine figures seem to shrink to even more diminutive proportions in the presence of his terrifying and imposing figure. Klesmer looms over them in the tiny drawing room, transformed by Eliot by virtue of his genius and artistic integrity into a positive image of Charlotte Brontë's Mr Brocklehurst looming over the quivering girls at Lowood School in *Jane Eyre*.

Mordecai is also a genius, but of a different Jewish variety. He is a visionary, and his presence in *Daniel Deronda* is distinguished from that of the Cohen family in two ways. He is Mirah's brother and therefore has a distinct function in the development of the plot, and he is the principal spokesman for the cultural consciousness which Eliot posits as an alternative to upper-class materialism. It is a cultural consciousness founded upon historical and racial awareness and upon the preservation of that awareness through the interpretation of records.

In his "Address to Working Men", Felix Holt pleads for the conservation of a "treasure of knowledge, science, poetry, refinement of thought, feeling, and manners, great memories and the interpretation of great records, which is carried on from the minds of one generation to the other". If one makes these minds Jewish, then one discovers a remarkable similarity between Felix Holt's political prescriptions for social order and Mordecai's philosophy of Jewish separateness with communication. Deronda becomes a proponent of this philosophy.

On a late autumn afternoon Deronda takes a wherry from Chelsea to Blackfriars Bridge, rowing himself to his destiny as Mordecai's "executive self": he progresses from west to east in a symbolic prefiguration of his departure from England, and he comes at evening, the Jewish holy hour, when all the significant events in his life occur. He meets his mother in Genoa at seven in the evening, and he returns to Mirah in London, his Jewish identity confirmed for him, at sunset. As he rows to meet Mordecai, Eliot describes a glorious Turneresque sunset with purple clouds spread across a saffron sky, and Mordecai's emaciated face is lit by the setting sun and by the spiritual eagerness with which he awaits Deronda.

Deronda has the face and bearing of Mordecai's visions; he is the elegant and refined embodiment of Mordecai's dream of a Jew who will implement his fevered fantasies of Jewish nationalism. He has been in search of someone whose description, needless to say, is matched exactly by Deronda:

> . . . he must be a Jew, intellectually cultured, morally fervid – in all this a nature ready to be plenished from Mordecai's; but his face and frame must be beautiful and strong, he must have been used to all the refinements of social life, his voice must flow with a full and easy current, his circumstances be free from sordid need: he must glorify the possibilities of the Jew, not sit and wander as Mordecai did, bearing the stamp of his people amid the signs of poverty and waning breath. (Ch. 38)

In his search for this healthy, upper-class Jew, Mordecai's mind has worked "constantly in images, moving in wide spaces". The workings of his mind are notably different from those of Gwendolen Harleth, incidentally, who is literally terrified of open spaces – they represent something unmanageable, uncontrollable, something which demands a giving up of the ego. But to give up the ego, the self, is exactly what Mordecai wants to do; he wants to relinquish his vision to a man who will accept the Jewish burden of textual exegesis, and who will strive for the establishment of a homeland for Jewish national consciousness.

The interpretation of texts and the establishment of a Jewish nation are imaginatively connected in Mordecai's wide-moving mind. His tutoring of Jacob includes the conventional study of reading and arithmetic, but he also recites Hebrew poetry to the boy, making him repeat to him the unintelligible lines, and believing that Jacob "will get them engraved within him . . . it is a way of printing" (Ch. 38). Despite Jacob's inclination to do something more lively and profitable than recite a mumbo jumbo of incomprehensible Hebrew, Mordecai perseveres, inspired by the belief that his "words may rule him [Jacob] some day. Their meaning may flash out on him. It was so with a nation – after many days" (Ch. 38). The meaning of a text, apprehended many days after an initial reading, is likened to the eventual establishment of a nation after the idea of that nation has been "read", so to speak, by those who will work for its implementation.

The forum for Eliot's most lengthy exposition of Mordecai's ideas is the working-men's club to which he takes Deronda. This is not specifically a Jewish club, but Eliot writes that "even to Daniel's little exercised discrimination, more than one of its members seemed to be Jewish" (Ch. 42). Miller, a second-hand bookseller, is descended from German Jews; Pash, a watchmaker, is a "small, dark, vivacious, triple-baked Jew"; and Gideon, an optical instrument maker, is a red-haired Jew who could pass for an Englishman. Eliot describes the company as "select of the select among poor men, being drawn together by a taste not prevalent even among the privileged heirs of learning and its institutions" (Ch. 42). This is, indeed, a select and unusual group, so select that it borders on the mythical.

To be sure, working-men's clubs were widespread in London in the last quarter of the nineteenth century, the cardinal qualification for admission being membership in the skilled, rather than unskilled classes. Mordecai's club is composed of serious, self-respecting, and industrious working men, principally artisans, who are fired with an intellectual ambition of remarkable scope. They discourse in a well-informed fashion about such matters as "the law of progress", "the main transforming causes of social change", and "the power of ideas". Their language is as ordered as their meetings, a correspondence which is nicely demonstrated by the following analysis of the distinctions between change and progress, articulated by one Lilly, a copying-clerk with a "well-filled forehead" who seems to have been reading Darwin and Spencer.

> Change and progress are merged in the idea of development. The laws of development are being discovered, and changes taking place according to them are necessarily progressive; that is to say, if we have any notion of progress or improvement opposed to them, the notion is a mistake. (Ch. 42)

Eliot is as detached from these Jews as she is from the Cohens, and they, too, work as a positive moral contrast for the reader and as a displaced way for Eliot to talk about proper working-class conduct. In the first place, their moral and intellectual seriousness opposes the upper-class frivolity and materialism which is so repellent to Deronda. In the second, and less explicit, place, it is significant that these lower-class Jewish men talk, rather than act. They are safely confined by Eliot to debate rather than to political action, to an expression of class consciousness which poses no threat to established social structures, nor to the cultural treasures which are housed by those structures and which are so dear to Felix Holt, Eliot's spokesman for the English working man.

Looking around "with the quiet air of respect habitual to him among equals", Deronda orders whisky and water for all, and listens to a discussion of whether the *diaspora* should be terminated by assimilation or by settlement in Palestine.[15] Gideon is the spokesman for assimilation: "I'm a rational Jew myself . . . I am for getting rid of all our superstitions and exclusiveness. There's no reason now why we shouldn't melt gradually into the populations we live among. That's the order of the day in point of progress." Mordecai wants no melting, but calls for a cultivation and solidifying of Jewish consciousness. He does not advocate Jewish nationalism as a means of establishing Jewish supremacy, and his vision of a non-competitive Israel is not unlike Felix Holt's vision of a society without class conflict. Mordecai declares that it is a "vain question . . . whether our people would beat the rest of the world. Each nation has its own work, and is a member of the world, enriched by the work of each" (Ch. 42). Felix Holt's social classes become Mordecai's nations. In the relationship between classes and the relationship between nations, however dissimilar the political meanings of each system of relationship, self-serving interests are put aside in the enrichment and conservation of a culture in the first instance, and in the betterment of the world at large in the second. In writing about class and in writing about nationalism, Eliot has the same vision of an organic whole composed of individual classes or nations who must exist in a mutually sustaining relationship with each other in order for man to move beyond gross survival, to be civilised in effect, and to create and preserve cultural treasures.

Mordecai's sister, Mirah, is also endowed by Eliot with a deeply conservative consciousness founded upon historical and racial awareness, both of her own past and that of her people. She has been brought up in the theatre, the daughter of a roving actor-manager and of a strongly religious mother. She is repelled by the preening, self-serving world of the theatre which she describes as one of cheap finery and disorder, with "men and women coming and going . . . loud laughing and disputing, strutting, snapping of fingers, jeering, faces I did not like to look at" (Ch. 20). She possesses a disdain for everything flashy and superficial and her values may be said to be in perfect accord with Felix Holt's distinction between "refinement of thought, feeling and manners" and "the indulgences of luxury and the pursuit of vain finery" as he describes it in his Address to Working Men. Applause is distasteful to her, and while her father is training her to become an actress/singer, she retreats to an interior life focused upon the Jewish faith instilled in her by her mother, which is kept alive by the reading of Jewish texts. For Mirah, "these books seemed a close companion with my mother: I knew that she must have looked at the very words and said them" (Ch. 20). It is not so much what those "very words" mean; their importance lies in the fact that they have been read by her mother, and by countless Jewish men and women in the past. These words possess a ritualistic significance – they are Felix Holt's "great records . . . carried on from the minds of one generation to another".

What is remarkable about Mirah Lapidoth's history is not so much its content of female spirituality in a predatory world of male materialism, but the manner in which she delivers this content. She presents a perfectly coherent narrative to Mrs Meyrick. Her father has been told by one of her teachers that she will never become a true artist, for "she has no notion of being anybody but herself" (Ch. 20). But for Mirah to be herself is, paradoxically, to stand outside her own experience and to tell her own story without self-consciousness. In this respect, and in almost all others, she is unlike Gwendolen Harleth, who cannot tell her own story. Gwendolen is guilt-ridden, hysterical and full of dread, and she latches onto Deronda whenever she can manage it, to spill out her miseries in fits and starts, so that he must read her, interpret her for herself. He never has to interpret Mirah. No one has to read her for she reads herself with perfect clarity and coherence. When she acts, she does best in parts in which she can be herself, and in telling stories she is best when she tells her *own*, ingenuously and with a fine sense of narrative order.

And she sings in the same way that she reveals the details of her troubled life, "with a subdued but searching pathos which had that essential of perfect singing, the making one oblivious of art and manner, and only possessing one with the song" (Ch. 32). Gwendolen Harleth, on the contrary, makes the listener conscious of her art and manner. She has a reasonably good soprano, a good ear, and can keep a tune. But her singing is designed to garner the attention and applause which are so distasteful to Mirah, and Klesmer sums things up exactly with his devastating remark, "It is always acceptable to see you sing" (Ch. 5). Mirah is an entirely selfless, socially conservative, religious Jewish girl – a perfect partner for Deronda and a perfect member of the lower classes for Eliot.

Mirah only becomes distanced from herself in a negative sense when she begins to love Deronda and to hear rumours of his attachment to Gwendolen after Grandcourt's death. She becomes unpleasantly conscious of the class difference between herself and Deronda. She compares his world, which she likens to "a portico with lights and lacqueys", to her own, a world of tents, "where the only splendour came from the mysterious inaccessible stars". But Deronda abandons the well-lit upper-class life and the class difference between them is dissolved by "ardent reverential love", which, Eliot declares, always creates its own hierarchy of "wealth and rank" (Ch. 63). This is the spiritual love which transcends class, the love story of a lower-class girl and upper-class man which is a familiar thematic item in countless novels, and which always requires a mythical dissolution of the social tension inherent in such problematic class relationships. Here, it is Deronda's Jewishness which dissolves the social tension, for he effectively removes himself from his class when he removes himself from England. His marriage to Mirah is the only marriage possible when he discovers himself to be Jewish and decides to go to Palestine. This journey, by the way, is facilitated in more ways than one by Deronda's male Jewish inheritance: he turns out to be Jewish *and* independently wealthy. Even though his mother has cut Deronda off from his Jewish inheritance, she has not cut him off from his monetary one. The Charisi merchant and banking fortune has been nicely invested by Sir Hugo during the years Deronda has assumed him to be his unspoken father, and the money from Deronda's *real* father facilitates his proper assumption of Jewish filial identity.

The only disreputable lower-class Jew in the novel is the Lapidoth father. He is unmistakably and unattractively Jewish, "a foreign-looking, eager, and gesticulating man" with bushy curls and an obsessive interest in money (negative qualities that link Eliot's portrayal of him with her sometimes implicitly anti-semitic descriptions of the Cohens). He is not only the quintessentially bad father, he is also the quintessentially bad Jew. And if his daughter possesses some of the qualities recommended by Felix Holt for the conservation of culture, he possesses none of them. He has no respect for the preservation and interpretation of records. He steals a purse in which is pasted an inscription memorialising the name of Mordecai and Mirah's mother, and the dates of her birth, marriage and death.

The significance of this family record fails to move Mr Lapidoth and he quickly pawns the purse. He is dead to the preservation of family history, and may be said, therefore, to be dead to the conservation of his own religious and cultural history. But Eliot dispatches this bad father and bad Jew very quickly from the novel. He makes off with a diamond ring belonging to Deronda on the same evening that Deronda reveals his Jewish identity and his love to Mirah. Deronda loses his ring but gains Mirah; Mirah loses her father but gains Deronda; and in a neat symbolic exchange Mirah finds the stable and religious Jewish man her father never was and Deronda marries a woman who is the positive obverse of his mother, unself-conscious, unassertive, and deeply religious.

When Deronda finally receives the solemn signal that his dying mother has arrived in Genoa and that he may be admitted into her presence, his first impression of her, "his chief consciousness", is that "her eyes were piercing and her face so mobile that the next moment she might look like a different person" (Ch. 51). She is a consummate actress and she implicitly stages the reunion with a son she has not seen for twenty-six years. She delays her entrance by keeping him waiting for several days, and she arranges herself in front of him, "looking at him as if she wanted him to observe her". She seems "not quite a human mother, but a Melusina, who had ties with some world independent of ours", and Deronda feels himself to be "in the presence of a mysterious Fate rather than of the longed-for mother". She appears, then, as a mythical and mysterious visitor from another world, but, paradoxically, her story is not a mythical or mysterious one: it is located in the exact circumscriptions and social codes of European Jewry which she had attempted to escape.

She has rejected everything that Mirah Lapidoth has found so comforting, so essential to her survival, and in a significant reversal of Mirah's distaste for theatrical performance, Jewish culture, for Deronda's mother, is one long, tedious drama in which she has been allotted the repugnant role of Jewish woman by a tyrannical director, her father:

> I was to be what he called "the Jewish woman" under pain of his curse. I was to feel everything I did not feel, and believe everything I did not believe. I was to feel awe for the bit of parchment in the *mezuza* over the door; to dread lest a bit of butter should touch a bit of meat; to think it beautiful that men should

> bind the tephillin on them, and women not, – to adore the wisdom of such laws, however silly they might seem to me. I was to love the long prayers in the ugly synagogue, and that howling, and the gabbling, and the dreadful fasts, and the tiresome feasts, and my father's endless discoursing about Our People, which was a thunder without meaning in my ears. I was to care for ever about what Israel had been; and I did not care at all. I cared for the wide world, and all that I could represent in it. (Ch. 51)

Mirah employs a series of participles to convey her abhorrence of the theatre (laughing, disputing, strutting, snapping, jeering), and Deronda's mother describes Jewish religious ritual as "howling" and "gabbling" and "endless discoursing".

Deronda, always sympathetically disposed to female distress, says that he can imagine the pain of her struggles as an artist and as a woman. But for all his androgynous sympathy, for all that identification with the deepest fates of women, and that "deeply-laid care for womanhood which had begun when his own lip was like a girl's" (Ch. 63), and despite his insistence that "what I have been most trying to do for fifteen years is to have some understanding for those who differ from myself" (Ch. 51), that is to say, from the age of thirteen when he read about the Pope's nephews, he cannot understand his mother. She declares, "You are not a woman. You may try – but you can never imagine what it is to have a man's force of genius within you, and yet to suffer the slavery of being a girl" (Ch. 51). It is ironic that he fails to understand her, in great part, *because* he is the English gentleman she wished him to become; that is to say, he is *so* English and *so* gentlemanly, that a tempestuous family drama conducted between an Italian Jewish father and daughter is beyond the range of his upbringing and his experience. Such impassioned family struggles are foreign to his comprehension.

After his second and final meeting with the woman about whom he has made so many fictions, and who finally eludes his understanding, Deronda is released for the problematic praxis with which Eliot dissolves her moral criticism of upper-class English life. The English gentleman is mythically transformed into an Italian Jew with a Zionist mission, but Deronda, of course, is never anything *but* the perfect English gentleman[16]. In all his dealings with family and friends, and especially with Gwendolen Harleth, he conducts himself as the decent upper-class Englishman that his mother wanted him to be. His only failure of sympathetic understanding in

*Daniel Deronda* comes in the two brief meetings with the woman who has made him what he is.

NOTES

1. This preliminary to suicide by drowning was, perhaps, suggested to Eliot by a story about Mary Wollstonecraft. Eliot wrote to Emanuel Deutsch (an assistant in the Department of Printed Books at the British Museum who taught Eliot Hebrew), "Hopelessness has been to me, all through my life, but especially in my youth, the chief source of wasted energy with all the consequent bitterness of regret. Remember, it has happened to many to be glad they did not commit suicide, though they once ran for the final leap, or as Mary Wollstonecraft did, wetted their garments well in the rain hoping to sink the better when they plunged." *Letters*, Vol. V, pp. 160–1.

   Deronda seems fated to rescue people from drowning, literally and metaphorically. He sacrifices his chance for a first-class degree in mathematics at Cambridge in order to tutor Hans Meyrick, and Hans regards this act as Deronda having "saved an ugly mongrel from drowning" (Ch. 16). And as Gwendolen Harleth struggles to articulate her dread to Deronda, he feels as if "he saw her drowning while his limbs were bound" (Ch. 36).
2. *Letters*, Vol. I, p. 254. In the 1840s, an association of sensuality with the mining districts is, of course, by no means peculiar to Eliot. Descriptions of working-class conditions in the mines are charged, directly or indirectly, with sexual meaning. For example J. C. Symons, one of the sub-commissioners investigating conditions in the West Riding of Yorkshire describes the dress, or rather the lack of it, of the young female workers: " . . . the chain, passing high up between the legs of two of these girls, had worn large holes in their trousers; and any sight more disgustingly indecent or revolting can scarcely be imagined than these girls at work – no brothel can beat it." *Parliamentary Papers*, 1842, Vol. XVI, p. 24.

   In *The Condition of the Working Class in England*, when Engels describes that condition underground, he often sounds like the nineteenth-century bourgeois moralist that he was. "In the dark loneliness of the mines men, women and children work in great heat and the majority of them take off most (if not all) of their clothes. You can imagine the consequences for yourself. There are more illegitimate children in the mining districts than elsewhere, and this in itself is sufficient evidence of what these half-savage creatures are doing when they get below ground." P. 284.

   When Eliot went to Leeds some twenty years after she wrote to Sibree, the English working class was as distasteful to her as ever. She described her visit to her close friend Barbara Bodichon: " . . . the Leeds work people, we were told, are sadly coarse beer-soaked bodies, with pleasures, mostly of the brutal sort, and the mill-girls 'epicene' creatures that make one shudder." *Letters*, Vol. IV, p. 476.

3. Carlyle's 1867 essay, *Shooting Niagara*, obviously comes to mind here. The relation of the political turmoil of the late 1860s to *Felix Holt*, *Shooting Niagara* and *Culture and Anarchy* has been analysed by Michael Wolff. See "The Uses of Context: Aspects of the 1860s", *Victorian Studies*, Supplement to Vol. IX, September 1965.
4. *Essays of George Eliot*, edited by Thomas Pinney (London, 1963), p. 420. "Address to Working Men by Felix Holt" appeared in the January 1868 edition of *Blackwood's Magazine*.
5. Ibid., p. 420.
6. U. C. Knoepflmacher notes that "despite their discrepant media, Arnold and George Eliot saw themselves in strikingly similar roles as the disseminators of culture". *Religious Humanism and the Victorian Novel* (Princeton, 1965), p. 64.
7. "Address to Working Men", p. 425.
8. Ibid., p. 426.
9. Comparison with another essay, written in January 1866 by James Greenwood, reveals a different impression of working-class ideas of common needs and national treasures. Not without its sensational aspects, like most of the pieces of journalistic social exploration which were popular in the latter half of the nineteenth century, *A Night in the Workhouse* describes a social group whose principal interest is to find a place to spend the night:

   > No language with which I am acquainted is capable of conveying an adequate conception of the spectacle I then encountered. Imagine a space of about thirty feet by thirty enclosed on three sides by a dingy white-washed wall, and roofed with naked tiles which were furred with the damp and filth that reeked within. . . . This far too airy shed was paved with stone, the flags so thickly encrusted with filth and I mistook it at first for a floor of natural earth. . . . My bed-fellows lay amongst the cranks, distributed over the flagstones in a double row, on narrow bags scantily stuffed with hay. At one glance my appalled vision took in thirty of them – thirty men and boys stretched upon shallow pallets which put only six inches of comfortable hay between them and the stony floor. *Into Unknown England*, edited by Peter Keating (Manchester, 1976), p. 37.

   The common need here is breakfast, a miserable concoction of oatmeal and water, in exchange for which the workhouse casuals are required to work a corn grinder.

10. *Essays*, p. 439. "Authorship" initially appeared in the first authorised edition of Eliot's essays, *Leaves from a Note-Book*, edited by Lewes' son, Charles Lewes, and published in 1884.
11. *Letters*, Vol. VII, p. 383.
12. *Essays*, p. 268. When it came to painting nature, Hunt clearly did a better job. In the Journal of a holiday at Ilfracombe in May and June 1856, Eliot records her impression that "almost every yard" of the banks of wild flowers in the Ilfracombe lanes "is a 'Hunt' picture – a delicious

crowding of mosses and delicate trefoil, and wild strawberries, and ferns great and small". *Letters*, II, p. 250.

13. Ibid., p. 271.
14. *Impressions of Theophrastus Such* (New York, 1879), p. 210.
15. Bernard Martin notes that by the 1870s, the Western and Central European Jew had achieved a degree of political emancipation and civic equality, but that also at this time, European Jewry was attacked by new waves of anti-semitism which provided a powerful impetus for the launching of an organised Zionist movement dedicated to the establishment of a Jewish homeland in Palestine. Martin writes:

> Even though hope for the ultimate ingathering of the exiles was one of the most deeply cherished elements in Judaism throughout the centuries of dispersion, non-messianic proposals to the effect that Jews themselves actually return as a nation to Palestine and begin colonising it were not seriously put forth . . . until the middle of the nineteenth century. *A History of Judaism* (New York, 1974), pp. 326–7.

Edward W. Said observes that underlying all Eliot's rhetoric about the East in *Daniel Deronda* "is the total absence of any thought about the actual inhabitants of the East, Palestine in particular. They are irrelevant both to the Zionists in *Daniel Deronda* and to the English characters." See "Zionism from the Standpoint of its Victims", *Social Text*, Winter 1979. In reading *Daniel Deronda*, it is clear that, for Eliot, the Arab inhabitants of Palestine do not exist and that Palestine is an "empty" territory to be filled by a restorative Zionist project.

16. In his discussion of the implicit relationship between Milly Barton's death and her passionate marriage (to Amos Barton in the first of Eliot's *Scenes of Clerical Life)*, Steven Marcus includes a footnote to the effect that Lennard Davis has:

> discovered a detail – or a missing detail – in *Daniel Deronda* that throws the whole central plot of the novel out of kilter. Deronda's identity is a mystery to himself and has always been. It is only when he is a grown man, having been to Eton and Cambridge, that he discovers he is a Jew. What this has to mean – given the conventions of medical practice at the time – is that he never looked down. In order for the plot of Daniel Deronda to work, Deronda's circumcised penis must be invisible, or nonexistent – which is one more demonstration in detail of why the plot does not in fact work. Yet this peculiarity of circumstance – which I think it should be remarked, has never been noticed before – is, I have been arguing, characteristic in several senses of both George Eliot and the culture she was representing. *Representations* (New York, 1975), p. 212.

It seems to me that this business about Deronda's penis is more complicated than Mr Davis suggests. If one considers Deronda's mother's intense hatred of all Jewish ritual and the fact that she only marries Deronda's father when she discovers she can "rule" him, and that her tyrannical father dies three weeks after she marries, and that she says to Deronda, "then I had my way", and "I said you should not know you were a Jew", (Ch. 51) then it seems entirely plausible that she would not have had Deronda circumcised.

And even if, in her independence from her father, she still felt she should have Deronda circumcised, it is possible she would have been influenced not to do so by the Reform teachings which flourished in Western Europe in the middle of the nineteenth century. (See Ch. x, "New Interpretations of Judaism", *A History of Judaism.*)

I realise that my hypotheses are of little pertinence to the sort of reading I have tried to make of *Daniel Deronda.* I only introduce them to quarrel with what seems an interesting observation on Mr Davis' part, but which is, on a close examination of the text, rather implausible.

# 9 Gwendolen Harleth as Heroine and Metaphor

Like Dickens in *Our Mutual Friend*, Eliot in *Daniel Deronda* concentrates upon the corrupt nature of upper-class society. There are, of course, many differences between the two representations – to mention the most obvious, at the end of *Our Mutual Friend*, fairy-tale bourgeois domesticity triumphs over upper-class greed and superficiality; at the end of *Daniel Deronda*, upper-class values remain unregenerated and are given no moral alternative, fabulous or other, within English society.

The respective experiences of Bella Wilfer and Gwendolen Harleth are also significantly different. Where Bella's dissatisfactions, primarily material rather than psychological, are dissolved by her transformation into fairy-tale princess, Gwendolen's miseries, predominantly psychological and finding expression in complaints about her economic situation, are not mythically dissolved by marriage to a fairy-tale prince. She is, in fact, abandoned by a hero who is more psychoanalyst than prince and left alone at the end of the novel with the psychological and moral enlightenment which he has brought to her. The absence of social regeneration and of marriage as panacea for female dissatisfaction points to the many imaginative connections that Eliot draws between the troubled consciousness of her heroine and the troubled consciousness of the culture she inhabits.

In describing Gwendolen's unhappiness, Eliot concentrates upon four symptoms of neurotic conflict – a fierce psychological imperialism, an obsession with performance, a fear of adult sexuality and recurrent fits of spiritual dread – and it seems to me that the structures of a disturbed psyche may be seen as analogous to the structures of a disturbed culture. Eliot means Gwendolen to be both heroine and metaphor.

In general, Gwendolen's psychological imperialism is analogous to the domestic and foreign imperialism of British politics; her obsession with performance is paralleled by the theatricality of social events; her arrested sexual development, which has its origins in a fixation upon her mother, is analogous to the arrested and sterile condition of upper-class life; and her fits of spiritual dread, which are a manifestation of her guilt for having wished both her father and her step-father dead so that she may have her mother to herself, bear an imaginative correspondence to the collective social guilt which Freud suggests has some mythic origin in a long-ago killing of the father and retention of the mother.

Gwendolen's psychological imperialism is suggested, for example, by Eliot's description of the terror which she experiences when she is alone, the immense solitude which impresses her "with an undefined feeling of immeasurable existence aloof from her, in the midst of which she was helplessly incapable of asserting herself" (Ch. 6). Self-assertion is only possible for Gwendolen when she has someone to dominate; it is only when she has "human ears and eyes about her" that she recovers her confidence and can feel "the possibility of winning empire" (Ch. 6). Gwendolen is a quintessentially novelistic, rather than epic, heroine, just as Deronda turns out to be an epic hero, rather than a novelistic one. She possesses none of that psychological certainty, that belief in a totality of correspondence between the individual and the cosmos which Georg Lukacs describes as an aspect of epic consciousness in *The Theory of the Novel.* Where the epic hero could gaze at the heavens and find, as Lukacs says, that "the fire that burns in the soul is of the same essential nature as the stars",[1] a "little astronomy" sets Gwendolen's imagination at work in ways that make her "tremble".

Gwendolen is an "exile" in the vastness of space, and she makes no connection between this feeling of alienation and religious awe. She shares this indifference to religious experience with her class. Like many, if not all, upper-middle-class English girls, she has been brought up with a proper religious education, but spiritual matters raise "no alarm, no longing" in her. And she is as indifferent to religion as she is to "the conditions of colonial property and banking" on which her very material existence is dependent. She is busy at her psychological colonising, establishing human territories for domination, such as her cousin Rex Gascoigne, and her mothers and sisters who constitute a regular colony of female subjects, while her class is at work building up the actual empire which, in part, determines and permits her exercise of domestic, psychological imperialism.

Gwendolen's ideal is "to be daring in speech and reckless in braving dangers, both moral and physical". She necessarily requires an audience for this daring, a doting Rex to stand by and watch her gallop across the Wiltshire countryside, a roomful of gamblers to watch her lose "strikingly" at the roulette table. But she feels she "falls behind" this ideal of moral and physical daring because of "the narrow theatre" which life offers to a girl of twenty. She understands herself and her society in terms of dramatic self-display and it is significant that Eliot describes most of the scenery in front of which Gwendolen arranges herself as social theatre. An afternoon devoted to archery, Gwendolen's wedding, an amble through an improved abbey, a New Year's Eve dance, all are events which Eliot describes, in part, in the language of theatre and of performance. And all are events representative of the upper-class English life which Eliot finds so lamentable, devoted to self-display rather than to intellectual and moral betterment, and which she rejects as virtually irremediable at the end of *Daniel Deronda*.

Gwendolen's mother is the most important member of her colony, the one to whom she is, paradoxically, most subject, and who holds her, albeit entirely innocently and unconsciously, in a condition of pre-Oedipal sexual arrest. The powerful presence of her mother in Gwendolen's sexual nondevelopment signifies, at least in part, an absence of the father; that is to say, what torments Gwendolen in great measure is her guilt for having taken her mother from *two* fathers, and, as I hope to show, what brings her to some sort of consciousness of the origins of her guilt is the death of a *third* father, Grandcourt, in a dreadful realisation of her wishes for his extinction.

Deronda is the agent of initiation for Gwendolen into two forms of history, that of her own psychology and that of the "great movements" of the world in which she plays so small a part. When she first meets him, all that Gwendolen really knows about herself is that she means to lead. Who or what is to be led is immaterial. Marriage is the one obvious arena of action which presents itself, and she feels that to "be very much sued or hopelessly sighed for as a bride" is "an indispensable and agreeable guarantee of womanly power" (Ch. 4). But to become a wife is something else entirely. Her mother's two marriages have taught her that women cannot do as they like, that they are the weak objects of male dominance, that they are constantly laid low by childbirth and debilitated by improvident husbands who take to pawning the family jewels. At the beginning of the novel the reader who is beguiled by Gwendolen's energetic narcissism may be misled into misreading her as an intelligent and vital young woman whose self-expression is severely curtailed by a male-dominated culture. But Eliot informs us that Gwendolen's passion to lead has "no disturbing reference to the advancement of learning or the balance of the constitution; her knowledge being such as with no sort of standing-room or length of lever could have been expected to move the world" (Ch. 4).

To be sure, Gwendolen toys with the notion that women are denied the adventures available to men. However, these adventures are desirable for the glamorous attention which comes with their execution, rather than for the execution itself. Talking about the restricted life of women is one of Gwendolen's flirtatious, and self-reassuring, strategies. She tells Rex that rather than be married she would prefer to go to the North Pole or ride steeple-chases, and in that verbal fencing with Grandcourt which constitutes their courtship, she says that women are not allowed to go in search of the North-West Passage or the source of the Nile, or to hunt tigers in the East. But to be in the vast, icy expanses of the North Pole or to be confronted with a tiger would send Gwendolen into hysterical fits, and it is as if in this articulation of what women are *not* allowed to do, she is articulating for her own psychological reassurance the impossibility of ever being *able* to do such things. Her flirtatious remarks about the restrictions imposed upon women do not signify a dissatisfaction with her culture. She does not stand in dissatisfied detachment, in rebellion against the patriarchal will, as does Deronda's mother. With Gwendolen's discontent, I think Eliot is trying to show that something different is at work. Gwendolen's discontent is not representative of an alienation *from* her culture; she *is* her culture, and her dissatisfaction with the self and with society is an expression of a world dissatisfied with itself, uneasy, aimless, and bored. All Gwendolen wants and means to do is what is "pleasant to herself in a striking manner". This is a life without an object outside the self, and if one examines the society in which Gwendolen puts herself on display, one can see a correspondence between an individual and a cultural narcissism which are both imperial in their very nature.

Eliot frequently describes Gwendolen's ideas about herself in the terminology of empire. When she gambles she fancies herself as "an empress of luck"; when Grandcourt proposes she feels she is "getting a sort of empire over her own life"; she imagines her marriage will afford her a large and rich territory in contrast with the "distasteful petty empire" of her sisters. In marrying Grandcourt, she hopes to colonise him, to subdue him under her practised management into an attentive and loyal subject. What she doesn't know and what is the miserable result of her misreading of him (and it is important to remember that she *does* misread him – her inability to assess him correctly, to see what moves beneath that languid and pale exterior, is an aspect of the moral deficiency of Gwendolen's character) is that he is a far more experienced and cruel manipulator of the conquered than she is. Her readiness to accept him, to see him as a way out of being a governess, to listen to the materialistic counsel of her Anglican uncle, has a larger, social meaning in the sense that her class, essentially composed of upper-middle-class Philistines, is all too ready to submit to the elegant blandishments of the Barbarians. One senses that the punishment dished out to Gwendolen is the punishment which Eliot feels is deserved by a class whose moral bankruptcy leads them to sell themselves to the aristocracy. Gwendolen is "sold" by her family to Grandcourt as much as she thinks she is selling herself. And she is sold into a kind of class slavery to a man Eliot describes in the terms of colonial management:

> If this white-handed man with the perpendicular profile had been sent to govern a difficult colony, he might have won reputation among his contemporaries. He had certainly ability, would have understood that it was safer to exterminate than to cajole superseded proprietors, and would not have flinched from making things safe in that way. (Ch. 48)

As one might expect, Deronda's sympathy is with the colonised. In a discussion at Grandcourt's country house of colonial disturbances in Jamaica (there was an outbreak of native unrest in October 1865), Eliot imaginatively conjoins the opinions expressed by each character, the fictive experience of these characters, and their relationship to each other. It is the first meeting between Gwendolen and Deronda after their encounter in Leubronn at the beginning of the novel. Gwendolen has become engaged to Grandcourt, and the party is at lunch. Grandcourt thinks the Jamaican negro "a beastly sort of baptist Caliban" – an expression of his distaste for lower-class Baptists, among other things. Deronda's sympathy, however lightheartedly he states it, is with Caliban, and when some ninny remarks that the half-breeds are to blame for all the trouble, he suggests that the English have only themselves to thank for that situation. Mrs Davilow merely offers the irrelevant information that her father had an estate in Barbados, which adds nothing to the discussion but which says a lot about the significance of the West Indies for her class. Gwendolen says nothing, looking at everyone in turn, so that she might more easily look at Deronda; she is only concerned with the impression she is making on him. She takes no part in this lunch-time chat because she is already beginning to see the paltriness of her own psychological imperialism, and because, influenced by Deronda, she is beginning to question the insidious colonial politics practised by Grandcourt and his class. And, in another sense, she is caught here in this scene as she is to be caught at the end of the novel – trapped between the presence of the moral enlightenment offered by Deronda and the absence of any place to exercise it. At the end of *Daniel Deronda*, she represents the only small hope which Eliot posits for English upper-class life, and this scene, which shows her mute between ideologies, prefigures her dilemma at the end as an individual, and implicitly as a representative of a class and of a culture.

When Deronda first sees Gwendolen at Leubronn, she is on display, a Victorian Belinda at the gaming table. She is part of a group who share a negative equality: countesses sit down with London tradesmen, and the shabby genteel mingle with the *nouveaux-riches*. Gwendolen's first response to Deronda's observation of her is that he judges her to be inferior, and it is a response which determines, in part, the dependent nature of her relationship to him:

> The darting sense that he was measuring her and looking down on her as an inferior, that he was of different quality from the human dross around her, that he felt himself in a region outside and above her, and was examining her as a specimen of a lower order, aroused a tingling resentment which stretched the moment with conflict. (Ch. 1)

This sense of being measured in scientific fashion, as if she were an insect under a microscope, exacerbates her compulsion to perform. She controls her facial muscles and sits down to lose her money in grand style. In this way she feels she can retain the attention which is so disturbing to her, but which is so essential for her confirmation of herself as a functioning being, for a confirmation, indeed, of her existence, "it was at least better that he should have kept his attention fixed on her than that he should have disregarded her as one of an insect swarm who had no individual physiognomy". For Gwendolen it is a "drama" in which she will play the role allotted to her in the most sensational style she can summon, even if she resents the fact that she is in the hands of a director, either Deronda in this instance, or the London financiers who direct her return to England because of a failure in the family investments.

When she comes home to the house which was once a "good background" in front of which she could arrange herself as St Cecilia at the organ, or pose as Rachel, the nineteenth-century tragedienne, she tries her best to reassert herself in the face of financial ruin. She fancies her chance as an actress but she has little besides her sinuous good looks to make a start. Like Deronda's mother, she resents being subject to forces outside her control; Deronda's mother rejects the role of "Jewish woman" and Gwendolen rejects the role of dependent governess, but Gwendolen clearly has none of the talent which facilitated the Princess Halm-Eberstein's initially successful, but eventually negated, defiance of the patriarchal will. Klesmer quickly demolishes Gwendolen's fantasies of being an actress and the problem with her performing self, which Eliot suggests as she describes Gwendolen's organisation of a game of charades, is that she has the costume but no word to fit it. She has the attractive trappings for her charade, indeed for her life, but she has no content with which to fill it, and one can connect this individual life with an upper-class culture which has all the proper, and seductively desirable, forms, but which is empty, in Eliot's view, of intellectual and moral content.

Gwendolen uses *her* attractive form to her best advantage on the afternoon when she first meets Grandcourt. It is the occasion of an annual archery meeting, and it is also the occasion for Gwendolen to be put on display by her relatives as an attractive commodity in the upper-class marriage market. She has had fantasies of making an immediate conquest of Grandcourt, of piercing him with her erotic arrow before he has time for thought; he is an aristocratic target which she will hit in the wealthy bull's-eye at first shot. But he is not so easily appropriated: he is as adept a performer as Gwendolen in this social theatre and even though he eventually marries her, gives her a co-starring role so to speak, he always remains producer and director of their performances on the social scene.

Eliot describes another highly theatrical and carefully staged event in *Daniel Deronda*, that of Sir Hugo's New Year's Eve dance. The chief tenants of the estate are invited so that Grandcourt, the prospective owner of the Abbey (Sir Hugo has no male children and Grandcourt is the son of his younger brother), "might see their future glory in an agreeable light, as a picturesque provincial supremacy with a rent-roll personified by the most prosperous-looking tenants" (Ch. 36). Eliot's satiric voice parodies Sir Hugo's reification of his tenants; she personifies in her description just as Sir Hugo reifies his tenants into a rent-roll. The scenes at the archery meeting and at the dance are splendidly managed theatre, "plays" in the sense that the upper-class participants play at bows and arrows and play at country-dancing with a captive audience of loyal tenants on both occasions. This is civilisation at its most appropriative. In the case of the archery meet, what was once vital necessity, hunting for meat with a bow and arrow, is transformed into distraction from the ennui attendant upon having absolutely nothing to do, and the dangerous animal becomes the archery target. In the case of the dance, aristocrats play at the country-dancing which was once one of the few forms of recreation available to those tenants who watch the aristocratic social theatre.

Gwendolen is unrivalled at this kind of performance: her sense and need of dramatic play thrives on an audience of attentive men and envious women. But she is, of course, never free from the necessity of that audience. When she is on display she must continually gratify the spectators for fear that she will lose them; her performance is both generated by and fraught with anxiety about, something not entirely under control. And in order for that society on whose stages Gwendolen gives her dramatic all to remain minimally at ease with itself, there are matters which must be kept out of sight, even if they are not kept out of mind. We are still ambivalent about knowing how the butcher cuts up the carcass, how the criminal and the lunatic are confined, how the dying meet their end; these were matters kept increasingly out of sight in the nineteenth century.[2] But what is kept out of sight does not always disappear from consciousness; the omnipotence of childhood wishes, the fantasy that once things are out of sight they no longer exist, does not work for the upper class in *Daniel Deronda* (nor does it work anywhere else for that matter). What is repressed in Gwendolen's consciousness, and what is repressed in the class and the culture for which she is a metaphor, makes itself felt as symptom, and sometimes as actual intrusion upon carefully staged social theatre.

Gwendolen's repressed fears manifest themselves in such ways as the fits of spiritual dread which overcome her without warning, in her inability to sleep alone, and in her fear of open spaces. What is repressed in and by her culture makes its appearance in the person of Lydia Glasher; the seamy sexual underside of upper-class life is revealed as Grandcourt's discarded mistress intrudes herself upon another carefully arranged social event, a roving archery meet wherein Gwendolen fancies herself as Rosalind in *As You Like It.*

The place of the meeting is very nicely selected, a grassy spot where a hanging wood creates the effect of an amphitheatre. A coachful of servants is on hand to arrange a picnic, and wardens are ready to guide the roving archers so they don't get tangled up in bushes or fall into streams. Eliot announces that she will not dwell on the glorious scenery or the food because she is "bound to tell a story of life at a stage when the blissful beauty of earth and sky entered only by narrow and oblique inlets into the consciousness, which was busy with a small social drama almost as little penetrated by a feeling of wider relations as if it had been a puppet-show" (Ch. 14). This is Gwendolen's life. She is indifferent to nature except as backdrop, and oblivious of her own small place in the wider relations of the world. At this Arcadian Vanity Fair Gwendolen discovers that she does not pull the strings. She is in the grip of a complex set of determinants outside her control, which have always been outside her control. Her flight from Grandcourt's attentions is precipitated by what happens in the woods on that summer afternoon – the woods are a festering Arden where lovers' quarrels are not resolved by marriage and where there is no comedic ending for the resolution of Gwendolen's troubles.

Roving malevolently among the peripatetic archers is Thomas Lush, Grandcourt's secretary-companion and implicit procurer. Fearful that a marriage between Grandcourt and Gwendolen will dislodge him from his easy life, he has arranged for Lydia Glasher to present herself and her case to Gwendolen. Mrs Glasher's manner is as direct as her intrusion upon the meticulous ordering of alfresco fun and games:

> My name is Lydia Glasher. Mr. Grandcourt ought not to marry any one but me. I left my husband and child for him nine years ago. Those two children are his, and we have two others – girls – who are older. My husband is dead now and Mr. Grandcourt ought to marry me. He ought to make that boy his heir. (Ch. 14)

There are no preliminaries here – Lydia Glasher makes a bald statement of fact and of moral obligation which forms a contrast to the verbal banter which both conceals and reveals the motives of Grandcourt and Gwendolen as they manoeuvre each other into marriage.

In making a connection between the sexual relationship between men and women and the relationship between all social beings, Marx suggests that the former is the paradigm for the latter:

> In the approach to *woman* as the spoil and handmaid of communal lust is expressed the infinite degradation in which man exists for himself, for the secret of this approach has its *unambiguous*, decisive, *plain* and undisguised expression in the relations of *man* to *woman* and in the manner in which the *direct* and *natural* procreative relationship is conceived. The direct, natural, and necessary relation of person to person is the *relation of man to woman*. . . . It follows from the character of this relationship how much *man* as a *species being*, as *man*, has come to be himself and to comprehend himself; the relation of man to woman is *the most natural* relation of human being to human being. It therefore reveals the extent to which man's *natural* behaviour has become *human*, of the extent to which his *human nature* has come to be nature to him. In this relationship is revealed, too, the extent to which man's *need* has become a *human* need; the extent to which, therefore, the *other* person as a person has become for him a need – the extent to which he in his individual existence is at the same time a social being.[3]

It seems to me that the relationship between Grandcourt and Lydia Glasher, distinctly sexual in its origins, has many of the social meanings which Marx here outlines. She has been, in Marx's thundering language, "the spoil and handmaid" of Grandcourt's lust, and the appalling sado-masochistic nature of their alliance expresses "the infinite degradation" in which Grandcourt lives entirely "for himself", for the gratification of his will. Grandcourt's existence as "a social being", his dealings with the world when he is not at Gadsmere with Lydia Glasher, his understanding of himself "as a *species being*, as *man*", perfectly express his being when he is at Gadsmere. To be sure, their alliance is no longer sexual, but Grandcourt remains bound to her in many ways; *not* out of some paternal attachment (his idea of paternal responsibility is to give instructions to the local bank), but because he has never really tired of her, and, of course, because he takes a perverse pleasure in making her suffer.

Grandcourt has secreted this woman in a part of England whose sombre topography is analogous to the imaginative terrain of her dark history. She lives in a coal-mining district, in a countryside "once entirely rural and lovely, now black with coal mines . . . chiefly peopled with men and brethren with candles stuck in their hats", in deep seclusion and with "no gentry in carriages to be met, only men of business in gigs". Her house is overshadowed by the mellow darkness of firs and cedars and guarded by stone lodges which look like "little prisons" (Ch. 30). She was once unspoiled, like the countryside, the lovely wife of an Irish officer, and she has been soiled, morally blackened, by her liaison with Grandcourt. It is interesting that Grandcourt hides her in a part of the country where some of the actual source of its economic wealth lies hidden, that is to say, in the colliery district. Lydia Glasher's sexual past is shaded among those firs and cedars just as one of the sources of wealth for men of Grandcourt's class, coal, is hidden in the dark and dirty mines.

When he makes his will, Grandcourt leaves everything to his son by Lydia; Gwendolen gets two thousand a year and the Gadsmere property. Her uncle, the Rev. Gascoigne, is offended by this shabby treatment and Eliot, creating an image which is wonderfully suggestive of upper-class sexual mores, writes that he remembers, "hints of former entangling dissipations, and an undue addiction to pleasure, though he had not foreseen that the pleasure which had probably, so to speak, been swept into private rubbish-heaps, would ever present itself as an array of fine caterpillars, disastrous to the green meat of respectable people" (Ch. 64). Grandcourt's society sweeps the objects of its secret sexual pleasure into private rubbish-heaps and these objects fester and breed caterpillars of resentment which make an unwelcome appearance on the plates of respectable society. Gadsmere is the gloomy residence of an exiled and discarded sexual object: it is also situated in the blackened terrain of the coal-mining districts, and Eliot, however unconsciously, makes an association between private and public exploitation. And, at the same time, she suggests how English upper-class society distances itself from the dirty business, both literal and metaphoric, which would offend its refined sensibility if kept in view.

The readiness of Gwendolen's uncle to close his eyes to Grandcourt's sexual dalliance is representative of his benign and jolly materialism. For him, Grandcourt is exempt from "the ordinary standards of moral judgments" because he is an aristocrat, and so long as Grandcourt doesn't make a public mess of his private entanglements, does not violate the prescribed social code, then he finds nothing to censure in Grandcourt's character. Eliot suggests the worldliness of this military captain turned clergyman, the son of a provincial corn-dealer who congratulates himself on the fact that he does not look it, when she describes his thinking as "ecclesiastical rather than theological", that is to say, concerned with administration rather than with contemplation. I think Eliot means such thinking, however benevolent, to be representative of a world more concerned with form than with content.

Gascoigne shares a concern for form with Sir Hugo Mallinger. Sir Hugo's country estate, the Abbey, has been improved in the best Victorian manner: what was once the refectory is now the dining room, and what was once part of the old church has been turned into stables. Horses inhabit the choir and it is as if Deronda's uncle has effected a reverse metamorphosis of Gascoigne's switch from the cavalry to the church.

When Sir Hugo points to a beautiful pointed doorway, a remnant of the east front of the church, he says it is more interesting, more decorative, to let it stand in the midst of what has been added than to reproduce the thirteenth-century building. This is a cultural attitude which appropriates what is, in effect, most ornamental and theatrical from the past: the doorway is dramatically and formally arresting as an isolated object, rather than being awe-inspiring because of its history as an integral component of a coherent religious life. And attendance at church in this upper-class social scheme is merely something that marks the beginning of the week as attendance at the opera marks the end of it. All is an occasion for self-presentation and display.

There appears to be one positive aspect of performance in *Daniel Deronda*, and it lies in Eliot's myth of the aritist. In the museum-like precincts of the Meyrick household art is sacred, and in the person of Klesmer art is given the status of the "social activity" which Eliot ascribes to writing fiction.

Catherine Arrowpoint marries Klesmer in defiance of her parents, and her action represents a rejection of their *nouveau-riche* values. Eliot opposes art to commerce, a common enough mythological opposition, but it seems to me that in *Daniel Deronda* art exists at the pleasure of commerce. Mr Arrowpoint bluntly announces to his daughter that "a man like Klesmer can't marry such a property as yours", (Ch. 22) but Klesmer and Catherine's property already exist in illegal cohabitation. Klesmer is engaged to come down to Quetcham ("to have a first-rate musician in your house is a privilege of wealth" Eliot declares in an ironic aside), and Mr Arrowpoint plans to draw "a large cheque" in Klesmer's name in the belief that this will "make him as safe an inmate as a footman" (Ch. 22). The businessman's patronage of the artist is the butt of Eliot's social satire, but she really offers no plausible alternative to what she satirises. She sets Klesmer up as an ideal figure of artistic genius living *in* the world, but when it comes down to it, Klesmer's role in *Daniel Deronda* is highly ambiguous.

Eliot sets up a mythical opposition between politics and art, between the Philistine values of Mr Bult, an expectant peer and party man who has "strong opinions concerning the districts of the Niger", is "much at home also in the Brazils", and speaks "with decision of affairs in the South Seas", and the sometimes melodramatically stated artistic values of Klesmer. It is as if she wants to have it both ways, to have artistic genius opposed to commercial materialism, and yet, on the other hand, to have artistic genius play an influential role in a society whose structures are, in great part, determined by that commercial materialism. Catherine Arrowpoint is, as it were, the territory for which Bult and Klesmer compete: it is a territory amassed from a fortune in trade.[4]

Klesmer laments "the lack of idealism in English politics, which left all mutuality between distant races to be determined simply by the need of a market", a singularly idealistic and naive notion, for *without* the British interest in creating markets there would *be* no discussion of "distant races". He delivers a speech which elucidates his theory of the mutually effective function of music and politics in society:

> A creative artist is no more a mere musician than a great statesman is a mere politician. We are not ingenious puppets, sir, who live in a box and look out on the world only when it is gaping for amusement. We help to rule the nations and make the age as much as any other public men. We count ourselves on level benches with legislators. And a man who speaks effectively through music is compelled to something more difficult than parliamentary eloquence. (Ch. 22)

The musician, then, has as great a political role in society as the politician, and this is all very fine, but if one examines Klesmer's activities in *Daniel Deronda*, the pronouncements become empty rhetoric for he does absolutely nothing to help "rule the nations and make the age". In actuality, he is "ruled" by ruling class patronage and he inhabits an age "made" by commerce. Eliot intends Klesmer as the ideal artist; she posits his musical genius as the "social activity" that she describes and prescribes in her essays on the integration of a decent moral life with the writing of fiction, but rather than showing how the artist might effect such an integration, she uses Klesmer as a spokesman for what turn out to be quite contradictory and confusing notions about art.

Gwendolen dreads him "as part of that unmanageable world which was independent of her wishes – something vitriolic that would not cease to burn because you smiled or frowned at it" (Ch. 23). To be sure, this is Gwedolen's constant fear of the uncontrollable at work, but Klesmer is also seen as some kind of mythical force, resistant to propitiation, by the women in the Meyrick household. And it is fitting that Klesmer, the spokesman for an ideally generous and benign imperialism, redeemed by a "banner of sentiment", should confront Gwendolen, a metaphor for the nakedly unsentimental imperialism of her class.

Klesmer tells Gwendolen that "the life of the true artist" is lived by "natures framed to love perfection and to labour for it". So art is, then, something natural; you have to have the right kind of nature for it, but Klesmer also tells Gwendolen that to be an artist she must subdue her mind to "unbroken discipline" because genius is "little more than a great capacity for receiving discipline" (Ch. 23). On the one hand, the artistic genius must have a "nature" framed to labour for perfection, but on the other, genius is really little more than the capacity for self-discipline. These are common enough explanations of the mystery of artistic genius; what is interesting to me is that Eliot seems to deflate art on the one hand, to bring it down to the level of "social activity", yet on the other, she represents Klesmer as some grand, ahistorical force that sweeps its way through upper-class drawing rooms making assessments of the "true artist", as Klesmer does when he pronounces Mirah Lapidoth one of the chosen.

Genius, in Klesmer's ambiguous pronouncements, is both a given and a learned social activity, and it is as if Eliot is groping around here for some displaced and satisfactory way to talk about the gifts and the responsibilities of the novelist. In *Daniel Deronda*, and elsewhere, she is always at pains to denigrate any imaginative distortion of reality. Gwendolen's indiscriminate reading in second-rate novels has not prepared her for the unfortunate actuality of having to work for a living. Such things have been made remote by fictive distortion: "What horrors of damp huts, where human beings languish, may not become picturesque through aerial distance! What hymning of cancerous vices may we not languish over as sublimest art in the safe remoteness of a strange language and artificial phrase!" (Ch. 14). Eliot has an ideal of proper mimesis, mimesis which must be as faithful as possible to the novelistic thing itself, faithful to the world as it mirrors itself in the novelist's mind, if one bears in mind her intentions as she spells them out in Chapter 17 of *Adam Bede*. But the mirror necessarily distorts, it is often scratched like the pier glass in *Middlemarch*, and those scratches are arranged into pleasing concentric circles by the candle of the artistic imagination. It seems that Eliot's consciousness of artistic subjectivity and consequent distortion is already apparent in *Middlemarch*; she implicitly includes herself in the collection of characters who seek to impose their own idea of order upon the randomness of social life, and who are the object of her criticism. In *Daniel Deronda*, she tries to resolve her dilemma, as she tries to resolve the dilemma of finding a place for Deronda's ideal social, political and religious consciousness. She displaces him from English society, and by never demonstrating how Klesmer, for example, might live a life which integrates social, political and artistic power she displaces herself from ever reconciling the artistic imagination with the voice of moral correction.

In his critical biography of George Eliot, Leslie Stephen says that the "story of Gwendolen's marriage shows undiminished power. Here and there, perhaps, we have a little too much psychological analysis, but, after all, the reader who objects to psychology can avoid it by skipping a paragraph or two."[5] For the modern reader, the inclination is to skip more than a paragraph or two of Mordecai's monologues disguised as conversation, and to savour every resonant sentence of Eliot's "psychological analysis" of Gwendolen and her relationship with Grandcourt.

It seems to me that Gwendolen's psychological conflict, which is expressed in her numerous neurotic symptoms, such as a fear of the dark, a fear of open spaces, a fear of being alone, and so on, is rooted in an infantile attachment to her mother and in a dread of adult sexuality. And it seems to me, too, that Gwendolen's sterile sexual arrest, caused by the fixation upon her mother, can be seen to have an imaginative correspondence to the sterile, unproductive upper-class English life in which she moves and which is the object of Eliot's social criticism.[6]

I use the term adult sexuality in the sense that I think Freud means it when he describes a child's pre-Oedipal attachment to the mother in his essay, "Female Sexuality". Freud describes the meaning of the Oedipus complex for male and female children:

> In that phase of children's libidinal development which is characterized by the normal Oedipus complex we find that they are tenderly attached to the parent of the opposite sex, while their relation to the other parent is predominantly hostile. In the case of boys the explanation is simple. A boy's mother was his first love object; she remains so, and, as his feelings for her become more passionate and he understands more of the relation between father and mother, the former inevitably appears as a rival. With little girls it is otherwise. For them, too, the mother was the first love-object; how then does a little girl find her way to her father? How when and why does she detach herself from her mother?[7]

The problems for Gwendolen is that she has not detached herself from her mother. I do not mean this as a glib reduction of the complexity of fictive characterisation to neurotic symptom, but rather that Eliot's descriptions of Gwendolen's relationship with her mother are so intuitively suggestive of what Freud formulates into theory, so rich in that psychological analysis which Leslie Stephen suggests we might want to skip, that one can make a psychoanalytic reading of Gwendolen Harleth without implying that this is all there is to be said about her.

Gwendolen is tormented by the terrible actualisation of her fantasies of wishing her own father and her stepfather out of the picture in order that she may retain her mother for herself. In marrying Grandcourt she displaces a wronged woman, Lydia Glasher, who in many ways resembles her mother, and at the same time she thereby situates herself in the position of a punished female; she *becomes* her mother in an unconscious attempt to be punished and to be consequently discharged of her guilt. And in a massively cathected act, *she* becomes the child's first love-object and

Grandcourt becomes *her*: he takes over the role of punitive male, which is the role she has played for so long in a household of women.

In describing Gwendolen's domestic tyranny, Eliot says that she is one of those people who possess "a strong determination to have what was pleasant, with a total fearlessness in making themselves disagreeable or dangerous when they did not get it. Who is so much cajoled and served with trembling by the weak females of a household as the unscrupulous male – capable, if he has not free way at home, of going and doing worse elsewhere?" (Ch. 4). Now Gwendolen cannot go elsewhere and do worse, and she is obviously not an unscrupulous male, but much of the time she certainly behaves like one, which is what Eliot is implying here. She is the daughter of her mother's first marriage, and she lords it over her mother and four half-sisters, the daughters of one Captain Davilow who joined his family during his lifetime, "in brief and fitful manner, enough to reconcile them to his long absences" (Ch. 3). Gwendolen's function in the Offendene household is quickly apprehended by the new housekeeper when she remarks to the lady's maid that Gwendolen is the one "that's to command us all".

As a child of twelve she asks her mother, "Why did you marry again, mamma? It would have been nicer if you had not," and as an adult she sleeps on a couch next to her mother's bed, described by Eliot as a "catafalque". In her notes to *Daniel Deronda*, Barbara Hardy suggests that this is a heavy-handed joke on Eliot's part about the Victorian best bed, but I think it is also an oblique reference to the bed as a memorial of the sexual demands which have been made upon Mrs Davilow, and which seem to have done her in. She is a worn and wasted woman, exhausted by the burden of four incipiently marriageable daughters, and alternately delighted and intimidated by the caprices of a fifth who behaves more like an "unscrupulous male" than a properly subdued young lady. Gwendolen has taken on the function of a third husband in her mother's household, one of the gratifications of such a role being that she thereby reconstructs, however unconsciously, that stage of pre-Oedipal sexual development when the father is out of the picture.

In "Female Sexuality", Freud describes one effect of the castration complex upon a girl:

> . . . she clings in obstinate self-assertion to her threatened masculinity; the hope of getting a penis sometime is cherished to an incredibly late age and becomes the aim of her life, whilst the

> phantasy of really being a man in spite of everything, often dominates long periods of her life.[8]

Gwendolen, if not exactly indulging in fantasies that she is a man, exhibits characteristics which are conventionally associated with male behaviour. She is aggressive in public (at least until she matches up with Grandcourt), and she is forceful in her private dealings with her family. Her fantasies are schoolboy ones of killing tigers and exploring the North-West Passage and her imperialistic way of handling the world is a cultural mark of male behaviour. I want to make a distinction here, by the way, between what might be interpreted as a feminist consciousness and a compulsion to situate oneself in the position of controlling one's mother. Gwendolen is no feminist self-projection for George Eliot: she wants, vicariously, to play the roles of husband and father.

Freud concludes his exposition of the difficulties experienced by girls in detaching themselves from their mothers and taking their fathers as a love-object by suggesting that a girl may follow "a very circuitous path whereby she arrives at the ultimate normal feminine attitude in which she takes her father as love-object, and thus arrives at the Oedipus complex in its feminine form".[9]

This is no place to introduce arguments about what constitutes "the ultimate normal feminine attitude", or to quarrel with Freud's teleological notion of the road to sexual normality. I am more concerned with a correspondence between Eliot's fictive female and Freud's hypotheses because that correspondence seems to illuminate some of the relation between cultural arrest in *Daniel Deronda* and the psycho-sexual arrest of its heroine. At the end of *Daniel Deronda*, Gwendolen puts her foot on Freud's path to the Oedipus complex: she has taken Deronda as an ideal love-object and invested him with all the moral authority and protective capabilities of the father. And Gwendolen's diminished egoism, her calm admission to Deronda that because of having known him she "may live to be one of the best of women, who makes others glad that they were born", suggests that she has also put her foot on the path to an improved moral life. Gwendolen and the culture for which she is a metaphor may, therefore, both be said to move, however slightly and ambiguously, from a point of stasis.

Gwendolen's dread of adult sexuality is demonstrated in her response to Rex Gascoigne's gentlemanly advances. His presence makes her want to curl up like a sea-anemone; she shudders and cries, "Pray don't make love to me! I hate it."[10] Her mother comes in to find Gwendolen sobbing bitterly and Eliot's description of Mrs Davilow's feelings suggests something of the unusual nature of the relationship between mother and daughter. She feels "something of the alarmed anguish that women feel at the sight of over-powering sorrow in a strong man; for this child had been her ruler". Gwendolen clings to her mother, crying, "I can't bear any one to be very near me but you," (Ch. 7) but in marrying Grandcourt she is obliged to have someone more than very near to her. He is an experienced sexual aggressor, and she is introduced to the marital demands which seem to have left her mother so demolished. It is interesting, incidentally, that Gwendolen does not become pregnant: it is as if a marriage which is partly founded upon the gratification of sado-masochistic compulsions can only end in sterility. And if one considers the class meaning of this match, the social advancement of the upper-middle-class girl to the aristocracy, it doesn't say much for Eliot's belief in class fusion as doing anything to invigorate a morally flaccid culture. Apart from Gwendolen's problematic enlightenment and implicit moral betterment, everything is sterile at the end of *Daniel Deronda*; the only fruitfulness lies in Deronda's mission to put an end to the *diaspora*.

With the decline of the Davilow investments, Gwendolen's hopes for a glamorous existence in which she will call the tune also decline. She has fled from Grandcourt when Lydia Glasher makes her uncompromising declaration of a wronged woman's rights, and she returns to England with the distinctly unglamorous possibility of becoming a governess in front of her. Grandcourt languidly represents himself in two meanings of the word: he reappears on the scene and he represents himself as a manageable lover. Gwendolen is determined to refuse him, but she is caught between her "disgust and indignation" and the thought of release from the Misses Mompert and what he will do for her mother. Her mamma has "managed badly", and Gwendolen succumbs with the conscious and mistaken belief that she will be able to govern Grandcourt more effectively than her mother has managed her two husbands. She sells herself to Grandcourt for the sake not so much of her own energetic, witty and attractive self, but for the sake of her mother's financial security: she undertakes the male function of providing for female dependants.

Grandcourt knows exactly what he is up to, and he brings along two gorgeous horses to put an expensive seal on the engagement:

"These beautiful creatures in their fine grooming, sent a thrill of exultation through Gwendolen. They were the symbols of command and luxury, in delightful contrast with the ugliness of poverty and humiliation at which she had been lately looking close" (Ch. 27). But horses in *Daniel Deronda* take on differing symbolic meanings: it depends on who holds the reins.

Gwendolen loves to ride; she can't wait to "lose" herself in a gallop when she finally accepts Grandcourt and his horses, but Eliot also imagines Gwendolen as the one who is subject to the discipline of the bridle. As she stands with her mother and sisters when they first arrive at Offendene, the image is positive, and Eliot says Gwendolen is like "a young racehorse in the paddock among untrimmed ponies and patient hacks" (Ch. 3). Her gauche sisters are the pony foil for her thoroughbred good looks, and her mother is the patient hack who has been broken and exhausted by familial demands. Gwendolen imagines that Grandcourt will be as "flawless" a husband as one can manage to secure, that he will allow her to "mount the chariot and drive the plunging horses herself". But Grandcourt is an experienced driver and rider, and he is not about to relinquish the actual and metaphorical reins. When Gwendolen marries him, "in spite of everything" (that is to say, with full knowledge of Lydia Glasher's claims upon him), he feels that she has been "brought to kneel down like a horse under training for the arena" (Ch. 29).[11]

But Grandcourt, although he imagines *himself* as a sort of omnipotent ringmaster of the social circus arranged for his own entertainment, is represented most frequently by Eliot as being in a condition of sluggish and parasitical stasis. By virtue of Eliot's imagery, Grandcourt seems to slither malevolently through the novel. In describing Gwendolen's misreading of his character, she says that he seems to be a "handsome lizard of a hitherto unknown species, not of the lively, darting kind. But Gwendolen knew hardly anything about lizards, and ignorance gives one a large range of probabilities. This splendid specimen was probably gentle, suitable as a boudoir pet: what may not a lizard be, if you know nothing to the contrary?" (Ch. 13). He turns out to be anything but a boudoir pet: on the fateful mediterranean cruise, for example, he is transformed into "a dangerous serpent" coiling himself "without invitation" in Gwendolen's cabin (Ch. 54) – a spot of sexual imagery that requires no exegesis. Lush, always trying to anticipate Grandcourt's movements, is constantly frustrated by his employer's unpredictable visage: he looks "as neutral as an alligator: there was no telling what might turn up in the slowly churning chances of his mind" (Ch. 15).[12]

Eliot consistently associates Grandcourt with water imagery, an appropriate prefiguration of his death by drowning, and it is as if he finally goes under in the Bay of Genoa by virtue of his life-long imaginative habitation of the murky depths. His mind works among the "ooze and mud" and his lazy malevolence and his fetid culture feed each other. His thoughts are "like the circlets one sees in a dark pool continually dying out and continually started again by some impulse from below the surface" (Ch. 28). This is an image similar to that employed by Dickens to suggest the workings of Eugene Wrayburn's mind as he walks by the river in *Our Mutual Friend*, as Eugene's conscious mind is disturbed by the suppressed impulse to seduce Lizzie Hexam. Grandcourt shares something else with Eugene Wrayburn, incidentally, and that is a similarity to John Stuart Mill's paradigm of the sluggish modern English gentleman. Grandcourt is an enervated type. He is extraordinarily pale, he has mere wisps of pale blond hair ("mealy complexioned male" is the opinion of his tenants), and his general languor suggests the moral languor of his culture. He is also quite stupid. He is only able to interpret Gwendolen's dread as jealousy, and he is unable to comprehend the remorse she feels for having displaced Lydia Glasher. He has none of Deronda's "plenteous sympathy", and in describing his essential dimness, Eliot declares that "there is no escaping the fact that want of sympathy condemns us to a corresponding stupidity" (Ch. 48). He also has none of Deronda's interest in language. He loathes writing letters (Lush is "as much an implement as pen and paper"), and he speaks in short sentences refusing amplification of his will beyond an unadorned assertion . As one of the spectators at his wedding reports, " . . . this Mr. Grandcourt has wonderful little tongue. Everything must be done dummy-like without his ordering" (Ch. 31).

On Gwendolen's wedding day she drives through the park at Ryelands in a state of febrile anticipation. Her susceptibility to changes in light and scenery gives her palpitations, and as she nears the house where she will literally have to hand herself over to Grandcourt, the approaching actualisation of her fantasies of being " 'somebody' . . . being in short the heroine of an admired play without the pains of art", brings her to a pitch of excited expectation. But Eliot also suggests the price in sexual compliance which Gwendolen is to pay for her social stardom: "Was it alone the closeness of this fulfilment which made her heart flutter? or was it some dim forecast, the insistent penetration of suppressed experience, mixing the expectation of a triumph with the dread of a crisis?" (Ch. 31). "Insistent penetration of suppressed experience" suggests, of course, the insistence of what is suppressed by the conscious mind making itself felt by whatever means are available to it; in Gwendolen's case what is suppressed manifests itself in her numerous hysterical symptoms. And the notion of penetration in this scene has an actual, sexual meaning. Gwendolen is to be penetrated by Grandcourt, and in the context of her psychological imperialism, her actual, physical acceptance of him represents her transformation from the coloniser to the colonised. The sublimated sexual penetration suggested by the civilised play with bows and arrows is to be desublimated for her, so to speak, and she is no longer the archer but the target.[13] When Grandcourt enters the room to claim his marital rights, he finds her in hysterics: she is explicitly shattered by a letter from Lydia Glasher returning the family diamonds and cursing her for having usurped her rights, and she is implicitly unhinged by the anticipation of sexual penetration. After she becomes Grandcourt's sexual property, she turns more and more to Deronda for spiritual solace.

Deronda's quasi-psychoanalytic relationship with Gwendolen is given its fullest expression in four crucial meetings between them. At the first of these meetings, which read remarkably like psychoanalytic "hours", Gwendolen is wearing the necklace which Deronda restores to her at the beginning of the novel. The necklace is made of turquoises that belonged to her father, and her easy relinquishment of it, it is "the ornament she could most conveniently part with", (Ch. 2) suggests the explicit unimportance of her father for her. She has never "known" him, that is to say, she has no conscious memory of him. This act, too, suggests the importance of her father in her unconscious; by pawning the necklace, she imaginatively disinherits him, refuses him as a love-object. Gwendolen wears the necklace wrapped around her wrist as a "memorial" to Deronda's act of restoration, and I think she also wears it as a memorial to her father. Wearing the necklace represents her incipient readiness to accept him into her consciousness, and perhaps, through the agency of Deronda as a displaced father figure, to free herself from her pre-Oedipal attachment to her mother.

This first meeting occurs on the occasion of the New Year's Eve dance at the Abbey, the first public appearance of Gwendolen as a new bride. Gwendolen and Deronda stand secluded by a window, and she asks, "What should you do if you were like me – feeling that you were wrong and miserable, and dreading everything to come?" He tells her that she must "try to care about something in this vast world besides the gratification of small selfish desires. Try to care for what is best in thought and action – something that is good apart from the accidents of your own lot" (Ch. 36). But this rather official, if admirable, advice does nothing for her, and a few days later she corners him in the library. The room itself becomes a confessional as Gwendolen demands consolation, even absolution, from Deronda: "An enormous log-fire, with the scent of russia from the books, made the great room as warmly odorous as a private chapel in which the censers have been swinging." Gwendolen repeats her plea for advice, and it seems as if Deronda is already reluctant to engage himself. He continues to talk to her in the language of self-improvement, to offer the counsel of selflessness and charitable enterprises, a mode which does not match Gwendolen's emerging consciousness of what is at work within her. She becomes insistent and quite explicit: life has become like "a dance set beforehand – I seem to see all that can be – and I am tired and sick of it". Deronda insists that her refuge must lie in "the higher, the religious life, which holds an enthusiasm for something more than our own appetites and vanities. The few may find themselves in it simply by an elevation of feeling; but for us who have to struggle for our wisdom, the higher life must be a region in which the affections are clad with knowledge" (Ch. 36). He is really talking to himself, *about* himself, rather than to Gwendolen, and it seems that the more he is pushed to come up with a *modus vivendi* for her, the more he moves towards abandoning the society which has become intolerable to her.

He feels helpless in the face of Gwendolen's dilemma, a dilemma which is representative in many ways of the materialism and moral vacuity of the culture he criticises, because he is in the process of discovering that he has no answer for *himself*. He is becoming increasingly discontented with his externality, and in the following chapter when Hans Meyrick confesses that he is in love with Mirah, Deronda begins to refuse the role of sympathetic adviser, of detached observer:

> He was conscious of that peculiar irritation which will sometimes

> befall the man whom others are inclined to trust as a mentor – the irritation of perceiving that he is supposed to be entirely off the same plane of desire and temptation as those who confess to him. (Ch. 37)

He has functioned as a critic of his culture and as a sympathetic confessor to his friends, but as these roles begin to be uncomfortably apparent to him, as all the demands for resolution which are integral to these roles are made upon him, he begins to withdraw from them. It is as if he becomes like Eliot as she writes her novel of social criticism; the more critical she becomes, the less she is able to resolve the tension which she represents. When Eliot says that a sort of education is being prepared for Deronda in his relationship with Gwendolen, it is an education in the consciousness that the roles of moral critic and sympathetic adviser are insufficient for him.

In the third meeting between Gwendolen and Deronda, Gwendolen dresses like a nun in a black dress with a large piece of black lace on her head. Deronda is to be her priest, and she confesses that she is afraid of "getting wicked". She is tormented by fantasies of Grandcourt's death, and at the same time she projects her wish for him to be dead into a fear that he will kill her:

> The power of tyranny in him seemed a power of living in the presence of any wish that he should die. The thought that his death was the only possible deliverance for her was one with the thought deliverance would never come . . . The thought of his dying would not subsist: it turned as with a dream-change into the terror that she should die with his throttling fingers on her neck avenging that thought. Fantasies moved within her like ghosts, making no break in her more acknowledged consciousness and finding no obstruction in it: dark rays doing their work invisibly in the broad light. (Ch.48)

Gwendolen's wish that Grandcourt die, which is freighted and cathected with her unconscious wishes that her father and her stepfather be put out of the picture, is projected into a terror that Grandcourt will throttle *her*, a terror which is an unconscious expression of her wish to be punished for her parricidal fantasies and consequently discharged of her guilt. Deronda can do nothing with Gwendolen's attempt to articulate some of this psychological conflict. He feels that words are useless, they have "no more rescue in them than if he had been beholding a vessel in peril of wreck". It seems as if there is not only a radical disjunction between what is going on in Gwendolen's mind and Deronda's ability to help her, and between Eliot's quite remarkably intuitive descriptions of fantasy and psychological projection and Deronda's rather commonplace advice, but that the disjunction between Eliot's moral criticism of upper-class English life and the implausibility of her alternative to this life which constitutes the end of *Daniel Deronda* and its thematic and formal problematic, is already coming into being.

In Genoa, Eliot conjoins the decisive experiences of Deronda and Gwendolen: he meets his mother and Grandcourt is drowned; he makes an explicit discovery of the meaning of his mother in his future, and she makes an implicit discovery of the meaning of her father in her past. Deronda is able to help Gwendolen to understand something of the meaning of her guilt merely in the articulation of it, and, paradoxically in helping her, he prepares himself to leave her. He returns from Friday evening services at the synagogue to see Gwendolen being helped ashore with "a wild amazed consciousness in her eyes, as if she had waked up in a world where some judgment was impending, and the beings she saw around her were coming to seize her" (Ch. 55). Her fantasies of parricide have been realised for the third time.

After the meeting with his mother which frees him for his ambiguous new career in the East, Deronda is able to properly respond to Gwendolen. As she begins in a fragmentary way to pour out her feelings of guilt, he sits motionless, feeling that he "must let her mind follow its own need", and saying "What I most desire at this moment is what will most help you. Tell me all you feel it a relief to tell" (Ch. 56). What she has to tell is described by Eliot in a manner which suggests the mechanisms of psychoanalytic free association. Gwendolen "unconsciously" leaves "intervals in her retrospect, not clearly distinguishing between what she said and what she had only an inward vision of". It is all a vision of wanting to kill Grandcourt:

> And then we got away – out of the port – into the deep – and everything was still – and we never looked at each other, only he spoke to order me – and the very light about me seemed to hold me a prisoner and force me to sit as I did. It came over me that when I was a child I used to fancy sailing away into a world where people were not forced to live with any one they did not like – I did not like my father-in-law to come home. And now, I thought, just the opposite had come to me. I had stept into a boat, and my life

> was a sailing and sailing away – gliding on and no help – always into solitude with *him*, away from deliverance . . . I knew no way of killing him there, but I did, I did kill him in my thoughts . . . I don't know how it was – he was turning the sail – there was a gust – he was struck – I know nothing – I only know that I saw my wish outside me. (Ch. 56)

In Gwendolen's imagination, Grandcourt is associated with the stepfather she did not like, the man she did not like "to come home", the man with whom she did not want to live. And she is condemned to sail away with this man who resembles her stepfather, and by association her own father, to glide on with no help, in an image which suggests an unwanted and repulsive sexual bondage. She is overcome with remorse not just for Grandcourt's death (and Eliot makes it clear that while Grandcourt is going under Gwendolen does not throw him a rope), but the guilt she bears in regard to her stepfather, and, again by association, in regard to her own father. She has refused them both as love-objects, as objects of sexual desire, preferring to remain attached to her mother in a state of pre-Oedipal arrest. Gwendolen says that she will be haunted forever by "the dead face – dead, dead", and one is reminded of the Edvard Munch-like picture of a dead face and fleeing figure which so alarms her when it is suddenly revealed during a game of charades at the beginning of the novel. It seems to me that this picture represents an image of the guilty child running away from the murdered father; it is Gwendolen in flight from her imagined deed and in flight from the sexual attachment which she dreads and which can only be avoided by the imaginative dispatch by death of the father from the family scene.

In *Totem and Taboo*, Freud makes a connection between a mythic killing of the father in primitive society and the modern, civilised symptom of free-floating guilt in neurotics:

> The earliest moral precepts and restrictions in primitive society have been explained by us as reactions to a deed which gave those who performed it the concept of 'crime.' They felt remorse for the dead and decided that it should never be repeated and that its performance should bring no advantage. This creative sense of guilt still persists among us. We find it operating in an asocial manner in neurotics, and producing new moral precepts and persistent restrictions, as an atonement for crimes that have been

> committed and as a precaution against the committing of new ones. If, however, we inquire among these neurotics to discover what were the deeds which provoked these reactions we shall be disappointed. We find no deeds, but only impulses and emotions, set upon evil ends but held back from their achievement. What lie behind the sense of guilt of neurotics are always psychical realities and never factual ones.[14]

Gwendolen may be interpreted as Freud's neurotic in search of atonement for her guilt, and if we understand her (and I obviously think we may) as a metaphor for her culture, then she may be said to express the collective social guilt which Freud describes for having murdered the mythic father. Now Gwendolen comes to understand something of the origin of her neurotic conflict: to be sure, this understanding is not spelled out by Eliot, it is imaginatively suggested. But it is in her confession to Deronda that Gwendolen is freed, at least and at best, to cope with her guilt, if not exactly to experience a psychoanalytic "break-through". If Gwendolen, then, is problematically liberated for some kind of moral betterment and may be read, in part, as a metaphor for her culture, then one has to consider how her culture is freed for its own and larger form of moral improvement.

What happens? Gwendolen is abandoned by Deronda, and English upper-class culture is abandoned by Eliot. It seems that the breaking apart of *Daniel Deronda* is a formal and thematic expression of what happens when a culture is made conscious of itself, when it is made aware of what ails it, so to speak. If we consider the Victorian novel as one expression of Victorian cultural consciousness, then the formal and thematic break in *Daniel Deronda* seems to suggest that in Eliot's mind English upper-class culture has itself irreparably broken apart. Gwendolen is dislodged from her egoism by Deronda's racial destiny, just as her culture is dislodged from a plausible regeneration by Eliot's pessimism. Social realism and moral correction can never connect here for Eliot because the culture she represents in *Daniel Deronda* has become disconnected, fragmented within its own structures. For Deronda, to know that he is Jewish means a termination of all his intellectual doubt and psychological uneasiness, of all that has bothered him throughout the novel: for Gwendolen and the culture for which she is, in part, a metaphor, to know what ails them, to have symbolically identified the origins of dread and guilt, means isolation and abandonment.

*Daniel Deronda*, then, ends in an image of sterility, despite Deronda's implicitly fertile quest in the East, and this sterile and celibate ending (to which I briefly referred at the beginning of this section) that violates the conventional, felicitous conclusions of much Victorian fiction, may be contrasted with the endings of *North and South* and *Our Mutual Friend* as a way of drawing some conclusions about the decisive differences in the mediatory performances of the three novels.

All the important family members present at the beginning of *North and South* are left out of its resolution of class and sexual tensions. Thornton's mother is left to contemplate the spotlessness of her drawing-room and Margaret's parents and brother have departed into death and exile. The novel ends with the establishment of a new middle-class family, whose most important wedding gift, in Gaskell's didactic imagination, seems to be the cooperation of the working class, and with the implicit generation of new moral values which will radiate out from the centre of that family to permeate industrial society. Dickens' novel, too, ends in the establishment of family, but unlike the union of John Thornton and Margaret Hale, which is sombrely dedicated to the improvement of a felt and distressing social actuality, Dickens' extended family, headed by the alliance of middle-class Harmon and working-class Boffin and including a former foundling and a convalescent upper-middle-class barrister, seems to retreat from the world in which most of *Our Mutual Friend* is situated to a West End fairyland where it devotes itself to innocent play, and to the dispensation of money made from rubbish collection to all the worthy characters who are enfolded within the circle of magical domesticity. Gwendolen Harleth and Daniel Deronda do not find a resolution of their respective struggles to discover, or to create, their psychological and social identities in marriage to each other. And no new moral values for English life are to be generated by the marriage of Deronda and Mirah, which seems to indicate Eliot's pessimistic assessment of the function of the family, whatever its class identity, as a positive force for social and moral change.

Despite the intriguing intricacies of Gwendolen's family drama and the decisive desire of Deronda's mother to transform him from an Italian Jew into an English gentleman, *Daniel Deronda* is, perhaps, in many ways more a novel of the critical imagination than of family life. Eliot also rejects the critical imagination as an agent of fictive mediation. If one considers the meaning of *Daniel Deronda* as social criticism in conjunction with its interest in the critical imagination, the fact that Eliot displaces her critical imagination right out of English society seems to reveal an implicit belief that the novel itself can no longer create resolutions of social tension with the formal and thematic coherence of *North and South*, and to a lesser extent, of *Our Mutual Friend*. The confident assurance of *North and South* is unsettled by the dark ambiguities of *Our Mutual Friend*, and *Daniel Deronda* seems to refute the implicit suppositions of both these novels that fiction can offer moral lessons, or alleviate social uneasiness, and it takes itself, as a novel that can perform these functions, right out of society. But ironically, *Daniel Deronda*, in the process of an implicit and obviously unconscious invalidation of the mythical resolutions of social tension offered by *North and South* and *Our Mutual Friend*, itself creates a resolution which is, if anything, even more mythical than those it may be said to refute. Eliot's hero, the social critic and ideal force for change, cannot, it seems, be contained within the conventional forms of Victorian fiction, nor within the conventional theme of marriage as the positive locus of social betterment. As he moves out of Gwendolen's life, he moves out of the world of the novel, so to speak, in a kind of regressive journey to a quasi-epic universe of religious and psychological certainty. The burden of Eliot's fictions of resolution seems to fall more heavily on Gwendolen than it does on Deronda in the sense that we wonder what will happen to her in the society that Eliot has so fully and effectively described; it is difficult for us to imagine what she will do with the understanding that she has so painfully achieved, but we never wonder what will happen to Deronda for he is made of the stuff of mythic, epic heroes and his prescribed destiny awaits him in a world ideally imagined as being without political and ideological conflict – a world far different from Gwendolen's, and, needless to say, far different from those represented in *North and South* and *Our Mutual Friend*.

NOTES

1. Georg Lukacs, *The Theory of the Novel*, p. 29.
2. John Stuart Mill's essay, *Civilization*, published in 1836, is the crucial text in this connection.
3. *Economic and Philosophic Manuscripts of 1844*, "Private Property and Communism", translated by Martin Milligan (New York, 1964), p. 134.
4. In a discussion of the country-house in the nineteenth-century novel,

Raymond Williams observes: "It is already clear in the country-house world of *Daniel Deronda* that a new and weak form is emerging: the country-house not of land but of capital." *The Country and the City* (London, 1973), p. 248.

Patricia Beer believes that Eliot intends Catherine Arrowpoint as an example of "the genuinely creative girl", a deliberate and significant contrast to Gwendolen's parasitical and sterile personality. Beer says that "what is fatally hampering to George Eliot's heroines is not society, not even provincial society, but their own lack of creativity, which includes creative intellectual powers". This seems to me to be wrong on at least two counts. Eliot is quite specific about the effect upon Gwendolen of her society: her restlessness is defined by its horizons, and her dreary future as a governess, occasioned by the failure of Grapnell & Co., determines, to some extent, her marriage to Grandcourt. And Catherine Arrowpoint is hardly creative; she is a competent musician, to be sure, but the most creative thing she does is to manufacture a comfortable outpost in Grosvenor Place where Klesmer holds forth as a prominent professor of music. See *Reader, I Married Him, A Study of the Women Characters of Jane Austen, Charlotte Brontë, Elizabeth Gaskell, George Eliot* (London, 1974), pp. 181–5.

5. *George Eliot* (London, 1902) p. 185.
6. Henry Auster remarks that in *Daniel Deronda* the reader has the sense "that for the English large concrete problems no longer exist, and in the absence of such problems, a more basic problem is taking shape as the society is sliding into a torpor of complacency and even decadence". "George Eliot and the Modern Temper", *The Worlds of Victorian Fiction*, edited by Jerome H. Buckley (Cambridge, Mass., 1975), p. 87.
7. *Collected Papers*, Vol. 5, edited by James Strachey (New York, 1959), p. 252.
8. Ibid., p. 257.
9. Ibid.
10. T. B. Tomlinson finds this scene to have "a probing, investigatory quality in it that is directly and positively in touch, through Gwendolen's sensitive but highly charged nature, with a certain threat that the universe (rather than *just* the intractable nature of middle-class country society) poses". *The English Middle-Class Novel* (London, 1976), p. 118. I think that Gwendolen and middle-class county society (actually it is upper-middle-class, not middle-class) cannot be separated in this way. She *represents* her society and one could, therefore, say that both Gwendolen *and* her society are threatened by what Tomlinson calls the "universe".
11. The connection between a well-trained horse and a pliable woman is given much more explicit expression in *My Secret Life* (New York, 1966). One of the innumerable exploits of its narrator is recorded in this way, "After the first fuck she was like a well-broken horse; she obeyed me in everything, blushed, was modest, humbled, indifferent, conquered, submissive . . . . " (p. 228).

    Anthony Trollope likens women to horses in several of the Palliser novels (in rather different language, needless to say). See especially *Can*

*You Forgive Her?*" Chapter 50, where Lady Glencora is described in the following way after engaging in a strenuous waltz: "Then she put up her face, and slightly opened her mouth, and stretched her nostrils, – as ladies do as well as horses when the running has been severe and they want air."

12. Lush is perfectly at home in Grandcourt's swampy culture. He is the son of a vicar who stinted to send him to Oxford, but instead of taking orders he becomes a travelling companion to the upper-class. His inclination to live a life of "dining with high discrimination, riding good horses, living generally in the most luxurious honey-blossomed clover – and all without working" is gratified in his role as secretary-companion and general steward of Grandcourt's dirty business.

    Lush's effect on Gwendolen is something like the effect of Solmes on Clarissa Harlowe. Clarissa is appalled and repelled by his squatting stance and inclination to press upon her hoop with his "ugly weight". See especially Volume I of *Clarissa* (Everyman's Library: London, 1932).

    Sir Hugo says Deronda is "a kind of Lovelace who will make the Clarissas run after you instead of your running after them" (Ch. 32). This strikes Deronda as a "tasteless joke", but it is an explicit reference to Richardson's novel and perhaps in naming her heroine Harleth Eliot had some of Clarissa Harlowe's fear of male sexual aggression in mind.

    Gwendolen finds Lush physically repulsive; his "prominent eyes, fat though not clumsy figure, and strong black grey-besprinkled hair of frizzy thickness" frighten and repel her.

13. Neil Roberts describes Gwendolen as Eliot's "first sexually alive heroine after Maggie Tulliver, who is one of the few heroines in Victorian fiction in whom passionate sexual feeling is shown operating independently of, if not in opposition to, the moral and social consciousness". *George Eliot: Her Beliefs and Her Art* (London, 1975), p. 208.

    This seems wrong on two counts. Maggie Tulliver uses her sexuality as a means of control and confirmation of "the moral and social consciousness". To refuse Stephen Guest, despite her strong sexual feeling which no one can deny, is to exercise power in the one area available to her, namely the moral life. And Gwendolen is dead to adult sexuality, rather than being "alive".

14. Translated by James Strachey (New York, 1950), p. 159.

# Index

*All the Year Round*, 62n, 109, 130n
Arnold, Matthew, *Culture and Anarchy*, 25–6
Austen, Jane, 12
  *Mansfield Park*, 45
Auster, Henry, 205n

Baker, William, 146n
Bedient, Calvin, 145n
Beer, Patricia, 205n
Bettelheim, Bruno, 86n
Blackwood, John, 155
Boswell, James, 3
Briggs, Asa, 9n, 26
Brontë, Charlotte
  *Jane Eyre*, 164
  *Shirley*, 42

Carlyle, Thomas, 7, 20–1, 173n
coal mines
  conditions in 1840s, 172n
coincidence
  in Victorian novels, 15–16
Colby, Vineta, 29n
Conrad, Joseph
  *Nostromo*, 19
Craik, W. H., 30n

Davis, Lennard, 174–5n
Dickens, Charles
  *Bleak House*, xi, 71, 75, 83, 117
  *Dombey and Son*, 106
  *Great Expectations*, 112
  *Hard Times*, 6, 34, 82
  *Little Dorrit*, xi, 83
  *Our Mutual Friend*
    bourgeois marriage, 73, 104
    class and sexuality, 77–9
    exploitation of working-class women, 123–5
    family, 65, 97–100
    industrialism, 82–4
    language and marketable commodities, 90–2
    lower-class characters defeated, 57–9
    marriage and social class, 55–7
    mimesis and novel, 84–5
    money and role-playing, 117–18
    mounds and economic power, 95–7
    narrative and profit-making, 107–8
    secrets, 92–4
    social discontent, 54–5, 63–4
    urban alienation, 71–2
    working-class women, 67–70
  *The Old Curiosity Shop*, 82

Eagleton, Terence, 42
Edgeworth, Maria, 6
Eliot, George
  *Adam Bede*, 152, 154, 190
  "Address to Working Men by Felix Holt", 155, 164–7
  "Authorship", 157–8
  *Daniel Deronda*
    East End, 151–3
    English anti-semitism, 141, 160–1
    English working class and Jews, 153–62
    female sexuality, 190–5
    interpretation and texts, 148–50
    Jewish lower-class life, 161–3
    Jewish women, 167–71
    marriage and social class, 139–40, 194
    myth of artistic genius, 187–90
    novel and epic, 140–2
    psychoanalytic free association, 200–1
    psychological and political imperialism, 177–1
    sexual exploitation of women, 184–6
    social theatre, 182–4
    split novel problematic, 135–7
    working men's club, 166–7
  *Felix Holt the Radical*, 154–5
  "How I Came to Write Fiction", 157

Eliot, George (*Contd.*)
*Middlemarch*, xi, 46, 190
"The Modern Hep! Hep! Hep!", 160
"The Natural History of German Life", 158–9
Engels, Friedrich, 22, 32, 71, 172n
English middle class
and the novel, ix
English working class
and birth control, 30n
characters in Victorian fiction, 38
opium, use of, 109

fairy tales
Little Red Ridinghood in *Our Mutual Friend*, 85–6n
family
affirmed in *North and South* and *Our Mutual Friend*, 136
rejected in *Daniel Deronda*, 203
father
and Eugene Wrayburn in *Our Mutual Friend*, 72–3
and Fledgeby in *Our Mutual Friend*, 101
and Gwendolen Harleth in *Daniel Deronda*, 178, 197–201
and relation to wills in *Our Mutual Friend*, 73–4
in Victorian novels, 13, 19
Freud, Sigmund, xii, 177
*Civilization and its Discontents*, 77–8
*Female Sexuality*, 191–3
*Totem and Taboo*, 201–2

Gaskell, Elizabeth
*Cranford*, 23–4
*Mary Barton*, 4–5, 27, 31, 36, 44, 77
*North and South*
competetive individualism, 20–1
family and class tension, 11–12
Irish workers, 44
myth of class cooperation, 39–40
plot, 14–16
sexuality, 44–5
social change, 47–9
strike, 40–4
threat to middle-class women, 42–4
unionisation, 33–5
relationship to father, 28n
*Ruth*, 124
Greenwood, James, 173n
Greg, W. R., 5–6
Guerard, Albert, 94–5

Hardy, Barbara, 145–6n, 192
Hobsbawm, Eric, 9n, 73, 130n
Hopkins, A. B., 10n
Houghton, Walter, 29n
*Household Words*, 9, 88n

industrial novels, 5–8

Jamaica, 180
James, Henry, 38, 122
Jews
and English working class in *Daniel Deronda*, 153–62
as epic characters in *Daniel Deronda*, 142
and paper mill in *Our Mutual Friend*, 84
Johnson, Samuel, 3
Jones, Gareth Stedman, 86–7n
Jones, R. T., 145n

Kay-Shuttleworth, Lady, 8
Keating, Peter, 7, 38
Kermode, Frank, 130n
Knoepflmacher, U. C., 173n

Leavis, F. R., 145n
London, x
casual labour market in 1860s, 86–7n
East End, 86n
embankment of River Thames in 1860s, 53
improvement of sewers in 1860s, 53
Lukacs, Georg, 7, 142, 177

McVeagh, John, 28–9n
Manchester, x, 4–5, 21, 22
working-class population in 1840s, 27
Marcus, Steven, 19, 70, 174n
Martin, Bernard, 174n
Marx, Karl, xii, 11, 32, 61n, 96, 128n, 185
Mathias, Peter, 9n
Mill, John Stuart, 74, 196
Miller, J. Hillis, 128–9n
Munby, Arthur J., 69
*My Secret Life*, 17, 70, 86n, 205n

Neff, Wanda, 88n

Oedipus complex, 191–3
Orwell, George, 10n, 98

Palestine, 167
paper manufacture

paper manufacture (*Contd.*)
  and Commissioners on the Employment of children and Young Persons, 82
  and Factory Acts Extension Act 1867, 82
  and *Our Mutual Friend*, 88–9n
Pinter, Harold, 129n
prostitution
  in Victorian England, 86n

Richardson, Samuel
  *Clarissa*, 206n
  *Pamela*, 55
Roberts, Neil, 145n, 206n

Said, Edward W., 174n
Shaffer, E. S., 146n
Shelley, Mary, 31
Smiles, Samuel, 17
Smith, Grahame, 117, 130n
Stephen, Leslie, 190
Stowe, Harriet Beecher, 141

Taylor, R. W. Cooke, 5, 26–7
Thackeray, William
  *Vanity Fair*, 45
Tocqueville, Alexis de, 21
Tomlinson, T. B., 205n
Trollope, Anthony
  *Can You Forgive Her?*, 129–30n, 205–6n
  Palliser novels, 136
  *Phineas Finn*, 130n

Ure, Andrew, 18

*Varney, the Vampire*, 49n
Williams, Raymond, 9n, 146n, 204–5n
Wilson, Edmund, 61–2n
Wolff, Michael, 173n
Wollstonecraft, Mary, 172n
Wright, Edgar, 28n, 35–6